Stories of the Greats,
the Near Greats, the Ingrates,
the Has-beens, and the Never Weres

Joe Franklin
with
R. J. MARX

Scribner
New York London Toronto
Sydney Tokyo Singapore

Up Late with

Joe Franklin

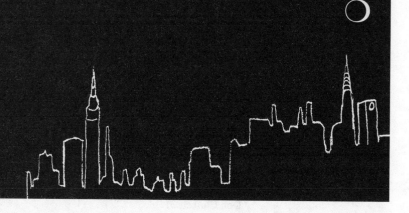

SCRIBNER
Rockefeller Center
1230 Avenue of the Americas
New York, New York 10020

Scribner and design are registered trademarks of
Simon & Schuster Inc.

Designed by Deirdre C. Amthor
Manufactured in the United States of America

1   3   5   7   9   10   8   6   4   2

Library of Congress Cataloging-in-Publication Data
Franklin, Joe.
Up late with Joe Franklin : stories of the greats, the late greats,
the near greats, the ingrates, the has-beens, and the never
weres / Joe Franklin, with R.J. Marx.
p.   cm.
1. Franklin, Joe.   2. Broadcasters—United States—
Biography.   3. Joe Franklin show.   I. Marx, R. J. (Richard J.)
II. Title.
PN1990.72.F7A3   1995
791.45'028'092—dc20
[B]   94-24310
                                       CIP

ISBN 0-02-540775-9

PHOTO CREDITS
All photos are courtesy of the *Joe Franklin Show*.
Al Naidoff: 17, 19, 20, 22, 23, 24, 25, 28, 29, 32, 33, 34, 37, 41
Alexander Kerry: 3, 6, 18, 21, 27, 39
Richard Sinclair Fraser: 14, 47, 48
Howard and Zausner: 2
Georges Zwirz: 15
Braun Fotos Inc.: 16
Irving Desfor: 35
Beryl Sokoloff: 42
Werner J. Kuhn: 43
David Allen: 51
Don Chokel: 31

To Kate Smith, Martin Block, and Eddie Cantor,
who believed in me from the start.

*I also dedicate this book to those who caused it to be: You kind
people who stop me on the street every day—every hour—doctors, scholars, astrophysicists, gypsy cab drivers—to tell me you
grew up with me; you shared thousands of nights with us, and
from my program you learned nostalgia, Americana, the culture
of show business (both high and low), and current events. (After
all, I did interview five Presidents of the United States.)*

*For me, hearing all of that from you is the real reward, and if
I ever have the good fortune to bump into you strolling down on
Broadway, please stop me, shake my hand, and tell me about
your favorite episode of the* Joe Franklin Show.

Acknowledgments

A special thanks to my longtime producer Richie Ornstein and my director Bob Diamond for their many years as a part of my life. I hope they will continue to be a part of my life in the years to come.

The authors would like to thank the following people for their cooperation and assistance:

Peter Abel
Al Adamson
Roger d'Anfrasio
"Wildman" Jack Armstrong
Walter Banks
Mark Birnbaum
Michael Block
Jonathan Braun
Irving Cahn
Dennis Carey/the Red Blazer,
   Too
Lisa Carroll
Leon Charney
Pamela Chiti
Chip Deffaa
John De Maria
Hans Dudelheim
Howard Extract
Leonard Finger
GiGi Foge
Art Ford
Brad Franklin
Lois Franklin
John Gambling
Brian Gari
Ed Gollin
Elan Golomb, Ph.D.
Grandma Rosie
Mimi Gutter

Kamarr the Magician
Katonah Public Library and
   Westchester Library System
Morris Katz
Barbara Laurence
Carol Lee
Lincoln Center Library of the
   Performing Arts
Charles Linton
Ronnie Littell
Eve Marx
Jamie Masada, the Laugh
   Factory
Gary Paperman
Michael Pollio
Tommy Ritacco
Sophia Orculas Robbins
Dick Roffman
Alan Rothenberg
Ed Sachs
Phil St. James
John Sanders
Richard Selkowitz
Sam Sherman
Ron Simon/Museum of Televi-
   sion & Radio
Gary Stevens
Hal Stone

And our special gratitude to editor Carlo DeVito, who conceived the project and whose input helped us immeasurably along the way.

Joe Franklin and R. J. Marx

Contents

Acknowledgments	7
Prologue	11

PART I: The Young Wreck with the Old Records

Radio Days	17
Youth	66

PART II: The Golden Age of Television

WABC	83
Women	118

PART III: The Joe Franklin Show

Life in Times Square	141
Intermission: The Joe Franklin Guide to Phone Etiquette	156
The Mets, the *Million Dollar Movie*, and Joe Franklin	159
A Typical Joe Franklin Show, 1977	171
It Ain't Just Paint	173

PART IV: The Great Joe Franklin

Family, Friends, and Enemies   205
A Night at WOR-AM   217
Lord of Hosts   222
Reflections on Collections   239
Where Am I Now?   244
A Joe Franklin Chronology   253

Index   257

PROLOGUE

You have to love Joe Franklin.

—Howard Stern

The press has been very kind to me over the years. To them, I'm huggable, lovable, kissable. They've helped keep me on the air, to preserve my image as wholesome, family entertainment, with an occasional devilish spin. I've seen talk shows go from class to crass. I've seen the Lettermans battling it out with the Lenos, the Cavetts against the Carsons, and before that, the Jack Paars and the Steve Allens. Who could be more harmless than Joe Franklin? Everybody said, Ah, Joe's on from midnight to four in the morning. Who's watching? Who's listening? Meanwhile, today I have no debts, I've just begun my career, I'm still going strong, with the highest-ranked radio show in its time slot, with a second show heard twenty-eight times a week in the world's largest radio market, I'm a regular guest on dozens of television shows, the founder and head of the largest collection of memorabilia and nostalgia in the world. Every third phone call I receive is an assignment I cannot or do not care to accept. As Jack Benny said, "The measure of your success is not what you accept; it's what you can turn down." If anybody ever personified the Frank Sinatra song "My Way," it's me. Nobody ever told me what to do. I never had a boss. I feel sorry for people; they get ulcers all the time because the boss smiles at them crooked, or does *not* smile at them at all.

When comedian Billy Crystal—or anyone—does a spoof on me, they're doing a spoof on a spoof. Right now, even though I'm being serious, it's tongue-in-cheek. I have to confess, I don't know who or what is the real me. Even my audience is eclectic. I'm greeted as enthusiastically in colleges and universities as I am in geriatric wards. I'm as close to Joey Ramone as I am to Bob Hope. I don't even know if there is a real me, a real "Joe Franklin." A psychologist friend of mine suggested this feeling might be a kind of denial, a defense mechanism. Could be. But as far as I know, I have no angst, no pain. I envy nobody. I've been double-crossed and triple-crossed and deceived. I'm an easy mark, but I have no nasty streak in me. I've got no vindictiveness, no revenge, no rage. I've been hurt, lied to, and deceived by the very best in the world, but I'm still content. I have an old recording at home called "I'd Rather Be a Lobster Than the Wise Guy." In the old days the word "lobster" meant sucker. And it's true. I *would* rather be the lobster than the wise guy.

It all evens out. Out of the five or six really cruel write-ups I've gotten from the press, the five people who were really vicious to me, evil, four of them never came back to life. They disappeared.

I used to have a man who would call me with a very rough voice. He sounded like a very good imitation of Marlon Brando in *The Godfather*. After I got one of these scathing, brutal reviews, he would call me and say he was "gonna take care of that guy, right, take care of that guy." He felt they were writing stupid things about me, nasty things about my guests, how I conducted myself, very negative things.

When the first journalist stopped writing and I asked around about him, an editor mentioned, "He isn't working at this paper anymore." When the second one who was busting my balls stopped writing, I asked, "What happened?" I got the answer. "He isn't working at this paper anymore, and no one knows where he is." I thought, That's too bad, and that's it. By the fourth time, I began to put it all together. I found out later, through some of my well-connected sources, that this gentleman had taken upon himself to be my defender. I had never met him, but he apparently had ways of persuading said detractors to cool it. He was my protector, my benefactor.

Remember when they were messing with Wayne Newton how things ended? Wayne had to go out there on his own, a lone man, and confront the people who were making fun of him. I've never had to do that. I have people calling me constantly who want to do me favors, who sometimes don't even ask; they go ahead and do them. They just eliminate a problem sometimes, anything that may surface. I've got people who like me and don't want to see people mess with me.

With that thought in mind, I hope you enjoy the book . . . *or else!*

☆

PART I
The Young Wreck with the Old Records

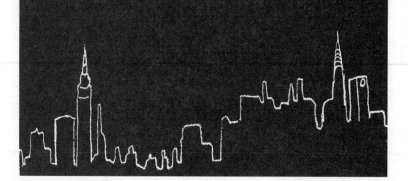

Radio Days

Another disk jockey of whom much is expected is 23 year old Joe Franklin . . .
— *New York World-Telegram*

When I started in radio, I wanted to start at the top. I wrote letters to Eddie Cantor, Kate Smith, Jack Benny, Fred Allen, all the greats of the time, and haunted their offices. At that time, 1945, CBS Radio was at 485 Madison; NBC was at "30 Rock" (Rockefeller Plaza), where it remains today; and WNEW was over at 501 Madison. These places were the mecca of the generation's wanna-bes, all of the radio stars blissfully unaware of the upheaval that television would bring in the next five years.

My first big thrill was when I sold a joke that I had probably heard in a burlesque house to the *Eddie Cantor Show*, and then a few more jokes. But those were few and far between. I wanted to be in the studios, making it happen, behind the mike, brightening the lives of the faceless millions.

When Ted Collins, Kate Smith's manager, wrote me back with a letter of encouragement, I went to visit him at his office at 1619 Broadway. I was in the office with him, just talking—I guess I was a pest—but at nineteen years old, he hired me to write the show called the *Kate Smith Hour*. He hired me! The *Kate Smith*

Hour, on Thursday nights between 8:00 and 9:00 P.M., was the most popular variety show in America, with guests like Clark Gable, Myrna Loy, Edward G. Robinson—all my childhood heroes.

I used to go to Kate Smith's house every day, and all I did was choose three records daily and write the intros. The job involved pulling out the music that was going to be played and writing two paragraphs of patter to go with the recording.

Ted Collins made me feel like a million bucks. I used to sit in his office, and his secretary would announce, "Mr. Collins, you're wanted on the phone," and he'd say, "Tell 'em to get lost, I'm talking to Joe Franklin." The phone would ring again, and the secretary would say to him, "It's General Marshall on the phone," and Collins would say, "Can't you see I'm talking to Joe Franklin?" It made me feel so important!

Many people thought Ted Collins was rough. But he was shrewd, and under his tutelage he made Kate Smith an international star. Ted Collins with Kate Smith was then what Colonel Parker later was with Elvis Presley. When she began in vaudeville in the late 1920s, she was heavyset, even as a teen, and she took a lot of ribbing for it. She played a chubby girl whose character's name was Tiny Little, and the rest of the cast was on her mercilessly. There were cracks like "What's eating her?" and "What's the matter, her boyfriend couldn't get both arms around her?" Georgie Jessel said at the time—much to his regret in later years—with her appearance, she'd never make it in show business. But Ted Collins didn't listen. He took over her career, and by 1932, now known as "the Songbird of the South," she was raking in $5,000 a week—this in the Great Depression. The phrase Songbird of the South became as famous as any title in the world. Kate Smith worshiped Ted Collins for his faith in her and admitted, "Without Ted, there would have been no Kate Smith— the Kate Smith the public has known for thirty years."

We had a lot of fun on the show. At one Kate Smith broadcast, I was watching in the wings, backstage. Kate Smith was standing on the stage behind the curtain, in front of an orchestra of forty, fifty, sixty men. In front of the curtain, her announcer, André Baruch, was engaged in a conversation and gestured with his hand, hitting the curtain—and Kate Smith behind it. Kate Smith was so astonished she squealed a high C and went up in the air higher than you can believe she could ever jump. When she came down, she tumbled, and all the musicians went down like dominoes with her! I never forgot that, one woman could knock the whole orchestra over. I guess she had never been goosed before.

I used to go to Kate Smith's house, where she sang for me privately. I can't tell you what a thrill that was. She used to sing on the radio to 60 million people and to me privately. I once met Irving Berlin at her house. Irving Berlin, who wrote "God Bless America" for her. He had written it twenty years before that but hadn't been satisfied with it. It took Kate Smith to convince him that the song was worthwhile. She was then *the* number one hit maker in all of radio, and she told me that no song ever caught on that phenomenally, that immediately. Berlin, incidentally, gave all the money he made from that song to the Boy Scouts, the Girl Scouts, and the war effort.

When a comedian referred to her as "the Songbird of the *Stout*," I was outraged. I was so in awe of her that I personally took umbrage and dashed off an angry letter to the comic. Roundabout, Ted Collins heard about the letter on her behalf and remembered me for it. I think he was about ready to write me into his will.

Ted Collins had an alleged romance with his star, but over the years he remained married to another woman. While not her lover, Ted Collins was most certainly her partner, not just an agent or manager. They split everything down the middle, fifty-fifty.

Not too many people liked Ted Collins. He refused to let Senator Robert A. Taft sing a duet of "God Bless America" with Kate Smith because he thought it would be used by the Republican politician for "publicity purposes." The usually hard-nosed, unemotional Taft was crestfallen. In another incident, the comedian on the *Kate Smith Show* was Henny Youngman. One week

☆

Henny wanted to take time off to make a picture in Hollywood. Considerately, Henny said, "Ted, I can get you a replacement for the week. He's a talented young comedian. I think you'll like him." Collins turned him down flat, refusing to let Henny take the time off to make the picture. By doing so, he missed out on introducing a brilliant young comic to the airwaves: Bob Hope.

But while he missed out on Bob Hope, he did introduce to the world Abbott and Costello, the Aldrich family, starring Ezra Stone, and many others. Ted Collins gave them a stage. He found new talent that he didn't have to spend too much money for, paying just a little more than a nightclub engagement. His main concern was that Kate was at her best when she sang. The purpose of the others was to give her a chance to rest. There was time for a change of costume, a stage wait, a chance for her to go to the john or get a glass of water. They were her seventh-inning stretch.

Later on, I kept in touch with Kate Smith and had her on my television show in 1963, 1964, and 1966. Toward the end she was confined to a wheelchair and was very sick. But both she and Ted Collins were tremendous influences. Ted Collins is the one who originated the line that was to be my credo for many years to come: "Sincerity's the key to success in show business. Once you've learned to fake that, you've got it made."

After the season ended for me with Kate Smith and Ted Collins, I got my first solo shot, a fifteen-minute program at WHOM radio, which was then managed by Frank White, later to become the president of CBS. The show was called *Vaudeville Echoes,* an old-time music show. It didn't pay anything, but I was behind the microphone professionally for the very first time. I was there for only four weeks when I met Martin Block at WNEW.

One day I had a date with Maureen McGinnis, a receptionist at the station. Who walked out into the lobby but Martin Block, the most famous disk jockey at that time. He said to me, "What're you doing up here, kid?"

I answered, "I'm waiting to have lunch with the receptionist."

☆

He said, "My record picker just got fired. Would you like the job? Select my records?"

I took the job.

In 1935, Martin Block was the voice of the first network hookup, during the Lindbergh kidnapping trial. That was the first time in history that the entire nation could simultaneously listen to one voice. Since broadcasters weren't allowed in the courtroom, he set up his broadcasting facilities in the men's room of the courthouse. Every few minutes he would get an update on the trial and broadcast it to the public. During the long court recesses, he played records, a tremendous innovation—until that point, the bands and singers had all been broadcast *live*. Along with Rush Hughes in St. Louis and Al Jarvis in Hollywood, Martin Block was to become one of the pioneering deejays. Walter Winchell was to coin the term "disk jockey," referring to Martin Block.

By the 1940s, he had become the voice of the *Chesterfield Supper Club,* featuring Perry Como. When I started working for him in 1945, he was host of WNEW's *Make-Believe Ballroom,* radio's most popular record show. Aired on Saturday mornings, Martin Block's countdown of the top thirty record hits in America was the major music event of the week. He also cowrote the show's classic theme song: "It's make-believe ballroom time / and free to everyone / It's no time to fret / Your dial is set for fun," which was recorded by Glenn Miller. Later, William B. Williams inherited the *Make-Believe Ballroom* and that theme song.

When Martin Block came to New York City from California in the 1930s, there were a lot of radio personalities. But he was the first to pretend that the big bands were live in the studio, in his make-believe ballroom. You would visualize, you would fantasize, chandeliers spinning around, lights, people gathering around the bandstand; he would paint a tremendous verbal picture. The great thing about Martin Block was that he did not ad-lib. All the critics wrote that he was the king of the ad-lib, but everything he said was written out. He had the knack of making it sound so spontaneous. And the power he had! One plug from Martin Block could make a singer's career, as in the case of Tony Bennett's first big hit, "Because of You," and Patti Page's "Tennessee Waltz." He cashed in on his success, becoming the world's first millionaire disk jockey. He wound up with millions—on a local station that had been nothing before he arrived. Salarywise, I think he gave me about $150 a week, which to me was gigantic money in those days.

Martin Block was the only man in town to be on two shows on two different stations at the same time. While the prerecorded *Make-Believe Ballroom* aired on WNEW, he rushed across town to broadcast the *Chesterfield Supper Club* on WNBC, leaving me in charge at WNEW.

During the day I pulled the records for the show. The process didn't take long. You know how I picked them? I closed my eyes. Martin Block said, "Go to the Harry James bin," "the Artie Shaw bin," "the Glenn Miller bin," and I would just reach in and hand him whatever I pulled out. I'd tell him what records I was playing, and he always said fine. There were no real charts in those days, so we ended up with lots of oddball selections.

After they were selected, he recorded the lead-ins for each song, one after the other. To record a show was no simple task. Since there were no tape recorders in those days, the voice and musical recordings were on what were called "transcriptions," big, round, glass-based records. Martin Block put his voice on a disk on one turntable, and then on a second turntable we placed the actual 78 rpm. You first heard Martin Block's voice saying, "Ladies and gentlemen, this is Martin Block, bla, bla, bla, here's the first record by Harry James," and as soon as his voice stopped, on the next turntable I segued to Harry James. I went back and forth like that, synchronizing the two machines as precisely as I could. We honed it to an art, and amazingly, there was never once a foul-up. Somehow the audience didn't seem to notice that he was on two shows at once, or they didn't care.

Martin Block liked my taste in music, erratic as it was, and followed me blind. Whatever I chose, he would play. He would play the exact same records that every other disk jockey would play, but the fact that he introduced the songs gave them a glow, a mood, a fragrance, a life of their own. At the end of the show, he would lean forward into the mike and say, "Good night to you and you and especially to *you*."

Martin Block was constantly being courted by the musical giants of the day, all eager for him to play their latest entries. This was the era of the big bands—Freddy Martin and Benny Goodman, Sammy Kaye, Harry James. Martin Block would say to me, "Joe, go into the lobby; Frank Sinatra is waiting out there. Give him a cup of coffee on the way in. Bring in Dinah Shore. Walk in Harry James." I was constantly in awe, but I learned how to deal with celebrities early on.

Martin Block was on twice a day, mornings and nights. And I was there morning and night, six days a week. In my downtime, I would answer his fan mail, go out and get him a sandwich, get his ulcer powder. Martin Block was the backbone of that station. Everyone else was just a fill-in.

I'll tell you one thing I did that he wouldn't have done by himself. When I found out that Al Jolson was in town, I got Al Jolson to be his guest. I reunited Jolson—in the studio—with a lady he had gone out with twenty-five years before. On the radio, Jolson exclaimed in his distinctive voice, "Brother Block and Brother Franklin, this lady was my girlfriend twenty-five years ago, and when I knew her she had very bad teeth. I spent five thousand dollars on fixing those teeth. I didn't mind the breakup, but I resented that she was laughing at me through my own teeth." Block fell over laughing.

Martin Block led the ratings in the whole city, even beating the network stations. Sponsors, of course, loved him. He could sell, as they say, an icebox to an eskimo. He could sell anything. The word for him was "unctuous." He made everything sound so mellifluous, so golden, persuasive. When I first knew him, he was in his early forties. Women adored him. His voice was so syrupy, even while selling tooth powder or refrigerators, I could hear female hearts throb. A challenge was thrown to him by an

☆

appliance dealer to see how many washing machines he could sell during a blizzard. Martin Block amazed the sponsor by going out on a live remote and persuading the listeners that this was one deal that wouldn't last. The washing machines sold out.

I learned everything at Martin Block's "voice steps." Not footsteps but *voice steps.* I studied his voice. How to talk on the radio. To sound natural. He had that knack of making you feel ashamed of yourself if you didn't buy the fur coat he was recommending; he had that great way of twisting it around so that if you didn't buy that fur coat, he pitied you—*pitied you.* He was the greatest commercial spieler that ever was. Great. If they didn't buy the stuff, he'd say, "Oh, do I feel sorry for you!"

Martin Block's show ran on WNEW from 1935 to about 1950, when he went to WABC, which doubled his salary. By that time I had my own shows, but I remained close to the man I considered my mentor. He made a brief foray into TV but was never comfortable with the medium. I believe he simply preferred radio. Like many radio personalities, he was stiff and uncomfortable in front of the cameras. For the last four years of his career, he returned to WOR-AM, where Bob Smith, his main executive producer at WNEW and one of the men who coined the term "rock and roll," had moved up in rank to become vice president. I did the tribute to Martin Block after he died during heart surgery. After the show, his wife called me, crying, telling me how beautiful she thought it was.

On the days when Martin Block was sick, he was replaced by a man named Maurice Hart, who had no fingers. Maurice Hart told me how it happened. He told me that he was cleaning his pants one time and put some cleaning fluid on them. He hung them out the window to dry, then shook them vigorously, before he realized what was happening. Can you visualize the scene? The pants exploded in his hands. Over the years he developed, from necessity, the talent of putting records on the turntable with his fists. Maurice Hart had a great voice, but he remained second to Martin Block.

The disk jockeys of the time—the announcers, the "platter

spinners"—were just regular guys with great speaking voices. A lot of them became famous later on. One man who became a famous television host later—I'm soul-searching whether or not to give the man's name, but I'd rather not; it would brutalize him—was one of the disk jockeys at WNEW. He was the staff announcer there. One time the employees at the station all collected money for him—I think his wife was sick or something—and I pitched in. Many years later I reminded him about that, and he got furious at me. He didn't want to think about that. He got really angry, way out of proportion, and started to scream at me. But that's what happens. "You never chipped in! I never took charity! They never passed the hat around for me!" But they did.

Martin Block grew to like me, and after a few months he said, "Joe, how would you like to have your own radio show?" I thought, He's got to be kidding. Sure enough, he got me a radio show. He talked to Ted Cott, the station manager, who would do anything to keep Martin happy. Martin Block's show went off at 7:30 P.M., and I did my own show, *Vaudeville Isn't Dead,* at 7:45 P.M.

Ted Cott was the big boss, the program manager. He had a son, and there was a contest around the studio to name him. I won the prize—with the name "Boy Cott." Ted Cott also had a program on WOR at the time, which he hosted, called *So You Think You Know Music.* I used to get him all his guests. He was the boss of WNEW, but oddly, the show aired on the WOR Mutual Network.

Ted Cott was kind of cocky and, like a few other station managers, had a reputation of being tight with the dollar. I loved the idea of doing a show, but there was money to take care of. I had to go to the bargaining table with him. He asked me, "Joe, what do you want to get paid?"

I said, "Mr. Cott, it's up to you."

He said, "Well, I'll give you double what you got paid when you were on WHOM."

My salary at WHOM had been zero. I was embarrassed to tell him the truth. I didn't want to say I wasn't getting paid, but I didn't want to make it too high, either, because I didn't want to bargain myself out of a job. So I said I got fifteen dollars a week. He said, "Okay, you'll get thirty bucks a night. If you get a commercial, we'll give you extra." So I was on for thirty bucks a night. And then, as young as I was, they immediately got a sponsor, and my fee went up to over $100 a night. I was soon on seven nights, so I was making a thousand, fifteen hundred bucks so fast I didn't know what it was all about.

Before I started my show, Martin Block half-jokingly warned me not to compete with him. He was the king disk jockey, and since he played all new records, big band, the equivalent of today's Top Forty, I thought I'd play old records. I already had a large collection of my childhood favorites and was constantly adding to it. I became obsessed, going all over the city buying old records of old-time singers and vaudevillians at junk shops for a nickel apiece. Then I'd bring them back to the station and play them that night. My squeaky voice hadn't filled out yet, but I would authoritatively announce, "Here's a record from 1921 by Eddie Cantor, it's worth five hundred dollars." When I went back to another store the next day for more records, I put down four nickels for four records. The dealer snapped, "Hey, come 'ere, kid."

"What do you mean, 'kid'?"

"I heard somebody on the radio last night saying these records were worth five hundred dollars apiece."

From then on, the records cost me a quarter.

Not very many people were collecting phonograph records in those days, and I turned it into a science. I hit every record store in town. Collecting became more than a hobby, it became almost an obsession. I wanted complete collections of the great vaudeville performers. I wanted records of all the greats, of Paul Whiteman, Bing Crosby, Bert Williams, dozens of others. In order to track down obscure disks, I used to go to the public library and request old phone directories from 1930. Then I'd scan the pages and compare which stores might still be in business. If a store was still around, I'd make the trip and ask the proprietor, "Can I go down to your basement and look at your old inventory?" He usually said sure, grateful to get rid of records that nobody wanted anymore. I'd buy whatever I found for next to nothing. I got those records in perfect mint condition. The acetate was glass; drop it and it would shatter. You couldn't look at them in except the shade, they were so shellacked. They were so shiny you could use them to shave.

With a wealth of material from my personal record collection, I found myself becoming a valuable commodity. I would carry a stack of disks from studio to studio, the old-time songs, Jolson, Rudy Vallee, Smith and Dale, Elsie Janis, Belle Baker, Sophie Tucker, Ben Bernie, Georgie Jessel, and Georgie Price—the list goes on and on. I was working for Martin Block on WNEW, and now I had my own show on WNEW called *Vaudeville Isn't Dead.* Then I got two more shows on WMCA called *Main Street Memories* and *Antique Record Shop.* I even took on another show in Paterson, New Jersey, for the fledgling station there, WPAT.

The reason I went to WPAT was because a man named Herman Bess, who had been the sales manager at WNEW, offered me virtually an open checkbook to go with him. Not only was I on the air three hours a day, he also made me program director. I was broadcasting on three stations at one time, WNEW, WPAT, and WMCA. Doing something nobody else was doing—playing old music. Listeners thought I must be forty, fifty, sixty years old. Even today, when someone asks my age and I tell them, they say, "Is that all?"

I was living out a fantasy, playing the records of the artists I loved, the vaudeville performers, singers, the music of the bygone days. There was an old-time singer who made more records than anybody else except Enrico Caruso. His name was Henry Burr. He was all but forgotten even then, in the 1940s. I ran across a Henry Burr record, and when I listened to his voice, it just did something to me, triggered emotions inside me.

☆

I was a fanatic of old songs and corny old tenors. Ballads like "Just a Girl That Men Forget," "I'm Sorry I Made You Cry," tearjerkers. They touched me, they gave me goose pimples, and they still do. I found that in some ways I felt closer to records and old songs than I did to real people. They were my escape. Most nights I go home, even now, and play my old 78s, songs like "I Wish I Had My Old Gal Back Again," "I Wonder Where My Baby Is Tonight," from the 1920s. "Am I Wasting My Time on You?" "Are You Lonesome Tonight?" Old, old songs. I've analyzed it over time. In some ways, I've concluded, the songs give me support. They make me feel safe, secure. Whatever else is going on around me, no matter how out of control the world is becoming, these old songs remain a constant. Those voices from the distant past remain alive, more than just memories. They were a part of my psyche, and this is what I brought—and still bring—to my radio audience.

Old music was, at the time, a totally radical concept. When I began with this nostalgia kick, nostalgia, nostalgia, people told me I was crazy! People told me you've got to stay with *now, now, now*, or the future. This was postwar America, 1946, when everyone presumably wanted to forget their pasts and forge ahead to the future, when babies were booming, suburbs were erupting over the landscape, when the public's mind was fixed on "progress." They told me nobody cares about the past. That was for scholars, the universities, not the public. I felt, They brought it to the elite, I would bring it to the masses. I would bring a human quality to it, while the others were starchy about it. They sniffed at me. "He's a kid, what the hell does he know about memory lane?" Yet today nostalgia, collectibles, are a billion-dollar culture, an untapped trillion-dollar industry. I pioneered nostalgia, and if I have any understandable pride, I think it's the fact that I was the first one to push it.

To show you how far we've come, at the time I started playing the music of the past, the word *nostalgia* itself meant "homesickness." I was frequently criticized by English teachers and grammarians who would write me, "Joe, you can't apply nostalgia to show business. Nostalgia means homesickness. Look in the dictionary, nostalgia means yearning for home, as in a homesick soldier. But nothing to do with Al Jolson, Kate Smith, or Rudy Vallee." People thought I meant *neuralgia.* But I stuck with it, and the public responded.

As for my style over the airwaves, despite the exposure, it took some time before I hit my stride. I felt as if I were just announcing until one day I just felt good. What triggered it was a chat I'd had a week before with a radio announcer named Paul Douglas, who became a big movie star later on. He said, "Joe, when you're talking on the air, don't think of a lot of people, think of one person. Think of your mother, think of your grandmother." Martin Block never even told me those words. That stayed with me, and I never lost that technique of staying very intimate, very cozy with the audience.

I was advised that in order to foster my budding career I should hire a press agent. In the late 1940s, the press wielded a power unheard of today. People today forget the astounding number of newspapers and columnists and the clout they wielded. They were the ones who indicated thumbs up or thumbs down, who could make or break a rising star, who could truly see to it that you never did "eat lunch in this town" again. People cowered in their wake. But if you played them right, you had it made. At that time, a nod from one of the top columnists—a Winchell of the *Mirror;* an Ed Sullivan, who then had a column in the *Daily Mirror;* a Nick Kenny; Danton Walker of the *Daily News;* Louis Sobol of the *Journal-American;* Sid White in *Radio Daily;* or one of many others in a city of a dozen dailies—was essential. I realized early on that cultivating them was as important as honing my skills behind the microphone. So I hired a man named Art Franklin—no relation—to help me learn the ropes.

I paid him the lordly sum of $1,000, and he carried me for six months. He was the PR man for Kate Smith and Jack Barry, the game show host who later got involved with the quiz-show scandals. He would give tips to the columnists, who would, if they

☆

deemed fit, mention my name and put a plug in their columns like, "Arthur Murray instructress Joan Denny and J. Franklin Have That Old Feeling . . ." I didn't even know Joan Denny, had never set foot in an Arthur Murray dance studio, and don't believe I have ever had "that old feeling" before or since. Or, in another column: "What singer waxes amorous for platter spinner Joe Franklin?" I wanted to know myself. At Art Franklin's behest, the literary lions of Broadway would immortalize my "quips," chestnuts like "Disk spinner J. Franklin says, 'Why do they call them First Nighters when more often they're First *Mourners*?'"

Among my closest friends was Nick Kenny, the radio-TV critic of the *Daily Mirror*. Winchell was on page 10, and Nick Kenny was toward the back. Nick Kenny, called the "Old Sailor," was tremendously popular. He was also referred to as "Needlenose Nick" because of his long, hooklike nose. I've got a photograph somewhere of him posing with Jimmy Durante. Nick Kenny's got the longer nose.

Nick was a very successful songwriter and poet. His poems were generally based on the exploits of his six-year-old daughter Patti; he called them "the Patti Poems." They contained lines like "Snow is God's dandruff." He wrote songs that were gigantically big, like "Love Letters in the Sand," which Pat Boone revived; he wrote "There's a Gold Mine in the Sky," "Cathedral in the Pines," big, big songs in their day. Getting a mention in his column was a reciprocal arrangement. If I played his songs on my radio show, he would give me a plug in his column. It was a matter of quid pro quo. It was a "recip."

He had a box in his column called "Today's Birthdays," a listing of celebrity birthdates. Nick Kenny liked me so much that one year he had my name in his birthday box four times. That's love, huh? Nick said about me to my friend the radio host–press agent Irving Cahn, "That's a smart kid, a smart kid. He has a *Yiddishe kop*."

Columnist Jack O'Brian of the *New York Journal-American* was another one of my early boosters. He took a liking to me and his constant write-ups brought me recognition I probably wouldn't have known. "Franklin Show Great—Gleason Show Terrible!"

The columnists could make you or break you. Ed Sullivan was second only to Walter Winchell in power and influence. And affluence. Later, he went on TV with the *Ed Sullivan Show,* but he had started as a sportswriter, and when I first met him, he was a very big columnist, very important, for the *Daily News.*

I met Ed Sullivan one time in my barbershop on West Fifty-seventh Street. He was getting a trim alongside me. When the haircut was done, he started to walk away, down the one flight of stairs to the street. So Roger, the barber, chased him. "The money, Mr. Sullivan! The money!"

Sullivan was offended. He turned to Roger and glowered, "Don't you know I'm Ed Sullivan!" I always liked Oscar Levant's line, "Ed Sullivan will last as long as other people have talent."

But nobody was as powerful as Walter Winchell. I used to say on my early radio show that when he was in vaudeville, in a sketch called "Gus Edwards' Kid Kabaret," with Eddie Cantor, Georgie Jessel, and Georgie Price, he was just tall enough to peek into a keyhole. And he never forgot how to peek into one. That's how he became the number one gossip columnist in history. I was shocked when I answered the phone one day and it was him. He told me he got a kick out of the story. I was very flattered that he knew I existed, that he deemed me significant enough to call.

You never wanted to cross Winchell! If a press agent ever sent him an item that was incorrect and it came to his attention, he would never deal with that individual again, he'd ban him, he'd send him into exile. Misinformation was called a "wrong-o." If a press agent was banned from Winchell for six months, it meant he was in deep trouble, because Winchell was the cash cow, the money machine for press agents. Without Winchell on their side, they couldn't retain their clients.

Every time I was in Winchell's column I would get calls to do more radio, to do more banquets. Just as Nick Kenny would take

☆

his "recips" out in song plugging, Winchell had his price as well. He wanted items for his column. If a press agent gave Winchell six strong items about famous people, he'd give him a payoff, an "orchid of praise." He could single-handedly turn a flop into a hit, as he did with the original *Hellzapoppin* in 1938. The drama critics panned it, so Winchell took it under his wing, and it played Broadway for years. He made multimillionaires out of Olsen and Johnson, because he pounded their show every day on his radio show and in the column. "I knew I was a big shot," Winchell once said, "when people who called me a son of a bitch behind my back began asking me for favors."

Winchell had a lot of enemies. That's an understatement, because he broke the careers of many, many performers. "I don't know why he's allowed to live," said the actress Ethel Barrymore. He was always fearful that someone might try to exact revenge. One night at the studio I saw him coming out of the building. I said effusively, "Hello, Mr. Winchell!" When I moved forward and raised my hand, he fell back, cowering against the wall. I guess it was just an automatic reflex.

I never forgot that—how, just when I raised my hand in a friendly salutation, in a cordial greeting, he went back against the wall. Then he recovered and said, "Oh, how are you, Joe." This was a man with such a high opinion of himself that he called other columnists his "wastebaskets."

In later years his power completely dwindled. In the 1960s I ran into him at a banquet for Allen and Rossi, the comedy team. I was on the dais, and I looked in the corner. Who's sitting there alone in the back of the room? Walter Winchell. The onetime most powerful man of the press, the dragon himself, sitting there alone because he didn't have a column anymore, or a TV or radio show. I couldn't believe it. He just sat there with a red face. At that point he was probably happy just to be invited and remembered. But only ten or fifteen years before that, he had been the most influential man in the media. He was the godfather of modern-day journalism, and now he was utterly neglected.

Art Franklin was in with them all—Winchell, Sullivan, Kenny,

★

the others. He also helped me to get profiled in national magazines like *Varsity* and *Coronet,* which played up my youth and created myths about me that still survive. Once the press gets hold of a story, they cling to it for years to come. Most performers think, Why bother to correct it? Myth becomes reality at the hand of creative publicists.

Art Franklin gave me a whole biography, none of which was true, but it made great copy. Art Franklin knew no bounds in stretching the tall tale. He told the press that I used to tell my classmates that Ben Franklin High School "was named after one of his least important relatives." In truth, Joe Fortgang (me) became Joe Franklin. The story of my meeting with George M. Cohan on a park bench was probably the tallest tale. It was printed time and again for forty years, telling all the world how I started my record collection in 1938 when I was wandering through Central Park at the age of twelve trying to dig up material for my school newspaper and I saw the songwriter George M. Cohan sitting on a park bench, feeding the pigeons. According to the apocrypha, Cohan and I struck up a conversation, and the legendary songwriter invited me up to his apartment, where he and his wife fed me a multicourse meal. Before I left, he let me select one item from his closet of souvenirs, and I chose a record hidden in the back called "Life's a Funny Proposition After All," from 1905. Unable to find something suitable to autograph it with, he at last settled on some white shoe polish. That cherished memento supposedly inaugurated my career of collectibles. (I actually did meet George M. Cohan once. I saw him in a movie theater about two years before he died.) But from that day on, so it goes, I took on after-school work and spent all my earnings on records by the vaudevillians.

None of it is true, although, as a teenager, I did actually meet an elegant, aristocratic woman whose name was Ethel Levey, George M. Cohan's first wife. She had been a superstar in her heyday. As an entertainer, a Broadway star. She, in turn, introduced me to a man who had been a friend of hers, the man who succeeded Enrico Caruso at the Met, Richard Martino. His real

☆

name was Richard Martin, but his name had to be Italian to be recognized at the Met.

Columnist Earl Wilson once wrote, "The participants of show business are rumpots, nymphomaniacs, prostitutes, fakes, liars, cheats, pimps, hopheads, forgers, sodomists, slobs, absconders—but halt. I understate it horribly." With my newfound success, I did find myself the prey of one or two scam artists. One of the slickest teams was called Fine and Nelson.

They saw that my show *Main Street Memories* was successful and came up with the notion of syndicating it nationally. I thought that was a great idea, so I was ready to listen to whatever they had to offer. Jack Fine told me they needed a pilot to sell the show on the road, station to station, on a syndication basis. To do so, he needed expense money, $1,500, which was a lot in those days. But, he assured me, the rewards would pay me back tenfold, no, hundredfold, if not more. So I shelled out the cash and said, "Call me from the road." I waited for his call. And waited. And waited. Then one day I met him in the bank. He never went anywhere. I'm very gullible, for I do things in a hurry, I sign contracts in a hurry, I sign affidavits, I sign testimony for people who are going into court. I'll sign anything, just to get rid of people. Frank Sinatra was a very close friend of mine; he has been on my show maybe ten times. He said to me that when he started out he was signed "exclusively" to three different bands. He told me, "Hearts and contracts were meant to be broken."

But while I made my mistakes, it was through the efforts of Art Franklin and the attention of people like Nick Kenny, Walter Winchell, Jack O'Brian, and others that I got the opportunity to work with my third major radio mentor, after Ted Collins and Martin Block, Paul "Pops" Whiteman.

Paul Whiteman, a rotund, mustachioed violinist turned bandleader, was the man who brought the term "jazz" into the mainstream of our lexicon. Paul Whiteman had a show on the "Blue

★

Network." The Blue Network was then a divested arm of NBC, which at that time was owned by Ernest J. Noble, the man who invented the Life Saver. As a result, the Blue Network was occasionally referred to as "the Life Saver Network," but in a few years, it would become far better known to the world as ABC.

Paul Whiteman's deejay show on a network was groundbreaking at that time. Paul Whiteman, the *bandleader*, was playing *records* on a network. Even Martin Block played records only on local stations, not over the networks. Nobody on network radio had ever used recorded music. Up to that point, the networks had prided themselves on being "live," but Whiteman's show changed all that. After a trial run called *Borden's Musical Review*, Whiteman convinced the networks that a national deejay show could make it. For thirty-nine weeks I pulled the records for the *Paul Whiteman Club*, the first coast-to-coast disk-jockey show. Broadcast over 228 stations from 3:30 to 4:30 P.M., the *Paul Whiteman Club* garnered the largest share of advertising revenue in the history of radio, nearly $6 million for the year.

Paul dubbed me "Little Joe, the Young Wreck with the Old Records," which stuck with the press as a handy label. Along with selecting records from his extensive library, I would bring recordings from my own collection. Paul looked to me to search out one or two unusual items for each show. For the opening broadcast, Paul's eyes lit up when I brought in Eddie Cantor's "That's the Kind of a Baby for Me."

It's a misnomer that they called him the "King of Jazz." He didn't really play jazz in the Louis Armstrong–Dizzy Gillespie sense. But he played damn good swing, show music, and the best of what you might call "society music." His greatest musical contribution was to bring improvisation into a cultured setting, to take musicians out of the honky-tonks and dives into the concert halls and nightclubs. He paid the highest salaries of any bandleader; that's how he kept such good talent. He discovered—I hate to use that word, but he can rightly claim to have discovered Bing Crosby, Tommy Dorsey, Jimmy Dorsey, Jack

Teagarden, Morton Downey, Sr., Johnny Mercer, Hoagy Carmichael, Mildred Bailey—the list of his protégés and discoveries is enormous.

Paul Whiteman was often in need of being hot coffeed, and I was usually the one to retrieve the beverage. At one time, his drinking exploits were notorious. Paul and his trumpeter, Henry Busse, drank a case of champagne every night for nineteen straight nights. Another time, Paul set a record by drinking a hundred bottles of beer in a single sitting. Though he was good-natured most of the time, his musicians held him in awe. His secretary, Dorothy Ross, used to tremble in front of him. Mike Pignatore, his banjo player, was hunchbacked, a dwarf, and used to take some wicked abuse from Paul. When he played at the Capitol Theatre, my job was to stand outside his dressing room while he was inside with a famous starlet, Marilyn Maxwell. He was "rehearsing" the next scene. I'm sure that's all they were doing. I'd stand there just to make sure nobody would walk in and interrupt their reading.

But he was the king. The King of Jazz. A big man, a very important man, and it's a tragedy that you can't find his recordings today. Paul came on my TV show in later years many times; we remained very friendly, and I kept in touch with him and his wife, Margaret Livingston, at their farm in Lambertville, New Jersey. Sadly, his drinking remained a problem but was more sporadic. He would lay off for several months; then something would set him off, and he would go on a binge. I went out to his farm many times, every Saturday for dinner. They served beautiful food, wonderful lamb stew, just nice country dining. He always put his arms around me and greeted me with "Little Joe, little Joe, my little Joe."

During my run with Paul Whiteman came one of my career's biggest breaks: a bad review. No, not for me but for one of my longtime idols, Eddie Cantor. Eddie Cantor created a radio show called *Ask Eddie Cantor* in the late 1940s, a record program. The show was reviewed in *Billboard*. The review was somewhat scathing in tone, concluding that "it's doubtful that the average listener could stay with it for a half hour." But there was a silver lining in this review, at least for me. The reviewer, Joe Martin, commented, "Only four recordings were used to liven up the proceedings. If there is a problem in obtaining enough old disks, then someone involved in the show had better latch on to Joe Franklin, whose collection of old recordings have made fine local shows around New York for a long time." To my delight, Eddie heeded the call, and I finally got a chance to work head-to-head, mano a mano, with the man I'd worshipped as a show business idol since my youth.

I loved him, he was so magnetic to me. I've often wondered why Cantor meant so much to me. He was a singer, but he was not really a singer. He was a dancer, but you couldn't characterize him as one. He acted in many movies and plays, but you wouldn't refer to him as an actor per se. He was a total performer, and that's why I think I gravitated toward him. He started in show business in vaudeville, with Gus Edwards' Kid Kabaret. The other members of the group included Walter Winchell, Georgie Jessel, and later, Groucho Marx, Ray Bolger, Eleanor Powell, and dozens of others. Among the best known of his many, many hit songs were "If You Knew Susie (Like I Know Susie)" and "Yes Sir, That's My Baby." He wrote the theme song for the Merry Melodies cartoon show, which you can still hear on the Cartoon Network about a hundred times a day. In 1920, Brunswick signed Eddie Cantor to a five-year recording contract at a salary of $220,000 a year, putting him in the top income brackets with Caruso, Galli-Curci, and the Irish tenor John Mc-Cormack.

A great vaudeville performer, Eddie Cantor was struck hard by the stock market crash. He was virtually wiped out, selling most of his real estate and assets at fire-sale prices. But he recovered from the financial blow, and by the fall season of 1931, he was on the radio airwaves with *The Chase & Sanborn Hour*, which ran on NBC Sunday nights until 1934. It became the biggest show of the early 1930s. Cantor introduced to radio the studio audience, a radical departure from the days of the 1920s, when audiences had been either forbidden from attending the shows or told to remain completely silent during the broadcast. Cantor played cheerleader to the crowd, rousing them to fever pitch with his comic antics.

Eddie Cantor's show stayed in the Top Ten for the entire decade, while he split his radio career by appearing in top-grossing films like *Whoopee, Kid Millions, The Kid from Spain,* and *Roman Scandals.* In later days, he was to introduce great performers to the world, among them Dinah Shore, the singer Eddie Fisher, and the late, great Sammy Davis, Jr., who was a child at the time performing with the Will Mastin Trio.

When Eddie Cantor was appearing at the Loew's State Theatre, he broke all attendance records. He was on the same bill as *It's a Wonderful Life.* He did seven or eight performances a day, between showings. Between the performances there were people lined up in double file for several blocks, and while the movie was playing, before his next show, he would go out on the street and serve them hot coffee while they were waiting. It was just amazing how he mingled with the public. Sometimes he'd take a seat in the box office with the ticket taker, selling tickets, to show how close he was with the fans.

Yet I had a reporter here recently from *The Wall Street Journal,* and we were talking about my favorite stars, and when I mentioned Eddie Cantor, he said, "Who?" He had never heard of him. He was twenty-six years old, a very sharp man. He asked brilliant questions. But it made me realize it's a different generation today.

I just worshiped Eddie Cantor. I used to love his radio shows. He was on at 9:00 P.M. for his east coast show, then at midnight for his broadcast to the West Coast. To me he was very handsome, virile, dynamic. Those shows became a permanent part of my own personal memory lane. I vividly recall going with my father to the NBC building at 30 Rockefeller Plaza. We'd go up to the eighth floor; the big Studio 8H. There would be hundreds of people waiting outside the studio with tickets in their hands, very proud and happy, very, very lucky to have those tickets, maybe twelve hundred to fourteen hundred people lined up in the hallway facing the entrance to the studio.

Eddie Cantor would stroll into the studio about a half hour before airtime, scan the multitude and scratch his brow, moaning, "Look at all these people! Oh, I gotta get more money! These people all came to see me, I gotta get more money!" He was so friendly and warm and nontheatrical. He mingled with everyone, moving through the line. He'd say, "Excuse me," and it was like parting the Red Sea. The audience was so excited to see the star of the show in their midst.

In the radio studio, the milieu, the ambience, was thrilling. To know that we were seated and that Eddie Cantor and Harry Von Zell and Bert Gordon—"the Mad Russian"—and Dinah Shore and guests like Cary Grant were onstage and were broadcasting to 30, 40, 60 million people! And I was there! Many times, in order to get laughs, Eddie would drop his pants, wave his arms, do something really silly. There was something about radio that just appealed to me; it was magical. Eddie Cantor epitomized that.

There was always a warm-up man who came out about ten minutes before the show and did jokes, then told the audience how important it was to have a good time, to let it all hang out, be loose, be outrageous. An applause sign would light up, and sometimes cue cards would tell us to "LAUGH!"

Eddie always opened up with a peppy, snappy song. Later in the show, the announcer, Harry Von Zell, would make an announcement, and Eddie Cantor would run behind him and look over his shoulder at the script, roll his eyes, and say, "Does it really say that?"

Eddie was known for his philanthropy, his willingness to perform two or three benefits a night. But he had a hard side, too. One time I saw a director on the radio show criticize something Eddie did at the rehearsal. So Eddie took him aside and said, "Listen, don't you tell me what to do. I've got two million dollars in the bank." You know what the man did? He went out and printed a phony bankbook. For two million dollars and *one cent*.

★

He had the gall to bring it in and show it to Eddie the next day. Whattya think Eddie did? Fired him.

Possibly my greatest thrill of all time, and I'm talking about my entire career, was producing the Eddie Cantor Show at Carnegie Hall, walking with him to the stage door, leading him onto the stage. All the money went to "the One World" foundation, and tickets for the benefit performance sold for up to $100 a ticket—the equivalent of $1,000 today. And every seat was sold out! In fact, it was *oversold,* and about three hundred people ended up sitting on the stage itself. Cantor would say to them, "I know you can only see my back, and you paid ten dollars to sit here. So here's a dollar for you, a dollar for you, a dollar for you . . ." He actually passed out dollar bills.

When I was going into the theater that night, I saw an old, old man talking to Eddie: "Mr. Cantor, I've been a fan of yours for many years, and I must see your show tonight. I must see it, if I don't see it—"

Eddie said, "I'm sorry, I don't have any seats for you."

So he said, "Well, then, do you have seats for Sonja Henie at Madison Square Garden?"

Then there was another man among the people waiting. An old man. He pushed his way through the crowd up to Eddie Cantor, who was about sixty years old at the time, and called out, "Mr. Cantor, I've been a fan of yours since I was a little kid."

Mr. Cantor said, "Yeah? And how old are you?"

"Ninety."

It was a one-man show, a huge, blockbuster, flag-waving success. They said it was the best show of the whole year. Ward Morehouse wrote a review that I couldn't have paid for:

It might even be the best play of the season. Cantor, performing before a huge audience at Carnegie Hall, with the overflow customers almost surrounding him on the stage, went all the way back to the days of his youth at Henry Street and came on through the years as he offered his very special bill. . . . He brought forth laughter and applause,

☆

contented sighs and chuckles. He turned back the clock and sang the old songs and talked of the great moments and the great people of his theatre career. He pranced and he danced; he wiggled and he squirmed; he jumped up and down, swung his arms, spread his fingers, rolled his eyes— and delighted a multitude. He paid his tributes to some theatre stars of today and yesterday, to Al Jolson and George Jessel, to Irving Berlin and Ted Lewis, and to Will Rogers, W. C. Fields, Marilyn Miller, Bert Williams, Gus Kahn and Walter Donaldson, George M. Cohan and the Great Ziegfeld. . . . Eddie Cantor's show is expertly organized; he is in command all the way. I wish he would bring it into a Broadway playhouse for a limited engagement. He would sell out.

Many years later, Steve Allen remarked that Eddie Cantor wasn't really that funny. When they asked Eddie what they thought of Steve's remark, he said, "Gee, if Steve said it, maybe I should give my money back. I've gotten paid a lot of money to be funny, but if he says I'm not, I owe a lot of people."

It looked as though I might have a budding career as an impresario. The success of the Eddie Cantor Carnegie Hall show led to other offers. They wanted to play the show on Broadway but he didn't want to work that hard.

One live show I jumped to host was the Al Jolson Remembrance Night. When I talk about my great idols, I guess my fans are aware that Jolson and Cantor are the top one and two. In the late 1930s and early 1940s, Al Jolson's career was in a severe downswing. After the success of *The Jazz Singer* and early films like *The Singing Fool* in 1932, he found himself unable to reproduce his success on film. More significantly, contemporary audiences viewed him as a relic, an object from the past. A line passed around the circuit: "Jolson couldn't get booked at a benefit."

But all that changed with the release of *The Jolson Story* in

1946, with Larry Parks. I had the honor of being asked by Columbia Pictures to help with the musical selections. I didn't get any money for it. I did it because I was a fanatic Jolson fan.

The movie won an Oscar for its score and single-handedly revived Joley's flagging career. To show you how far it had fallen, Jolson was attending a screening of the film, gauging audience reaction. The audience cheered wildly as the curtain lowered; it was an unmitigated smash. Jolson was beaming with pride until he heard one lady say to another, "It's too bad Jolson couldn't be alive to see this."

Jolson called me whenever he was in New York, and he and I would sit and talk about old records. He would come into the studio when I was with Martin Block. My own personal favorite from his collection was called "Movin' Man, Don't Take My Baby Grand," about a moving man who empties out an apartment after somebody didn't pay the rent. "You can take my wife, my whiskey, but don't take my baby grand . . ." As the song came to an end, he called out, "Brother Franklin! Break that record!"

I never saw Jolson at the height of his powers. I wish I could have. He was probably the only entertainer in the world who, when he was starring in a Broadway show, which was most of his career, about twenty minutes into the show, would say to the other actors and performers, "Go home." The vehicle didn't matter, nobody ever came to see the play, they came to see him. He would just sing for the audience for two hours. That was a thrill. I don't think anybody in the world has ever had that kind of power; the vehicle didn't matter. The play's the thing, but in his case, the play was *not* the thing. The thing was *him*.

Jolson never had money problems. When someone asked Groucho Marx what he thought Jolson would do about television, Groucho answered, "He'll probably buy the whole thing and give it to his wife for Christmas." Jolson would have been sensational on TV, but he died in 1950, just about a month before he was supposed to make his TV debut. His style would've been electric, dynamic. "On the nights when everything is right,"

★

wrote a critic, "Jolson is driven by a power beyond himself." But Jolson never had a chance to prove himself.

One year later, in 1951, I produced the Al Jolson Remembrance Night at Carnegie Hall. I ran big ads, listing the multitude of stellar talent I was sure would attend. I made the mistake of listing one performer without clearing it first. I headlined Milton Berle, the number one star of TV at the time, "Mr. Tuesday Night," on the bill. Probably a rash act, but I was certain he would attend to honor the memory of Jolson. Unfortunately, I was wrong. Milton wasn't coming, and I didn't have any permission to use his name. He didn't show, he threatened me, and he sent his brother to read me the riot act. Later on, of course, we became very close friends, but at the time, it was very embarrassing.

Even without Berle, Al Jolson Remembrance Night was a special evening. Eddie Fisher, who was then the hottest singer around, hotter than Sinatra at the time, sang his current number one hits. Jimmy Durante came. Al Jolson's young widow, Erle Chennault Galbraith Jolson, flew in from the coast, and during the intermission her fur coat was stolen. She was up in the box, and she put the coat over the railing. When she came back from intermission, the coat was gone. It was a $10,000 coat.

Ruby Keeler, Al Jolson's second wife, had totally distanced herself from the memory of her legendary husband. She was very bitter after their divorce. In the movie *The Jolson Story,* they paid Ruby Keeler $25,000 *not* to use her name. She didn't want to be associated with Jolson. She even changed the last name of their son. For years she wouldn't speak about Jolson to anyone.

Many, many years passed, and I remained wary of calling her, even when she was the toast of the town in *No, No, Nanette.* One day I found out she was waiting for me, wanting to come on my show. We finally scheduled a date. Her publicist, her manager, her agent, warned me, "Don't talk about Al Jolson! Whatever you say to her, don't talk about Al Jolson!" But I loved Al Jolson and broke the barrier. For her, time had healed the wounds, and the memories flowed. We did a big, big hour talking about nothing *but* Jolson. Ruby Keeler and I became very close. She was made into a star through Jolson.

Despite the successes of the Cantor show and the Jolson tribute, my days as an impresario were numbered. I ran other shows, variety shows, benefits, at Carnegie, at theaters in Brooklyn, featuring a potpourri of comedians and performers, but somehow I got less daring. I was not about to become the master showman like Billy Rose that I occasionally fancied myself to be. (Billy Rose's advice to me, incidentally, when I met him in Ted Collins's office, was: "Learn to type, kid.") Besides, my sights were set on other fields.

Costs had increased, and salaries of radio stars were going sky-high. Many of the half-hour shows had been reduced to fifteen minutes. The hour shows had either completely disappeared or been halved to thirty minutes. Yes, radio was faltering, as silents had with the appearance of *The Jazz Singer* and as vaudeville had with the closing of the Palace Theatre almost twenty years before, in 1931. Poignantly, radio genius Fred Allen observed, "When a radio comedian's program is finally finished it slinks down memory lane into the limbo of yesteryear's happy hours. All that the comedian has to show for his years of work and aggravation is the echo of forgotten laughter." I was determined, at the grand old age of twenty-five, not to be left behind on "memory lane." I was going to create my own. The new medium called "television" beckoned.

Ronald Reagan

I had Reagan as a guest five times, never as a government official. He was very charming. When I was a kid, I used to go to a

☆

theater every week called the Loew's State. It was a vaudeville theater at the time. One week the bill was called the *Louella Parsons Holiday Review.* On that bill was Louella Parsons, the famous Hollywood commentator, and she had about five or six budding actors and actresses in her company, maybe eight, and I used to wait by the stage door for autographs. The day I was waiting was a rainy, rainy day; all the stars whizzed right past the fans except one: Ronald Reagan. He stood in the rain and signed. Every autograph. He was a young actor then. I thought, There's a charming guy! So sure enough, look how charming he was. He charmed his way into the White House!

Lucille Ball

Eddie Cantor told me one day he was making a movie called *The Kid from Spain,* and he had all these gorgeous Goldwyn girls behind him in one scene; they included an all-star lineup of Betty Grable, Paulette Goddard, and a young newcomer named Lucille Ball. There was one scene that called for Eddie to receive a pie in the face. He was to duck, and one of the girls would get the pie in the face. The only glamour girl who volunteered was Lucille Ball. No other girl would dare expose herself to that "belittlement." Eddie Cantor said to me later on that he knew that day in 1932 that the then unknown actress Lucille Ball would someday be a star because she wasn't afraid to be outrageous.

Mack Sennett

Mack Sennett died in the 1940s. I wish I could have met him. I own his private archives. He had an unrequited love affair with a lady named Mabel Normand. Very big star. I have part of their estate, pictures signed "To Mabel with love," "To Mack with love." They are part of my archives. Mabel died in 1930, at twenty-eight years of age. She burned out from drugs, just as the silent-movie era, of which she was a major figure, was dying.

Bing Crosby

I had Bing Crosby on radio twice and TV once. He came to New York only once, maybe, in the last twenty years before he died. The day he was on my show, he was in such a good mood that he went out on the street, walked up to a girl, and said, "My name is Crosby. Do you want to do a road tour with me?"

Bing once told the whole story of how he fought a courageous battle when he was younger. The producers at the studio wanted to pin back his ears. They said that they were so wingy, they stuck so far out, if the camera shot him head-on, he'd look like a taxi with both doors open. So, despite his gigantic radio fame at that time, Bing finally did what they asked. They told him that he had no future in movies because of his ears, so he went along with them, and he did pin back his ears. But the heat, the heat used to always loosen the stickum that he used, so one day he said, "So long. I'm gonna leave my ears the way they are; they're just going to have to take me the way I am now." He told them, "If you want me, I'll be at the golf club." He was the hottest property at Paramount, and pretty soon they needed him back. They agreed to let him appear with his ears au naturel. But when the movie, *She Loves Me Not*, with Kitty Carlisle Hart, was released, he warned his fans, "In the first part, my ears are pinned back. I look streamlined. But in the second part, they're flapped out. I look like Dumbo the Elephant."

Bing's hair was thinning. He hated toupees because they used to make him itch. He became very self-conscious about his hair

☆

loss and always tried to do all the scenes outdoors so he could wear his hat. They promised him they'd buy him a script where he could play a rabbi—then he could keep his hat on all the time! He just hated that toupee. He went along with it even when he had to meet a girl in a railroad station, a scene in which he had to kiss the girl. They told him, "Bing, take off the hat." But he rationalized leaving it on with some impeccable logic. He said, "No, I'd be so emotional, I'd forget to take off the hat."

I loved Bing Crosby. He won the Academy Award for *Going My Way.* In fact, to the best of my knowledge, the sequel to that movie, *The Bells of St. Mary's,* was one of the few times in history where the sequel made more money than the original.

All radio shows were aired live, but Bing Crosby was on the Philco show and wanted to tape his shows. One reason was that he wanted to be able to take more time off. The second was that he owned the company that made the tape, Ampex, which he formed with his partner, John Mullins. Mullins developed the technology from German magnetic recordings found immediately after World War II.

Before magnetic tape, on wire recordings or transcription disks it was impossible to edit. If you screwed up something, you had to go back and start the whole show over. On magnetic tape you could edit. NBC refused to let Bing tape his show, but ABC, which was still the Blue Network, told Bing he could do anything he wanted, for they had no big names. So Bing switched networks, and they taped his show, and that was the beginning of the end of live radio.

Fred Astaire

It was through Bing that I met Fred Astaire, who became a good friend. I asked him on my radio show to name his favorite dancing partner over his long, illustrious career. He had danced with Ginger Rogers, Rita Hayworth, Vera-Ellen, Eleanor Powell, some of the very best, but not to embarrass any of them or to show class, he named a man! He said, "Gene Kelly." When Gene Kelly and Fred Astaire danced together in the *Ziegfeld Follies,* of course, they did a great dance number, directed by Liza Minnelli's father, Vincente Minnelli.

Fred Astaire told me that when his legs got tired, he just decided to stop dancing. He went into dramatic parts. He was in *On the Beach, The Towering Inferno.* Gene Kelly, too, when his legs got tired, performed dramatically in *Marjorie Morningstar* and *Inherit the Wind* and directed many films.

Inger Stevens

I had Inger Stevens on my show many times. She came on once when she was plugging her TV show *The Farmer's Daughter.* You know, she was madly in love with Bing Crosby. They made a movie together called *Man on Fire,* and she couldn't put him out of her mind. Soon after he married Katherine Crosby, Inger Stevens committed suicide.

Georgie Jessel

I loved Jessel. He was on my show maybe 150 times. He would come on my cruises all the time and was the main entertainment. Toward the end he was in a wheelchair, but he still came on my cruises. One of his girls was the famous madam Xaviera Hollander. She was at the bon voyage party several times, on the day of sailing. He had a few ladies. I don't think he paid them money; they were just happy to be with him.

He was always broke, always broke. I used to give him a hundred bucks every time he was on my show, and my show was a "no pay" show. I had him on one time with Cardinal Spellman. Spellman was amazed at the way Jessel quoted so intelligently from the Bible. It was just incredible the way Georgie Jessel remembered passage after passage. Spellman listened in awe. At last, Spellman says to him, "You're a Jew, you never went to school? Where'd you learn all that?"

So Georgie says, "Your Eminence, when I was in vaudeville, I went around from city to city doing one-night gigs, and I'd wait in the hotel room reading the Gideon Bible until the hooker got there."

Georgie Jessel would wear his medals whenever he went on a talk show to demonstrate his patriotism. Jessel was controversial, very unorthodox in his political leanings and statements. The main thing is, he would go around flaunting all kinds of medals; he'd always wear a uniform with about twenty medals. He was the subject of many, many takeoffs and spoofs. People used to make fun of his lisp. They didn't know he had that lisp from a minor stroke. So it was kind of cruel. He told me one time on my show, "Last week, I was impersonated on eleven network shows." But he couldn't get a job on a network show; he couldn't get a booking. A kind of pathetic, ironic life.

When I knew him, he had a lot of girlfriends, a lot of hookers, but at various times in his life he had been married to the most beautiful women in the world. He had a girlfriend once, Lois Andrews; he married her when she was sixteen years old, and it made all the headlines. Georgie Jessel jokes were a hundred times more plentiful than Joey Buttafuoco jokes or those about Seinfeld and his young girlfriend. Georgie Jessel was forty-six, and Lois Andrews was sixteen, which was big news then. Eddie Cantor used to crack, "Georgie Jessel was to be here tonight but couldn't make it because his wife was teething."

☆

Georgie Jessel, George Burns, and a Toupee

George Burns used to break up Jack Benny. George Burns just had to wink or belch and Jack Benny would fall over laughing. Georgie Jessel used to break me up the same way. I guess it's no secret—a few people in the industry knew it—that George Burns, when he got tired of his toupees, would send them to Georgie Jessel. Jessel would wear them for a year or two. Jessel had seven different toupees, one for every day of the week. Each one with a little more hair—he was trying to make people believe that his hair was growing naturally! And when Jessel got through with *his* toupees, he would send them to a singer named Sid Gary, a short man with a booming voice. Sid Gary had been the vaudeville partner many years ago of George Burns. So it had all sort of gone full cycle.

Sid Gary and Harold Gary

Sid Gary, in his heyday, was a very popular recording star. He had been big in vaudeville, and Milton Berle loved him, would use him on his TV show, on club dates, banquets, various gigs, engagements. Sid Gary had a brother named Harold Gary, a very fine actor who was in a lot of big Broadway shows, *big* Broadway shows. If you go to the library, through the archives, you'll see his name in *Hello Dolly!* and *The Price* by Arthur Miller.

Harold Gary used to ask to come on my show, beg to come on my show, and I did have him on once or twice. But he always called fifty times for every one appearance. He'd call me when he had a little time in between jobs and say, "Joe, can I come on your show?" I guess I didn't have him on for a while, so he finally stopped calling.

☆

One day I got a phone call from the police, and they said, "Mr. Franklin, do you know someone by the same of Sidney Garfinkle?" I didn't know that name, so they said, "Well, it also says on the wallet Sid Gary." Apparently he dropped dead on the sidewalk, on Seventy-second Street and Broadway on the traffic island. The cops took out his wallet, and among the clippings was one of him on my recent cruise. I thought, Oh, Sidney Garfinkle must be Sid Gary.

They said, "Mr Franklin, we just want to tell you, he died on the street, and we thought maybe, maybe, you could tell us how to reach the next of kin." So I looked in the phone book fast for Harold Gary, and I found it. I said, "Harold! This is Joe Franklin!"

Harold answered testily, "Well? What do you want? What do you want? I'm busy."

I said, "Harold, I just wanted to tell you, your beloved brother dropped dead on Broadway." He called me thirty or forty times to be on my show, and the one time I call him, he acts annoyed.

Charlie Chaplin

Chaplin was on my radio show, and at the peak of his fame, he was criticized for his marriages, his political leanings, and also because he never found time to become a U.S. citizen. He was a little bit left-wingy, and he didn't want to live where he wasn't wanted. So he went into self-imposed exile in Switzerland until they invited him back for an honorary Academy Award in 1972. There's one scene in a movie called *The Gold Rush* where he sits starving in his Alaska cabin during a big snowstorm and carves up his shoe—to eat as a delicacy. Remember that scene? That's one of the most charming moments in cinema history. He was the first one to mix comedy with pathos.

He grew up a street urchin, his mother dying in the poorhouse. He wound up dancing on the street, passing around a hat for pennies, in an orphanage for destitute children, so I guess his career was kind of an echo of his impoverished childhood. I asked him on the air about people who analyze his movies. There are whole books written by people analyzing Charlie Chaplin movies, frame by frame. They see Freudian significance in every frame. Every time he kicks a fat man from behind, he's supposed to be knocking the Establishment, and there are a hundred more theories. Chaplin swore to me that although people read all these shadings, all these meanings into his movies, all he had in mind was to make people laugh. I never forgot how he told me that people can overanalyze what was never there in the first place.

Gene Autry and Cliff Edwards

Gene Autry told me that when he came to New York and was poor, he tried to get help from a man named Cliff Edwards. Cliff Edwards was a big, big Broadway star. His nickname was "Ukulele Ike." He made the ukulele into a national rage, long before Arthur Godfrey or anybody else. Gene Autry told me that when he was just starting out in show business, Ukulele Ike gave him a cold shoulder. Later on, Gene Autry became a billionaire, and Cliff Edwards's career fizzled. Cliff Edwards came to Autry looking for work. Autry could have given him a job, but he didn't.

Edward G. Robinson

When Kate Smith played in vaudeville in *George White's Scandals* at the Palace, she was on the same bill as Edward G.

Robinson, who later made a hit in the movies. At the end of the bill, at the entr'acte, she lifted him up and swung him all around. Kate Smith swinging the tough gangster! She made a big hit, and he did, too. That was his first appearance ever in vaudeville.

Edward G. Robinson was in the Theatre Guild as a legitimate actor, but they didn't want actors then; they wanted "types." They wanted to give him rootin'-tootin' parts, but he refused to accept them. So later, after becoming one of the world's most famous screen gangsters, he separated from Warner Brothers and worked independently and did very well as a straight actor. He was a very fine actor. His real name was Emmanuel Goldenberg, and he came from the Bronx.

Billy Rose

One of the men who probably influenced me the most was Billy Rose. He was short, five feet two inches tall. And he used to send for me to sit in his office at the Ziegfeld Theatre, next to these long-legged, tall, tall women.

He owned Billy Rose's Diamond Horseshoe, nightclubs; he was a master showman. He was one of the richest men in the country; financier Bernard Baruch had told him to buy AT&T when it was ten cents a share. He began as a stenographer, a typist. He told me, "The only way you could get ahead in business in those days was to be a stenographer and typist and get a job with the boss. The boss'll get to like you, and you'll move up in the ranks. A lot of bosses had male secretaries at the insistence of their wives, so I studied typing, went to business school after regular school, and I was, in the army, classified as a clerk typist."

☆

Rudy Vallee

I was very close with Rudy Vallee. I would travel with him to nightclubs in different states in his car and stayed in his house on Mulholland Drive when I was in Hollywood. By the 1960s, he was not such a big star; his career had tapered off. He wanted to play General Patton in the film *Patton*, he wanted that part badly, but it went to George C. Scott. Rudy hadn't had a film in a long time, and he was very bitter that the parade had passed him by.

Rudy was, like me, a very untheatrical, very unpretentious man. He felt unappreciated. He had a big, big comeback in a Broadway show called *How to Succeed in Business Without Really Trying,* a big, big hit; he almost didn't get that part because during rehearsals he had a big fight with Frank Loesser, the composer. He antagonized everybody, for they resented the fact that he was supposed to be very, very wealthy but he was very, very cheap. I used to tell these people, "Look, it's his money. Let him spend it the way he wants." Instead of a tip, he'd give a fountain pen with his name inscribed on it to a waiter. But how can you tell anybody how to spend his money? The waiters would take it, they'd have to be polite.

People forget that in his heyday, in 1930 or 1931, Rudy Vallee was bigger than Michael Jackson and Bruce Springsteen and the Spin Doctors combined. He was gigantic. One time he picked up the phone in his house, and on the extension, he heard his wife, Fay Webb, saying, "Hi, lover, I'm gonna poison him tonight." It made front-page headlines. It was bigger than World War I and II put together. Rudy heard it, and it leaked to the press. That marriage didn't last long, naturally.

We'd go down to Rudy's basement and listen to records all night. He loved that. I was just goose pimply to spend time with him. He would drink a lot, Jack Daniel's, every night. By then, his voice was gravelly and gruff; he didn't sing right, he didn't sing correctly. But in his heyday he had a gorgeous voice, but then his voice got very gruff through misuse. Growly, gravelly, but not from smoking; he just didn't sing right.

His popularity tapered off toward the end. He'd go into night-clubs and do bad jokes and work with a tape recorder, sing to a taped record. Toward the end, he was notorious for giving bad shows.

His estate, called Silvertip, went on for miles and miles. The estate, the acreage, stretched as far back as the eye could see. He used to play tennis there with Ginger Rogers; he had outdoor tennis courts. Jack LaLanne was his best friend; he lived two houses down.

After Eddie Cantor died in 1964, Rudy Vallee became, per-haps, my best friend in the world. Rudy died on July 4, 1986, in bed watching TV. His death was not that well publicized; he wasn't that big anymore. Fame is fleeting. But Rudy Vallee was a mega-star before that term was created.

The Motion Picture Home

I went to the Motion Picture Home and saw all my idols there—Jerry Colonna, Mary Astor, Rose Hobart, Mae Clarke—but I hated the way they looked. I don't go to funerals. I don't want to see people in caskets. I'm not ghoulish. Mary Astor went a little tiny bit off the wall. I don't want to see them old and wrin-kled and shriveled. I want to remember them the way they were.

Milkman's Matinee

Art Ford was probably my first friend in the business. He was on all night on WNEW with a show called *Milkman's Matinee.*

Actually, he was the *second* Milkman; the original Milkman was named Stan Shaw, who would say, "This is your velly, velly good friend, the Milkman." Nobody in those days knew if anyone was listening all night; it was one of the first all-night shows. During one show, at about three or four o'clock in the morning, Stan Shaw thought no one was listening, so he broke wind on the radio. You can't hide that, and he got canned. That's when Art Ford took the job.

Art Ford was very very popular; he was a nice guy. He had a romance with a girl named Nancy Walker, later known to many as the Bounty towel girl. She was a radio actress at the time, and Art Ford gave me fifty dollars to write a script for her. Their romance never developed into anything; he was very, very tall, she was very, very short.

Art is still around. What a nice guy. I always was most envious of his speaking voice. I learned a lot from listening to his technique.

Telly Savalas

Telly Savalas was the director of my radio show in 1950. A lovely guy. He had half a finger; he pointed at me with half a finger and said, "Start the show." He returned many times after he became a superstar. I was crushed when he died.

Ben Hecht

The journalist and screenwriter Ben Hecht told me that when he was sixteen years old, he was working in the photo department of the *Chicago News*. The regular caption writer got sick, and he was required to fill in. The lead story was about a dentist who had had sexual relations with one of his patients while she was under. Hecht's caption read "Dentist Fills Wrong Cavity." He was fired the next day.

The Real Old-Timers

What I've always tried to highlight are silent-screen and vaudeville comedians like Jack Duffy, Billy Dooley, Snub Pollard, Neil Burns, and Walter Hiers. And Charles Ray, who had been a superstar until sound came in, then afterward could only get bit parts. Charlie Chase would be, I guess, an in-betweener; also Fatty Arbuckle and Harry Langdon. They probably would fall into the category of bread-and-butter favorites. Charlie Chaplin had his own little company of stock comedians and comediennes—every one of them was so familiar to the public—and later on they branched out and made their own little shorts.

As for the noncomedians, the dramatic performers, in my personal collection I've got maybe three hundred full-length silent films, which of course include the Valentinos and the Swansons, but the ones I love are the forgotten heroes and heroines, the kings and queens, princes and princesses, of the Saturday afternoon serials. Even the *Our Gang* kids of the silent era who sort of paved the way for the famous *Our Gang* kids later on. (Elizabeth Taylor's first movie part was opposite Carl "Alfalfa" Switzer.)

These performers paved the way for everybody. The point that I want to put across is that aside from the Greta Garbos and the Charlie Chaplins and the Richard Barthelmesses and the superstars, the Lillian Gishes, there were a tremendous number of

☆

people who were the backbone of the industry. Their faces were as familiar all over the world as those of presidents or kings. They deserve recognition; no one remembers them.

In my search for old-timers, I was duped once or twice. There was an old-time song-and-dance man who made a lot of movies as a juvenile named Johnny Downs. This man kept calling me and calling me, saying that he was Johnny Downs and wanted to be on my show. So I had dinner with him and put him on my show. Later on, I found out he was a doorman. It must've been some kind of practical joke somebody wanted to play on me. I fell for it, although he really looked like the Johnny Downs type.

Johnny Mercer

I had Johnny Mercer, the great songwriter, come on at nine o'-clock in the morning so drunk he actually fell down on the show. He was really, really drunk, but a great, great talent. He came on looking perfectly nice; I thought he knew how to hold his liquor, but we just cut away to a commercial.

Joan Crawford

I had dinner with Joan Crawford a couple times at a restaurant called Le Voisin. She was still very vital. I told her that one of my great regrets in life was that I never answer my fan mail. She scolded me, telling me how horrible that was. She said she always answered her mail and that it was very wrong of me not to. Every time I don't answer it, she said, I lose a fan. Which is true, but I just can't write letters. She answered every letter, she told me, every single one that she'd ever gotten, thousands, if not millions, of them over the years.

I don't answer a letter. That's one of my regrets; I feel so bad about that. Once I tried a mimeographed postcard. It said: "Dear Friend, thank you for your kind words. I hope I can continue to please you." Then I sent it to someone who had written to tell me how much they hated me!

I'm a big fan of Jackie Cooper's. I'll never forget when he told me one time, after the show, not on the air, that when he was about sixteen, he was on a movie lot with Joan Crawford. She was apparently in need of a little biological push, and he was elected. He went to her house many, many times and made love. She was very businesslike about it, in and out, until one day she said, "It's all over now, no more."

He met her many, many, many years later, on a movie set again, and he said, "She glanced at me for a moment, and I think she remembered." That was very poignant to me.

I loved Joan Crawford. I was always intrigued by her big, sexy mouth. To me she was very, very sexy; I think she was one of my secret fixations. I had Douglas Fairbanks on my show, and I asked him about the book called *Mommie Dearest,* for he was once married to Joan Crawford. He said, "I don't want to know it! Don't discuss it! I don't want to hear it! I never knew her to be that way; she was very kind, sweet," and he chopped me right off.

Errol Flynn

I was in a cab a few months ago with Richie Ornstein, my producer. The cabdriver was a young lady, a very beautiful, gorgeous redhead. She said to me, "I just saw Errol Flynn last night on TV in *Captain Blood.* If you can introduce him to me, the ride is on the house."

I said to her, "I'd love to, but he died thirty years ago."

Cary Grant

Cary Grant was in town to promote a movie he had coproduced called *Houseboat*. He had a list of maybe fifteen or eighteen radio and TV personalities he wanted to call to promote the film. He called me up and said, "Helloo, Mr. Franklin? This is Cary Grant."

I said, "Mr. Grant, what a pleasure!"

He was very frustrated, and he said, "The pleasure's all mine. You're about the thirteenth one I've called this morning, and you're the first one who didn't say, 'If you're Cary Grant, I'm Napoleon, I'm Josephine, I'm Adolf Hitler.'"

I went to see the screening of *Houseboat,* and he got to like me and came on my show. It was one of his few TV appearances ever.

Cary Grant told me that when he was in his later years, he went to a charity event but forgot his tickets. At the door, he said, "I'm Cary Grant!"

The lady said, "You don't look like Cary Grant."

John Wayne

I had John Wayne on once. I asked him why they called him Duke. He said he once had a dog named Duke, and they named him after his dog.

Greta Garbo

I loved Greta Garbo. In a way, I'm glad she quit movies so that people remember the way she was instead of seeing her grow old. Now she's gone, of course. She was a watcher of mine, a listener of mine. I would've loved to get her on the air, but it just never happened.

I know she was listening because one time I was playing some of her old soundtracks on my radio show from an old M-G-M album of soundtracks. Her companion called me and said, "Miss Garbo appreciates what you're doing, Joe." And I could hear a woman sobbing in the background. I thought it was a joke. I thought someone was playing a joke on me, but then, I like to believe that it really was her.

Willie and Eugene Howard

There was a great comedy team once, very big, called Willie and Eugene Howard. Very big comedy, they were like Dean Martin and Jerry Lewis, Dan Ackroyd and Bill Murray. They were in a Broadway show, and I was interviewing them backstage for my high school paper. While I was backstage with them, there was a whole table filled with sandwiches from the Stage Deli, and they were eating the sandwiches and belching *so loud,* I never heard anybody *belch so loud!* I mean like the Second World War; it was a gas attack!

Then it came time for them to go onstage and do their routine; they were great, they did their routine great, the audience was shrieking! The minute the routine ended, they came back and started to belch again! I never saw such control! To belch like two old pigs, then to go out there and do their show so impeccably, immaculately, and then start to belch again.

Bob Hope

Bob Hope is a very close friend of mine and did a lot of my shows. He would always kid me and say, "I remember you, Joe. When I was a kid, I used to love you." And he's twenty-five years older than I am.

People forget what a good singer he was. He introduced a lot of big songs on Broadway. "I Can't Get Started with You," "Smoke Gets in Your Eyes," "It's de-Lovely," all written for his various Broadway shows as a singer. We know he sings "Thanks for the Memory," "Two Sleepy People," and "Penthouse Serenade" but tend to forget he was a hit maker, too.

When I talk to Bob Hope about the old days, about Fanny Brice, about the *Ziegfeld Follies,* he'll pretend that he forgot, but he hasn't. He only wants to think and be *modern*—which is the secret of his success. He never went in for nostalgia. I asked him about being with Fanny Brice with the *Ziegfeld Follies,* and he acted like the name was a long, distant memory. "Oh, yeahhhh, Fanny Brice," like he read about her in a book, and that's about all. He's shrewd; he's cunning.

On his TV shows, all the old-timers hated him because he never put any of them on. It was always Brooke Shields, Donny Osmond, the stars of the moment. That's the secret of his success. It always worked. He was likable.

The Three Stooges

When I see the Three Stooges, I fall on the floor. Other people make me smile, maybe, maybe, but to laugh out loud, only the Three Stooges can make me do that. Slapstick. I never met them, no, but I still get hysterical when I watch them. There was a skit where Curly gets a goldfish bowl, falls down, and the bowl gets stuck on his head. Moe attempts to shoot it off with a gun, but can't. Whenever I see that scene . . .

Louis Armstrong

Louis Armstrong was on my show about four times. I loved him. He always used to give out cards, and on his card was a picture of him sitting on the toilet. He was the only guy I ever knew who gave out cards like that.

Tallulah Bankhead

I was in a taxicab with Tallulah Bankhead once, and somebody came up to the cab when we stopped for a red light and asked her for a dime. She opened up her pocketbook as the light changed. The driver said, "I gotta go. I can't wait, mister, because the cars are honking their horns behind me," so she tossed the whole pocketbook out the window. The cab took off. She was an amazing lady. She didn't go back for it. Just spontaneous.

Guy Lombardo

I had him on the show maybe thirty or forty times. I used to tell Guy, "When you die, you're going to take New Year's Eve with you." He was Mr. New Year's Eve. Every New Year's Eve program I would always play a lot of Guy Lombardo. Very nice man. And kind of detached. He announced the song titles wrong.

☆

If the song was called "Is That All There Is?" he would say,
"That's All There Is."

Jimmy Durante

Jimmy Durante always loved that lyric by Cole Porter "You're
the top, you're the inferno Dante / You're the nose on the great
Durante." He came on my show about twenty times. I used
to visit him at the hotel. He would lean out the window of the hotel and wave to the people on Forty-fifth and Broadway. He
never knew how to say no. If anybody asked him for a favor, he'd
say yeah, yeah, yeah, but when the time came to show up, he
couldn't do it because he was booked, he was out of town.

I think I was the one who created the phrase "the Wizard of
Schnozz." He married a ballet dancer. He used to tell me on his
program that he fell in love with her toes, and she fell in love
with his nose. I could do hours on Jimmy. When he was in town,
he'd sit in my office with me and we'd talk about old times. He
had very vivid recall.

George Raft

George Raft told me on my show that he spent all of the $10
million he made on women, horses, gambling, and whiskey—
and the rest he spent foolishly.

☆

Orson Welles

There's one thing I never forgot about Orson Welles. I went to an advertising agency once, and they were auditioning people for a dog-food commercial. About nine or ten men were auditioning, and one of them was Orson Welles. He was on his hands and knees barking like a dog to get a dog-food commercial. That was one of the great humiliations I've felt for another human being in my whole life.

Claudia McNeil

Claudia McNeil was on my show and told me that the night she won the Tony Award, she couldn't get a cab to take her home because she was black. She had won a Tony Award, had received a standing ovation, a whistling, cheering audience shrieking for her, for *Raisin in the Sun*, but she couldn't get a cab home. I cried.

☆

Youth

Dear Diary: Robbed $1 from Pop's coat pocket and bought 3 new records. By Bing Crosby, Tony Martin and Connie Boswell.

—From my diary, February 8, 1940

In my press material, I've announced that I was born in 1928. I'm going to come clean and admit that my real birthdate was March 9, 1926, in the Bronx, the son of Martin and Anna.

My birthday was a slow news day. The *Daily News* headlined, in that year of Prohibition, the seizure of five hundred cases of scotch whiskey in Jamaica Bay. The Sixth Annual Radio Show was in progress at the Pennsylvania Hotel, and the death of the oldest woman in northern New Jersey was announced. There were two robberies in midtown, one at the Cohan Theatre, the other at a restaurant called Janssen's Hoffbrau. Luther Burbank, the plant wizard, was seventy-seven that day. You could get a five-room home in Brooklyn for $5,850, and a swanky place in Forest Hills went for $7,250. Film stars included Rudolph Valentino, Wallace Reid, Richard Dix, Harold Lloyd, and Leatrice Joy; people danced to the Daffodil Dip and the Bambalino Charleston. Willie and Eugene Howard were headlining at B. F. Keith's Palace Theatre on Forty-seventh and Broadway; and Eddie Cantor was, as usual, doing benefits. With him on the bill were the singer Harry Richman, Georgie Jessel, Phil Baker, and Sid Silvers, with musical accompaniment by Ted Claire and his band. Little did I, a screaming infant, know that these would be the names that would influence the direction of my life.

I called my father "M.F.," based on his initials. He had a thriving business, and he brought us, my mother, Annie, and my younger sister, Meg—her name we pronounced "Mechhhh," to her horror—into Manhattan, the east Seventies. We called her Mech, Mecha, Maddy, Meg, and Madeline, but mostly Mechhhh.

In those days the East Side was not all carriage trade. Fifth Avenue may have been Peacock Alley, but once you got east of Park, things could get dicey. On First and Second Avenues there were some of the worst slums in the city. We lived in one of the better buildings in the region of the city known as Yorkville. Our apartment, on the second floor of a luxury building, had beautiful rooms and was well appointed. It was a palace compared to some of the tenements my school friends lived in. From the outset I was ashamed to be the only kid in my whole class who lived in an upper-middle-class apartment house, replete with elevator man and doorman. I downplayed our reputed money and begged my parents to "move into a tenement!"

I played dice with the elevator man down in the basement. Every time I lost, which was usually, he kept the money. But when I won once, he never gave me the keep. I couldn't complain to my parents, the police, or anybody because I couldn't admit to gambling.

We always had a sleep-in maid. I remember a German lady when I was about seven or eight, a tall, blonde German who used to sleep in the room with me. I must confess, I used to get turned on, as young as I was. That may have influenced my taste in later years. I've always liked tall blondes.

Both born in America in 1900, my parents were the children of Austrian immigrants. M.F. was the same age as James Cagney and a classmate of his at P.S. 158. I went to the exact same school later on. M.F. started business as a newspaperman, in 1920, working at the *New York Evening Mail,* on the same floor, next desk, as the very young Ed Sullivan, then a sportswriter. But M.F. got sidetracked, unable to make enough money in the newspaper business. He went into the paper and twine business and, working seven days a week, built a thriving company called the Second Avenue Pushcart Mart. All the women bought pushcarts from my father, and shopping bags to put their merchandise in. I worked with him on Saturdays, standing outside, selling shopping bags to the women shoppers for two cents each.

M.F.'s main interest, though, was stamps. He was a serious-minded philatelist; that's probably where I got my interest in collecting. He had a first-rate collection, Every night he could be found leaning over his stamps, magnifying glass in hand, trying to replate one-cent Benjamin Franklin stamps. The Franklin stamp is a legend in stamp-collecting circles: the first prepaid U.S. postage stamp, issued in 1847. Replating is the process of finding 100 of these stamps and placing them in panes of 100 to match the original engraved sheet. It was a specialized branch of a specialized field.

M.F. tried hard to get me to start a collection, but I just wasn't interested. I reluctantly went with him to stamp conventions, where he would make speeches and get awards and plaques and medals. But I could never understand the thrill of stamp collecting. What I was collecting as a boy and in later years—old movie programs and souvenir books—was only junk compared to what he saved.

Knowing of my love of radio, M.F. tried to win me over to stamp collecting by taking me to Macy's to watch *Captain Tim Healy's Stamp Club,* a radio show broadcast from the department store three days a week with a focus on stamps. Captain Healy would give out tips for kids on beginning their collections. But I was far more interested in an old-time recording star, a ballad singer named Irving Kaufman who made thousands of records, who used to broadcast in another department store, Hearns.

☆

Much to my parents' dismay, I became a big fan of cowboy singing. It certainly wasn't my Old West heritage. I begged my parents to take me to a place in the Village called the Village Barn, which broadcast a radio show called *Cowboy Tom's Gang,* sponsored by Sunsweet prune juice. One of the stars was Tex Ritter, who became a big movie star and the actor John Ritter's father. Tex Ritter had a big record later on, called "High Noon"—"Do not forsake me oh my darling." When he left his place at the Village Barn, it was taken by a fellow named Tex Fletcher.

Those were people I really loved. I worshipped Gene Autry the way some people have an orgasm over John Wayne. I've always been a sentimentalist, into sad songs, and these songs touched me. One time, many years later, Gene Autry was on my show and he brought a record with him called "The Flowers That I Picked for Her Wedding Are the Flowers I Placed on Her Grave." So sad! It reminds me of a joke. Somebody says, "Whattya get when you play a country song backwards?" Answer: "You get your wife, you get your house, you get your money, you get everything back." Very sad songs.

I try to be cheerful talking of the early days, the childhood days, but I had no reason to be particularly cheerful as a boy. My father called me "Cracky," or "Crackpot," because of my interest in radio performers, crooners, silent movies, vaudeville shows. He thought they were an utter waste of time. One night, to punish me, he took away the handle to my Victrola, making it impossible for me to listen to records. I raised a riot at night for my handle, so he smacked me. I tried to hold him off, but he kicked me in the crotch. I walked out on him. The next day, Annie broke my Victrola because I'd pestered them for the handle.

At other times, M.F. said I'd never amount to anything, and my mother more or less went along with him. By pursuing nostalgia as a career, by entering broadcasting, I always felt I was going against their wishes. It's not that I had great love and encouragement from my parents. M.F. was always very unemotional. He

☆

didn't show me any love, no kisses. He was very "masculine." Those were the days when a man had to hide his emotions. He would never kiss me the way I kiss my son now.

Although M.F. never, never talked, showed no emotion, he had one side that I remember fondly. He was very charitable toward bums. He would bring them into the house, real bums, what they'd call homeless people now. They'd take a bath in our bathtub; he'd give them a meal. My mother was always angry at him for it. But he was the head of the house. I'm the same way; I give out handouts all day long.

My grandfather—my mother's father—Aaron Heller, came around every Saturday and gave my sister and me a nickel. We waited the whole week for that nickel; it meant so much to us. The minute we got the nickel, we loved him, hugged him, and kissed him, but the minute he gave us the nickel, we ran out of the house. A nickel was a lot of money! To put it in perspective, there was a life insurance salesman who came to our door once every two weeks to collect his premium *in person*. The premium was a half dollar. Although the man was suave, elegant, and handsome, he was collecting a mere fifty cents. Imagine a businessman today coming to the door to collect that sum, saying, "Life insurance man."

We had a low-key, quiet family. My favorite dinner was always on Sunday night. If we were good, my mother would make lamb chops and green peas and chocolate pudding. We licked out the bowl. Maybe every third Sunday we went to the Horn & Hardart Automat; the four of us had dinner for about seven dollars. You put a nickel in and got coffee, a nickel in and got soda, ice cream—the food was sensational. I miss it. The last one closed recently, on Third Avenue. They're gone forever. Those were great days.

Sometimes on Sundays we went to see my grandmother on 142nd Street and Riverside Drive, riding on a big open-top bus. The family played cards all day; my father loved it. They played pinochle and poker, but I had no interest in either. My father, no matter where we visited, always went in the next room and fell

★

asleep. No matter what house he was in, he always fell asleep. I guess maybe now when I visit somebody, I say, "Do you mind if I go to sleep?" It's something that I got from him. Very very rude, very, very antisocial.

When I was little, I made up funny shows based on *Snow White and the Seven Dwarfs* or *A Christmas Carol.* I played all the parts myself. For a stage, I took a big bamboo curtain rod or pole, put it on both sides of the bed, and hung a big blanket around it. I rehearsed a one-boy show and, when it was ready, brought my parents in to watch. I guess down deep I was a performer.

When I was six, seven, eight years old, my favorite radio program was *Uncle Don.* I couldn't eat my dinner if he wasn't on. If the radio had static, I became hysterical. He was my must. Uncle Don Carney was a big children's favorite. The word got out that one night, when he thought the microphone was off, he said at the end of the show, "I guess that'll hold the little bastards until tomorrow." It ruined his career. The irony is, he never did say it. Somebody made it up, some columnist who had a lot of space to fill one day.

The same story also floated around about two other kids' show hosts, Jack Keogh of radio station KPO and "Uncle John" Dagget of KHJ, Los Angeles. In each case, it was just vicious rumor. From Soupy Sales to Pee-Wee Herman, the public expects their children's hosts to be pure, lily-white. The public seizes on anything; they're willing to believe gossip and innuendo; they become rabid. As a result, my boyhood idol Uncle Don was crucified for a dirty mouth that wasn't. He was eventually cleared, but the damage was already done. He lived on for a short while, but his popularity faded, and he moved to Florida, where he died at a young age.

I avidly listened to *Dr. I.Q., the Mental Banker.* The host asked a lady in the balcony a question. If she got the right answer, she'd win $5, $10, up to $25. If she got the wrong answer, she got a box of Snickers.

As I got a little older, I took it into my head that I wanted to be a comedy writer, a gag writer. I was crazy about the comedy shows, even when I was a little kid of nine, ten, or eleven years old. At about nine I listened to the radio and jotted down notes to the jokes as fast as I could. I wrote down Jack Benny jokes, Eddie Cantor jokes; there was a comedian named Ken Murray I avidly studied, and Bob Hope. I figured someday, when I was older, I'd recycle their material and use it myself.

I religiously tuned in to a man on the radio known as "the Voice of Experience." "Parents of America," he warned, "the future of the world is in your hands!" People sent him their problems, and he gave them guidance. A typical letter would come from a mother saying that she had given up her baby when she was young. Now she wanted the baby back, and the new mother wouldn't give the child up. The Voice of Experience replied, "Maybe someday you'll get lucky and have another baby, all over again." I just loved his simplistic, commonsense advice and warmth. A kid would write to him that his mother had died and he didn't have money for a tombstone, so he stole a tombstone. I wanted to meet the Voice of Experience one day. Later, I found out he committed suicide, after he had solved everybody else's problems in the world but his own. His marriage had failed, and he ended his life with a gun on a street someplace in California. I have all the books he wrote, all the movie shorts. He was like King Solomon to me, with a gorgeous, sympathetic voice.

But my *everything* as a kid was Al Jolson. Once, broadcasting from Hollywood, Al Jolson made an announcement: "Ladies and gentlemen, I'll be in New York for the next two weeks. I'll be living in the Hotel Martha Washington." The next day, I hurried down to Twenty-eighth Street and stood outside the hotel. It seemed a little strange that so many women were coming in and out, but I didn't really give it a second thought. I stood outside the hotel for ten days until the doorman finally asked me if I was waiting for somebody. I told him Al Jolson, and he fell over laughing. The Martha Washington was a women's hotel!

I finally tracked Jolson down. I used to follow him around to restaurants. I stared through the window, my face pressed

☆

against the glass while he dined. He used to eat loads and loads of bread, eight or nine pieces before the meal, at Lou G. Segal's or other restaurants. I used to gaze at him through the window until he got up.

I was intrigued, fascinated by radio. I think it might have begun one day after I met a man when I was very young named Fred N. Tracy, who was known by his initials, "F.N.T." I asked, Why the initials. He said, "In the pioneering days, radio announcers were ashamed to have people know their names, radio was so new, so daring, so risqué. Nobody wanted to admit it; they were embarrassed to be known as a radio personality." It was almost like in the old days of theater, where it was "life upon the wicked stage." Nobody would ever let their daughter go on the stage. It was considered a vagabond profession, a Gypsy profession. There was nothing worse than being on the stage or being in the movies in the early days. For decades stage and screen performers were treated very poorly, as were musicians. Paul Whiteman was the first one to insist that his musicians walk in the front door instead of the back door, like poor slaves or kitchen help. Later on, show business performers became the royalty of the world, princesses and queens who all wanted to be stars.

F.N.T.'s wife's name was Maude. In those days, every old lady was named Maude; it was such a typical name for an old-time lady. F.N.T. lived in an old, broken-down apartment with papers piled up to the wall. I must've been eleven or twelve years old when I met him at a junk shop. He invited me to his house. I thought maybe he was gay. I had met people at movie theaters who were gay, who would give me a stick of chewing gum, put their hand on my knee. I didn't know what it meant, but I thought this might be the same kind of man. Instead, he was friendly. He just wanted to talk about the old days of radio. This was 1938, 1939, and radio then, of course, was beyond its infancy. It was already big time. He had been an announcer in about 1921, 1922, and now he was an old, old man with white hair, his body all bent over.

F.N.T. was my first encounter ever with any kind of show

business. He showed me photographs of himself at the peak of his fame, old radio scripts, told me about the old crystal sets, carbon microphones, pictures of WOR radio when it was located in the basement of Bamberger's Department Store in Newark. It was ironic that many years later I went full circle, broadcasting on WOR in the modern era. I wonder what F.N.T. would have thought.

As soon as the school day was over, I went to the movies, five days a week. I caught the 3:30–5:30 P.M. shows. You got music, a film, newsreels, bingo, screeno, dishes, orange juice, all for twenty cents admission. Georgie Jessel once commented that the customers were mad if they didn't strike oil under their seats.

The first movie I remember seeing was called *What! No Beer?* with Jimmy Durante and Buster Keaton. It was a movie about Prohibition and I remember when beer came gushing out of barrels. I thought it was going to gush into the movie theater, and I got scared.

When I was a kid, Tony Curtis was my best friend. His name was Bernard Schwartz then, and Bernie and I would go to the movies every single day. He came to my house, and we told my mother we were going out to play basketball. My mother would give us each a dime, for a soda or a soup, but we'd go straight to the movies for a dime. We frequented a theater on Seventy-fourth Street called the Annex and one on Sixty-seventh called the Rex, today the location of the Channel 5 building.

On weekends, she gave Bernie and me an extra dime to go from Seventy-seventh to Ninety-second to the YMHA. I wanted to take the bus, per her instructions, but Bernie insisted we walk both ways to save the fare. Occasionally, she gave us each a quarter, and we stretched it to the limit, to the distant environs of Times Square. It cost a nickel for the subway, a nickel to go home, a dime for a movie on Forty-second Street, and a nickel for a hot dog.

Forty-second Street was elegant and clean then, with nice double features, John Wayne double bills, not like today. In the

★

summertime, you'd see men wearing coats and ties and jackets. Our favorite theater was called the Laff Movie. We went whenever we could to see a comedy. They played the Three Stooges, the Ritz Brothers, Laurel and Hardy, the Marx Brothers.

There was such a thing as "poor" and "poor poor." Bernie Schwartz was poor poor. Bernie's father, Manuel, was a hardworking tailor; they called him "Mano" for short. I used to call for Bernie, and we went to the York Theatre on Sixty-fourth Street and York Avenue, right below their apartment. But even though Bernie didn't have a suit and couldn't afford a haircut, all the girls used to flock around him, even when he was only twelve or thirteen years old. The other kids were so jealous of him because of his popularity with girls that they would punch him. There was a kid named Milton who hit him for no other reason than that he was jealous. Bernie got all the girls.

Bernie and I belonged to a social club called the Silver Streaks. The Silver Streaks took hikes, played basketball, wholesome stuff. Dues were a nickel every Saturday night, and over several months, we had accumulated about thirteen dollars. Bernie was the treasurer, and I suspect he was dipping into the funds. The treasury never grew larger than thirteen dollars. He was penniless. He needed the money, I guess, to buy food for his family or for clothes. We laugh about those days now.

The only real influence on me in high school was the dramatics class. It was taught by an actor named Judson Laire, who played Papa in *I Remember Mama,* opposite Peggy Wood. He was in Broadway shows like *The Patriot,* and he was our drama coach. He was a tall, distinguished man with a deep, brittle, British kind of speaking voice, and he motivated me to do more dramatics. His passion for the theater rubbed off on me, just by being close to him and soaking up his wisdom, his vibrations.

I've had so many offers to do plays, then and now, but I've got a mental block about rehearsing. I'm sure if I tried I could learn how to memorize, but I just have that fear of trying to remember lines, that I'd forget them and be panic-stricken. If I ever did take a part in a play, I'd always take a minor one. I went to Camp

Anawana, then Camp Windsor, every summer. The camp season was about nine weeks, and when I got there, they put me in a play the first week. They thought, Joe is so great, he's got a great voice, he's gonna be the star of all the plays. But I fizzled out. I was good for about an hour.

I was such a radio bug, such a movie bug, I never did homework. I don't know how I got away with it. You were supposed to hand in your homework, and I never did, and still graduated. I guess I was a good faker. Once in a while, I would be punished. The teacher put me under her desk, and I looked under her dress and up her legs. Well, I was young. You could call that one of my first sexual experiences.

One of my thrills as a teenager was sneaking into burlesque shows. Ironically, I was probably the only one in the audience who went to see the comedians, not the dancers. I went to my first burlesque show when I was fourteen, at Coney Island. To get in, I used to wear a hat and dark glasses, somehow convincing the ticket taker that I was eighteen. I lowered my voice an octave, "One, please."

The days of the stripper began with Ann Corio and Gypsy Rose Lee, and then there were Margie Hart and Rose La Rose. Gypsy Rose Lee starred in all the big shows for Mike Todd, *Star and Garter Revue* and others. But compared to today's concept of burlesque, these women were well covered. They would never show their dingle. Couples, men and women, went to these shows. They were respectable and respectful.

I've been very close through the years with Georgia Southern, whose husband was a friend of mine. She twirled her tassels in opposite directions, she was great at that. She would throw cigarettes out into the audience. I remember one time I caught one. She tossed them out indiscriminately (not lit!). I used to love the candy barkers who sold their wares during intermission. "Tell you what I'm gonna do! I'm gonna sell you this candy bar! You're gonna find a ten-dollar bill inside one of these bars!" Those spielers were great, those hucksters.

But best of all, I loved the comedians who entertained the

☆

crowd between numbers. They made me laugh till my back hurt. For me, it was always the comedians first, the dancers second. At sixteen, seventeen years old, I sat there, just as I used to sit in front of a radio, and jotted down the jokes from burlesque. There was a theater then on West Forty-second Street called the Eltinge, named after Julian Eltinge, the famous female impersonator of the 1920s and 1930s. Some of the great comics of burlesque were Red Skelton, Phil Silvers, who began in burlesque, Joey Faye, a lot of old-time stars. Abbott and Costello began in burlesque before they were discovered by Ted Collins, and Eddie Cantor was in burlesque when he was a kid. By the time I was watching, I just saw little-known comics, old-time slapstick comics, nobody famous. But almost everybody began in burlesque in the old, *old* days. It was a world unto itself. When the comedian was finished with his act, I usually walked out. I wouldn't even stay to watch the next dancer. They were great days, fabulous days. I loved burlesque shows. I just wished they'd stayed the way they were.

I finally got a chance to meet my idol, Eddie Cantor. After several letters, Eddie Cantor granted me an audience at his suite in the Sherry Netherland Hotel. I was lucky: Eddie was like me today. If anybody called, he would say, "Come over, sit around with me." I sat in the luxury suite, just grateful to be in the same room as the great man, content to watch as he chatted with cronies or as tailors fitted him with suits. Eddie was always being measured for suits. Somehow I managed to talk him into buying a few of my jokes for his radio show. It was the first money I'd ever made in the entertainment business.

I got my first "real" after-school job working for Bloomingdale's. My task was to pick up the receipts from the various departments and bring them to the central office. While I should have been making the rounds, I spent at least half my time in the record department playing records. (I think that's why I got fired.) My boss was named Mr. Zimmerman, and he was in charge of maybe 150 kids. I thought of him as a tyrant until one day I saw his paycheck: thirty-five dollars for a week. I had hated him up until then, but when I saw how *little* he was making, I was stunned. I couldn't believe it; this was 1940! How people could support a family on that kind of money in those days was incredible.

Then came the war years, and there was plenty of work on the home front. Though I didn't last at Bloomingdale's, part-time jobs abounded. I quickly found a new spot with Celebrity Service. Earl Blackwell is the owner; he's quite ill now, he's got Parkinson's. I used to get on the phone and try to find out where celebrities were living. A lot of my compilations are still being used today, though most of the celebrities are dead, or half-dead, by now. I was one of the pioneer workers for Celebrity Service. At Celebrity Service I spoke with radio stars like Fred Allen, Ken Murray, and Joe Howard, the old-time singer who wrote "I Wonder Who's Kissing Her Now." Much later, I had dinner with him a few times, and he told me how he got the inspiration for that song: he overheard somebody at the next table in a restaurant saying, "I wonder who's kissing her now." Joe Howard introduced me to the Brill Building, the famous address on Broadway that was home to Tin Pan Alley, where all the composers and lyricists had offices and talked shop.

I got very close to Irving Caesar, who wrote "Tea for Two," "Swanee," and "I Want to Be Happy." He was George Gershwin's first partner, before Gershwin teamed with his brother, Ira. Once, I met Irving Caesar on the street in front of the Brill Building, and he sang me a song about his lost dog. I couldn't help laughing; the song was so corny, so bad, embarrassingly gauche. I thought, This is the man who wrote "Tea for Two" and "Swanee" and "Just a Gigolo" and all those great, great songs, and then this! I couldn't believe it!

I was already onto my next part-time job, working for a radio syndication company called Harry S. Goodman, when at last I graduated from Benjamin Franklin High. My most famous classmate was Daniel Patrick Moynihan, the senator from New York. He was a great debater, always fighting with the social science teacher, Mr. Weinstein, about whatever the topic was. He would outdo him, outduel him on any subject. Daniel Moynihan was a brilliant, brilliant orator. Joe Galiber, current Bronx state senator, was also a classmate. My own best subject was probably English, I got 100 on my Regents exam. My worst was Spanish. I took Spanish four times and flunked it as many times, my score hovering around 42.

Then I was drafted.

I just wanted to do my part. I felt patriotic. In those days, everyone was for God and country, for your land and my land; there was no such thing as dissent. Believe it or not, my father was on the draft board; he could've held me back, but I didn't want that. I wanted to go.

But oh, I hated the army with a vengeance. I guess I have two recurring dreams to this day—I'm late for my TV show, and the other recurring dream is that I'm back in the service. I hated the army. They hated me. They called me "New York." They hated all New Yorkers. There was a captain in the army, in McCloskey General Hospital, who was named Captain Crank. I'll never forget that name.

He was not cranky; he was nice. He knew that I hated army life, he even bent over backwards to make life more endurable for me. But he, too, called me "Mr. New York," like the others. Anybody from New York was bad news, fair game. I dreaded getting up in the morning. You can never know how much I hated army life.

I was always doing KP, kitchen police, as a punishment, but also because they knew I didn't want to go out on field maneuvers. I was not athletic; I couldn't shoot. I used to lie and tell my parents and friends that I had just won a medal for sharpshooting. When I came home I wore my uniform for ninety days with a couple of sharpshooting medals all over me that I bought in the five-and-dime store, my "Purple Heart." I drank beer at night, but the beer in Texas was always hot. I think it was called 3.2. It was always 110 degrees. People were passing out like flies; they'd pile 'em in trucks and pack 'em into trucks, send 'em back to the barracks, like sardines, like lox, drenched!

I fell down during maneuvers. During the obstacle course I twisted my ankle. I was sent to the infirmary, McCloskey General Hospital, in Temple, Texas, where I finally began doing something useful. I played records over the hospital radio station. I didn't mind being there after a while; they treated me well and seemed to appreciate what I was doing. The music was piped into the rooms of the sick soldiers. This was my first time on the radio. I filled my playlist by going into the town of Waco and buying what I could find in junk shops. My mother sent me a few from my own collection in the mail. I announced over the air, "This is Joe Franklin, the young wreck with the old records." I really hammed it up.

During my time in the infirmary, they discovered I had third-degree flat feet. When you've got third-degree flat feet, you can't be in the army. They told me I was going home.

The day I got out of the army was the happiest day of my life. I was a terrible, terrible soldier. I was so happy to get back, I didn't take my GI insurance, and I didn't take my pension for being wounded. I took nothing.

My sister had corresponded with some of the soldiers. They continued writing letters back and forth. She discovered that my company was soon sent overseas. Out of my company of about 144 men, *142* were killed in the Battle of the Bulge, a classic battle of World War II. By my ending up in the infirmary— Well, I know I wouldn't be here today if I'd gone over there. It was just a wholesale slaughter, a sacrifice of those young men. They were very courageous, very brave, very matter-of-fact about it, but they were sacrificed for the sake of a defensive maneuver.

In the 1960s, when I read that they were going to draft seventeen-year-olds to serve in Vietnam, I went crazy. I was going to have Brad, my son, move to Canada. I was going to move there myself. All the kids, all the GIs my sister was corresponding with, everyone, was killed. They went right from Camp Hood to the Bulge. All the letters she sent came back marked "DECEASED."

☆

Part II
The Golden Age of Television

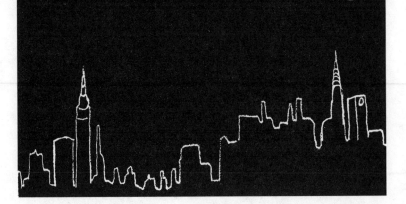

WABC

Channel 7's Joe Franklin Show *will be expanded to a full hour, Mondays through Fridays, effective December 17, 12:30 p.m.* Romper Room, *a children's program now seen in this time spot, will be dropped.*
       —*New York Daily Mirror*, November 21, 1956

Television in its infancy was very, very primitive, strictly black and white, no tape. Everything was live. Occasionally they would make "kinescopes," a very expensive way of filming television shows during the broadcast. It was impractical and beyond the budgets for 99 percent of the shows, costing about $45,000 in 1957. As a result the entire era is almost lost to the world forever. Not a single one of my shows from the 1950s is still in existence. People call me all the time and say, "My father was on your show in the 1950s, the 1960s. Can I get a tape?" I tell them there are no tapes, and they don't believe me. I never saw myself on TV until after I'd been on for fifteen years. Compared to today, we were in the Stone Age. Make that the Jurassic period, technologically in the dark. When they told me, "One day television's going to be broadcast in color, when they show the tomato juice, it's going to be in red," I said, "You're out of your mind! You're insane!" Who ever thought they'd show tomato juice *red* on TV?

A lot of people thought that TV was just a fad. Like radio, like talkies, television was given little chance of catching on. The official opening of NBC, the first network television station, was in 1939, at the New York World's Fair. Early TV was primitive, using huge, stationary cameras that needed enough lights to illuminate Yankee Stadium. World War II put a halt to further development of the television industry. Cameras on dollies weren't even conceived of until 1946, and the lights remained so hot that temperatures on the set remained at 115 degrees or higher. Special television "viewing glasses" were sold to consumers to "reduce bright light glare." Televisions were bulky and unreliable, and there were virtually no television repairmen to fix a damaged set. Nevertheless, by the turn of the decade, the medium was beginning to catch on.

I was one of the first ones to own a TV. I was at WMCA, and there was a chief engineer named Oliver Penny. He *built* me my TV. Handmade. I think I paid about $1,200 for it. In those days, that was enormous money. That set is gone now, but I loved it. Believe it or not, it was maybe a 15-inch screen. That was incredibly large for that time. Black and white, naturally. I knew that TV was going to change the world as soon as I saw it. I knew I'd be part of it. I just had that feeling in my bones.

The first shows I remember watching were on Channel 5, then called the Dumont Network, after their owner, Charles A. Dumont. They also manufactured sets themselves. Their programs ran locally for fifteen minutes each. One was called *Bob Howard, the Jive Bomber.* Bob Howard, a former vaudevillian, a recording artist years before, was what was known as a "jive singer," and the show's name was a takeoff on "dive bomber." His show was followed at night by Vincent Lopez, a famous old-time bandleader, playing the piano.

Most major performers were afraid at that time to make the transition to television. They figured it would ruin their careers. It was viewed as potential career suicide. Darryl Zanuck, the head of 20th Century-Fox, told me, "TV will never catch on. You can never convince me that after a long, long day of working in the kitchen, the woman's going to want to sit at home and watch a box. After a long day in the kitchen, she's going to want to go out and go to a movie theater. Nobody's ever going to sit home and watch a box!"

Milton Berle became the first superstar of the new medium. He was the first to muscle it out, to become "Mr. Television." He really earned that sobriquet. He deserved it, for he did something the others were afraid to do. He tried television and beat a path to the hearts of the American public. He was so dynamic that the night between Monday and Wednesday became known as "Berle's-day"; that's how popular his show was. He was on the cover of *Time* and *Newsweek* the same week. He had 92 percent of the viewership, the highest ever. That will never happen again. He brought vaudeville to television, and everybody followed. As the joke goes, Berle was responsible for the sale of more television sets than any other performer. I sold mine, Irving sold his, Myron sold his.

While prime time was flexing its muscles, daytime TV remained a wasteland. Channel 7 was still dark. Only a smattering of programs were listed in the fledgling *Television Guide*. At 10:00 A.M., *TV Shopper;* at 11, *Rumpus Room with Johnny Olson.* Dennis James had a variety show, and a program called *Man on the Street* solicited opinions at 12:15 P.M. Horse racing came on at 2:00 P.M.

I was on several radio shows at the time, but I was interested in finding out what television was all about. I was in the Stage Delicatessen when I was approached by a man named Dick Randall. His main business was called the Clara Lane Introduction Service, a dating service he owned with a stout lady, the real Clara Lane. Dick Randall told me that he was renting out space in the basement of the Hotel Wentworth on West Forty-seventh Street and asked me if I would like to have an office, free of charge, free rent. He would give me the office free in exchange for his using the prestige and the power of my name as a radio personality to help rent out the other spaces.

I went with him right from that delicatessen to the Wentworth basement. There were about twelve or fourteen cubicles, you could almost call them closets—cells. He'd rent out space to Broadway Danny Rose–type impresarios—they really did exist in those days, those kind of producers, promoters, agents. I took him up on his offer, and that was my first office.

One day, Dick said to me, "Joe, why don't we do some TV?"

I said, "I'm afraid of TV. I can't rehearse. Besides, I don't exactly look like Alan Ladd in a pinstriped suit."

But he convinced me to give it a try. We made a fifty-fifty deal. I'd be the TV personality, and he'd be the producer. I knew that deejays playing records wouldn't make it alone, but I had a notion of what I wanted to do: play old records and bring back the actual old-time stars in person. So we went to Channel 7, WJZ, the local ABC affiliate, and he got me on TV. When Channel 7 opened up in the daytime, they asked me if I wanted to be part of their lineup. "We'll give you the hour, Joe. What kind of show do you want to do?"

I thought about it and said, "I want to do a show of kids dancing to records." They told me, "That will never go." Of course, Dick Clark made millions with *American Bandstand.* So then I said, "How about a show of people singing old-time songs with the words on the screen?" They said no, and later came along a show called *Sing Along with Mitch,* which was very popular. Then I said, "If I can't do that, why don't I do a talk show? With people talking, nose-to-nose, eyeball-to-eyeball." Then they said, "The word's tele-VISION; you've got to give 'em vision, seltzer bottles spraying, pratfalls, baggy pants, you gotta give 'em burlesque skits." Anyway, I defied them. I thought, Well, I'll give it a six-month run. I debuted on television on January 8, 1951, with a show that was listed as *Joe Franklin—Disk Jockey.* In my time slot I was preceded by *Kitchen Kapers,* starring the six-foot six-inch cooking expert Tiny Ruffner. Following my show was still more cooking, with Dione Lucas. On opposing channels, I was going head-to-head against *Shopping News*, with Kathy Norris; the *Early Bird Matinee;* and the news with John Wingate.

★

At any hour of day or night, there was very little else of what would become known as the talk-show circuit. The *Tonight* show began as *Broadway Open House* in May 1950, hosted by Jerry Lester. But *Broadway Open House* wasn't a talk show as we know it today. It billed itself as a variety show. Jerry Lester had his own group, his own little coterie, including a young writer, Neil "Doc" Simon, and the five-foot-eleven, well-endowed blonde Dagmar, who sat on a chair under a large sign that read Girl Singer. In later years Dagmar would come up to my office, when she could fit through the door. She'd come in sideways.

Morey Amsterdam, the cellist-comedian who later became so well known as "Buddy" on the *Dick Van Dyke Show*, hosted *Broadway Open House* for a while, and a few years later, he got his own morning show. Another of the first television personalities was Wendy Barrie, an English actress. Her debut had been in the film *Henry VIII*, with Charles Laughton. A heavy drinker, she hosted her show seated on the floor, and her catchphrase was: "Be a good bunny!" She called all her guests "Sweetie" or "Dearie." Her show took place in an imaginary Manhattan apartment on the twenty-first floor. Why the twenty-first floor, nobody knew.

Martin Block ventured onto the airwaves, emceeing a music show with Perry Como, and deejay Art Ford ("the Milkman," whom I'd known from WNEW radio) hosted a variety show on TV. Barbara Walters, daughter of nightclub owner Lou Walters, made her first appearance on TV in 1949, covering the Easter Parade. A number of radio personalities crossed over from radio to television as well, including Kate Smith, Don McNeill, Virginia Graham, Zeke Manners, and Garry Moore, who debuted as host of *I've Got a Secret* in June 1952. But out of all these contenders, I believe I may safely claim that my show was the first TV talk show as we know it today.

Believe it or not, a few weeks after I was on the air—I'd made a few pennies, he'd made a few pennies—Dick Randall said to me, "Joe, I need money. I'll let you buy me out for a hundred dollars." I thought he was crazy, but I didn't ask questions. I gave him $100, and I belonged once again 100 percent to myself. If he had stayed with me that first year and a half, he would have made $20,000–$50,000. Instead, he sold out for $100.

This kind of behavior was characteristic of Dick, who was always sort of a sharpshooter. As a matter of fact, he's out of the country now. He was always skirting the edges, the fringes, of respectability. A little bit slick. He was a fast talker, a promoter, like a Mike Todd. Not a womanizer like Mike Todd but always in some kind of trouble. He still lives in Europe, producing movies.

The ABC studios were in an old building at 67 West Sixty-sixth Street. It used to house stables, and we came into offices that reeked of horse manure. We broadcast from the basement, cold in the winter and boiling hot in the summer. The air-conditioning never worked right, and the lights blazed. In that basement were the makeup department, film department, a lounge with a small television set, and a couple of makeup rooms. I remember a vending machine that routinely devoured our quarters. Every time somebody put a quarter in, it would disappear. One day, after months of annoyance, somebody kicked the machine, and quarters started pouring out. It was like a jackpot in a casino. Everybody stopped working and ran in. They felt they deserved it.

Leonard Goldenson was the president of ABC, and he would come visit us in the basement once a year. When he appeared, it was like General Schwarzkopf arriving; people cleaning corners that had never been cleaned, the ceilings, places I had never seen before.

Today, whenever I go past the building and think of that dingy basement and the people who went there to meet me, I shake my head in amazement. Elvis, Ann-Margret, John Wayne, the Kennedys, Jerry Lewis, Eddie Cantor, Georgie Jessel, Bob Hope, James Cagney, Mario Lanza, all came into our dingy basement. Today ABC has beautiful studios, but in those days they didn't spend the money. Whatever the station earned they spent on equipment or funneled the money into the big shows, like the

★

U.S. Steel Hour, Pulitzer Prize Playhouse, and the *Voice of Firestone.*

The station's biggest daytime show became the *Mickey Mouse Club,* broadcast at five in the afternoon. WJZ bought libraries of syndicated programs, and you could always see *Mark of Zorro, The Bowery Boys, The Dead End Kids,* and Chubby Jackson hosting *The Little Rascals. Jim the Wrangler,* hosted by Jim Wyler, featured western stars like William Boyd as Hopalong Cassidy. *Time for Fun* was hosted by Joe Bova, a very charming man who is now a Broadway actor. He played a character called "Jolly Jellybean," or "Johnny Jellybean," I forget which. My memory only goes so far.

A show called *Tinker's Work Shop* was hosted by Bob Keeshan, the future *Captain Kangaroo.* After he went to CBS, he was replaced by Henry Burbig, with his mustache and overalls. Henry, a comedian and dialectician, was famous for a routine called "What would William Tell?" He was, incidentally, in the same class as my father at P.S. 158.

For adults, a star of the new daytime lineup was Claire Mann, a charming, sophisticated talk-show lady. Tom Poston hosted a two-hour afternoon program called *Everything Goes.* Tom was one of Steve Allen's protégés, very underrated, clever, funny. He and I were close, and in years to come, our sons went to the same summer camp. *Everything Goes* was a variety show with a singer named Marion Colby and a famous opera star, the tenor James Melton. Melton had one of the biggest collections of antique autos in the world. They found his body on a New Year's Day frozen to death on his balcony. The show was taken off abruptly after rumors of payola among the show's managers and producers.

Scheduled alongside Tom Poston, Claire Mann, and the children's shows, I was the first to fill Channel 7's noon-to-one slot. Among this group and my rivals across the dial, I was soon dubbed by the press New York's "King of Daytime Teevee."

The set for the first daytime *Joe Franklin Show* was spartan: a table, no couch, two large chairs. The backdrop was a blown-up photo of the Essex House. We had two cameramen, a floor manager, and a boom man—that was the entire crew. The shows were not slick; there was no precision. It was all organic, from the bones.

My first guest was Fannie Hurst, the author of *Back Street* and many other best-sellers of the 1930s. We talked for the entire hour. As I was looking through her books—*Humoresque, Back Street*—I thumbed through one called *Great Laughter.* Chapter 1 was called "A Long Bunch of Memory Lanes," and I said to myself, That's a nice sound, a nice phrase. "Memory lane," I said, pondering it in my mind, remembering how my radio idol Fred Allen had used it as well. "Can I borrow that?"

She said, "Sure, Joe."

So I called my second show *Joe Franklin's Memory Lane.*

For the ensuing shows, I gathered about eight or nine people—singers, comics, acrobats, a whole troupe of performers—like those Steve Allen had assembled on NBC. Regulars included now-obscure names like Tony Lane's Trio, Lee Fields, June Natelson, Enzo de Mola, Alan Gerard, Miss New York City, and Rosalind Page. With these and others, I envisioned myself putting together a long-running stock company. That concept came to an end when I got a phone call the next day from AFTRA, the actors' union, that I owed about $6,000 in fees for all those guests. I didn't know they all had to get paid. I paid the $6,000, and I learned fast: Don't do too many live acts.

My old friend the bandleader Paul Whiteman was the president in charge of music at the station. He had a music contract with Frank Vagnoni, who was responsible for signing musicians for ABC shows. The terms of the contract meant that the musicians would be paid even if there was no show for them. There were about forty or fifty top musicians, and there was not one network program left for these men to play on. They still had about a year to go on their contracts.

Whiteman sent them over to my new little local show, giving us a live orchestra. It was unbelievable; I can't fathom it. If I'd had to pay that band, it would have cost me $20,000 a week!

★

Every single player was a star: Bobby Byrne, Morey Feld, Billy Butterfield, Rocky Colucci, Bob Haggert, Yank Lawson. I'd bring in Connie Francis, Eddie Fisher, to sing. I scratched my head at my good luck. In later years, I was grateful to have an organ or piano or synthesizer, a ragtime pianist or a Jew's harp, a ring-a-ding washboard. I just can't believe what a break it was that I was the beneficiary of all those great musicians under contract, and they stayed with me until their contracts expired. Naturally, they were not renewed. There was no need for them or any use for them on a show like mine. There I was, with just a local show and a zero budget, and I had that kind of musical talent.

Eddie Fisher, a brilliant young singer from Philadelphia, made some of his earliest appearances on my show, and I watched his career with fascination. In his era he was gigantic. He was far and away the biggest of the big. I had him on when he was starting out. Eddie Cantor, who "introduced" Eddie Fisher at Grossinger's resort in the Catskills, brought him to me when he was virtually unknown. Eddie Fisher was very, very pleasant but not too articulate. In the early 1950s, he had one hit after another: "I'm Walking Behind You," "Bring Back the Thrill," "Turn Back the Hands of Time," "Anytime," "Downhearted."

I was amazed that Eddie Fisher, who looked so shy and innocent and unvirile, married Debbie Reynolds, Elizabeth Taylor, and then Connie Stevens. He was deceptively a ladies' man, because he didn't look the type. He was rumored to be the third largest in the below-the-belt department in Hollywood, behind Milton Berle and Forrest Tucker.

Later on, Eddie Fisher got in trouble with Dr. Feelgood. Remember Dr. Feelgood, Dr. Max Jacobson? He wrote out prescriptions for pep pills, shots for your nerves. His patients became strung out, utterly dependent on his mixtures of amphetamines. He had a lot of celebrity clients, including Eddie Fisher's manager, Milton Blackstone, who came on my show himself many times to promote new talent. In the 1960s, Dr. Jacobson lost his license in a landmark case. His practice fell apart, and he died shortly thereafter. His fall from grace and the identities of his high-profile clients were front-page news. It marked one of the first crackdowns on prescription-drug abuse.

Eddie Fisher got his own show, *Coke Time*, and became known as the "Coca-Cola Kid." I didn't see him much anymore. It really hurt me that he didn't come back. It was the first in what would be a recurring undercurrent in my career. People I helped to promote or to whom I gave initial exposure often didn't return. Nobody wants to be reminded of the times when they were broke. It's human nature. At first I was confused, disappointed, but today I sympathize with them. They don't want to remember the days when they were struggling.

I've got to confess, Eddie Fisher was, and remains, one of my very favorite singers. I play his records on the radio all the time. Not the ones that he might have made ten or fifteen years ago when he had his assorted comebacks, but when he was at his peak, when he was twenty-two or twenty-three years old.

On radio, I had become famous for playing old records. On TV, I wanted to become famous for old movies. At that time, silents weren't the antiques they are now; they were only twenty-five years old and readily available. I went out and bought every old movie I could get. I found them sitting in bins at old camera stores, film stores. I bought them on safety film, but many of the original films were nitrate, very flammable, and thousands have been lost forever. Even as I write there's a desperate race against time to preserve what's left. Films are crumbling into dust, decomposing into nothingness. They can be copied onto safety film, but it's a very expensive process. Works of art that are two thousand years old are preserved, but films that were made fifty or sixty years ago are gone forever. Isn't that sad?

I worked with a film editor named Hans Dudelheim, who cut the movies, timed them, and made up the log for the programming department. Hans got a lot of ribbing for his name. One day a man came up to him and said, "Hans Dudelheim, that's a pretty funny name."

☆

Hans said, "Well, what's your name?"

The man answered, "Fendel Yirksen."

We played at least two to three films a day, of varying lengths. If they were good clips, I'd let them run on. Sometimes I'd play a fifteen-minute two-reeler, comedies starring Ben Blue, Ben Turpin, Charlie Chaplin, Fatty Arbuckle, Charlie Chase, B. S. Pulley, all the great comedians. *TV Guide* heralded selections like *Cured by Excitement*, with Billy Bevan, Madeline Hurlock, and Vernon Dent: "Two-reel top-rated comedy. Joe does the commentary, with honky-tonk pianola music background." Billy Crystal recently told me that when he was a kid, he would fake being sick so he could stay home and watch *Memory Lane,* especially for the clips. They gave him his first exposure to those great comedians of the past. He said, "Faking illness to watch Joe was my first acting excercise."

The station had what they called a continuity department, a euphemism for network censor. Grace Johnson was the woman in charge, and if anybody ever looked like a censor, it was Grace Johnson. She wore a black dress and stalked the basement floor like Margaret Hamilton as the Wicked Witch of the West. She used to scare everyone. She was the self-styled Will Hays of ABC. She would criticize almost everything, labeling it as "lascivious, lewd, ribald, racy," pulling out every adjective in the book. She had such power! And nobody and nothing were immune. I wish Grace could see modern TV!

Old cartoons were the first to be cut. Politically correct did not originate in the 1990s. *Betty Boop* and *Felix the Cat,* among others, stereotyped Jews, blacks, gays, and large segments were deleted. In many old films the Jews had long, exaggerated hook noses. The *Our Gang* comedies showed black kids eating watermelon, their eyes glowing in the dark. After I played one of those, I had to leave town for about a week.

But most of the censor's comments were, I felt, petty and insignificant. Nowadays, in a day and age when the standard talk show consists of tossing dwarfs, making love to doorknobs, and

☆

how to put on a condom, they seem completely tame. Your show could be lily-white, 99.9 percent clean, but if one guest said something off-color, they would take you off the air. You couldn't say the word "pregnant"; you certainly couldn't say the words "orgasm" or "climax," "hell," "damn." Forget it, that was profanity! I made the joke to one of my guests "Did you hear they merged Stop and Shop with A and P? It's called Stop and Pee." I got a three-day suspension. When we featured the Ubangi Dance Company, I mischievously let slip "U-bangi me, I-bangi you." My punishment was another three days. Though each suspension stung at the time, compared to what might have happened, I consider myself lucky. Jack Paar parted ways with NBC after what seemed to me an equally petty offense, a long, innocuous story involving the term "water closet."

A frequent guest on my show, the director Otto Preminger, got into big trouble with a censorship organization called the Legion of Decency when he used the word "virgin" in his movie *The Moon Is Blue.* He rightly pointed out that the word is used every day, at every mass of the Catholic church. They didn't care, and the movie was boycotted. It was said that if the Legion of Decency sneezed, Hollywood caught a cold.

To avoid having Grace Johnson chop my cherished silent comedies into incomprehensibility, I'd hold them back until two minutes before the show, figuring we could always slide them through. They wouldn't have time to screen them. That's how I got in a lot of hot water, but I would've never been able to show them any other way.

Probably the most disgraceful aspect of that era was the McCarthy witchhunts. The careers of many of my peers were destroyed by gossip and innuendo. A group called AWARE published *Red Channels: The Report of Communist Influence in Radio and Television,* pointing a finger at 151 of my peers, labeling them "commies," "subversives," and "dupes."

I was very upset about the fate of a friend of mine, John Henry Faulk, an announcer and storyteller, whose career was ru-

ined. Among the allegations against Faulk were that he had once
had dinner with Soviet ambassador Andrei Gromyko. Faulk
readily admitted this was true but pointed out that the secretary
of state and Eleanor Roosevelt were attending the same affair.
CBS fired Faulk, anyway. Faulk sued for libel, but the case took
six years. By the time the lawsuit was settled, Faulk was broke,
selling encyclopedias. The case pitted another friend of mine, attorney Louis Nizer, against Roy Cohn, ironically also a frequent
guest on my show. At last Faulk was awarded $3.5 million, but
by that time AWARE had folded and was unable to pay.

Like John Henry Faulk, the actor John Garfield was destroyed
by charges. At one time I walked down Broadway and saw his
name on four marquees. He was playing in four movies at one
time, among them the classics *Gentleman's Ageement* and *Body
and Soul*. He was the number one actor, a rising luminary. But
one year later, he couldn't get a job because of the red scare.
They accused him just because he'd read the *Daily Worker* when
he was a kid. It was a sad time.

I quickly began to shape the show with my own style. I never
had a studio audience. Maybe I felt embarrassed; if I couldn't fill
the house, I'd be humiliated. I've always had that insecurity
about filling the audience for five days a week. I'm always dis-
comfited when I see a show on TV, and at the end, during the
crawl, the announcer comes on and says, "If you would like tickets to the show, please write to so-and-so." Even worse is when
they ask the viewers for ideas.

The only downside of playing without an audience was that
we could never have a comedian perform his act. If you've ever
heard a comedian do his act in front of a camera, you know what
I mean. They die. I mean, *die*. Canned laughter is even worse.
Most comedians understood that. They got the idea and didn't
even try. We would just talk about their upcoming performances,
dates, and engage in the lively art of conversation.

The comics of that period came out of what was then called the borscht belt, so named because hotel guests drank the Russian soup borscht three meals a day. Some of the greats to come out of the borscht belt were Van Johnson, Danny Kaye, John Garfield, Sid Caesar, Phil Silvers, and Red Buttons. Resort owners like Jenny Grossinger were like second mothers to these young performers. They offered a paid training ground to these kids. It was a place to eat, to sleep; even getting $150 for the season, they'd love it. In those days you had some tremendous kids with talent, potential; they'd go up there and polish off the rough edges. Georgie Burns recently said, "There are no places left to be lousy." The borscht belt gave young talent that luxury. Some people consider my show the Catskills, the borscht belt, of television. Some performers would be terrible, some would be so-so, some pretty good. But once in a while you'd find a gem. It was the potential of discovery, of finding that gem, that made every show exciting.

I never rehearsed my show, never read the authors' books, just glanced at their jackets. I guess I was the only talk show on the air that was not rehearsed. If you see a talk show today and somebody says, "How do you feel?" it says on the cue card, "Fine." I'm not saying I did it the right way, but my philosophy always was, you don't rehearse your dialogue before you're going to have dinner with guests. Why would you do it on a talk show, where the commodity is verbal communication? A good dinner conversation flows spontaneously, and I wanted my show to do the same. I wanted to use that same technique on the air, for better or for worse.

It was very important for me to keep the guests isolated before the show. I wouldn't talk to them before a show, and I didn't mingle beforehand. They always tended to talk too much and shoot their load, and by the time they got on the air, they were dry. They forgot, when they spoke in the green room, that they were talking to one person. When they got out onstage, they were afraid of repeating themselves. I went out of my way to keep them from socializing with each other, but sometimes I couldn't control it. I wasn't there to supervise. I pleaded with them, "Please don't talk to each other too much in the green room before the show." But many times, they talked and talked and then came out and had nothing to say.

In those early days, it was easy to get great guests. For one thing there wasn't very much competition. Every movie studio had a PR person, eager to showcase their latest stars. I'd get Burt Lancaster, Lee Remick, Jack Lemmon, Paul Newman, from the PR people. Along with the up-and-coming stars, I sought out the old-timers. I used to look in telephone books and see which ones still lived around town.

Some of them were real old-timers, in their eighties, nineties, flattered to be remembered. One of my very beautiful highlights of that year was when I discovered that upstairs in the Hotel Wentworth lived a lady named Nita Naldi. She had been Rudolph Valentino's leading lady in movies like *Blood and Sand*. She told me about Valentino's days as a professional gigolo. Though he turned her on, she regretted that she could never do the same for him. From her private collection she gave me an incredible picture of Valentino, which hung in the lobby of the Paramount Theatre in 1926, when that theater opened. Today that picture is worth maybe $20,000 or $30,000 to a collector.

I brought a lot of the silent stars to my show. I had Buster Keaton, Gloria Swanson. I had as many as I could get. Sadly, many of the ones I liked were dead by the time I began. It's amazing about these old-time actors: Walter Connolly, or Charles Butterworth, or Warren William, great names you saw in old movies. They looked sixty or seventy. But when you read their obituaries, you see that they died when they were forty-two or forty-five. Somehow they aged more quickly in those days. I had as many as I could, but most of them were gone by the time I broke in.

I had opera stars, politicians, people who had their own shows on WABC, or people who were in town for a show. Soon they were all calling me. We had New York City mayor Robert Wagner four times; Bess Myerson, when she was a beauty queen; Ed Koch, when he was a congressman; Bishop Fulton Sheen, a very good guest, a very funny man. I had Bishop Sheen on one time

☆

with Milton Berle. They had appeared opposite each other on Tuesday nights. So Milton Berle said to the bishop, "We both have the same sponsor, Sky Chief."

Elvis made his very first television appearance on my show, before he was famous. He was a lovely guy, very shy; he called everybody "Sir." The colonel was standing in the back, watching his every move as Elvis sang a live number. The other guests on the panel were Ann-Margaret Olson, who later dropped the Olson and became Ann-Margret, and Jimmy Rogers, a singer-songwriter who came on with his test record of a song called "Honeycomb." It was quite a panel on one show—Jimmy Rogers, Ann-Margaret Olson, and Elvis.

After Elvis was on my show, he was picked up for the Tommy Dorsey summer replacement show on Dumont Network, the *Dorsey Brothers' Show*. From there, he was picked up for the *Ed Sullivan Show*. I don't get credit for being the first to put him on because there are no kinescopes; none of it is documented.

I had a network of friends and press people who would bring me guests. One of my best sources was Irving Cahn, who co-produced the *Luncheon at Sardi's* show and had had the first review show on the radio, *News, Views and Reviews*. Irving had started in the earliest days of radio, on WBNX in the Bronx, then went to WHOM radio when it was in the basement of the Hotel President. Irving was talent coordinator for a show called *20 Questions,* first on radio, then on TV. The late publicist-attorney Dick Roffman brought me authors of undiscovered gems. Along with Irving Cahn and Dick Roffman, I was fortunate to get talent through Gary Stevens.

Gary Stevens was a public relations man who was later hired to promote Johnny Carson. Gary is sophisticated, a brilliant mind, a man of letters with impeccable connections in Hollywood and on Broadway. A former executive at Warner Brothers, he and his partner Sid Rubin brought me Anne Bancroft, Fred MacMurray, Kim Novak, Eddie Cantor, and many others.

All my bookers worked on a freebie basis. Occasionally, I'd let them print business cards with my name on them. I was sometimes careless passing out those cards. Once in a while I'd get a call from a garment house. One owner said, "Mr. Franklin, where's the fashion show?"

I said, "What fashion show?"

He answered, "Somebody walked in with your business card yesterday. He said he's your talent coordinator and he was going to do a fashion show on your program, so I gave him twenty-four dresses."

So I said to the owner of the garment house, "If you're that dumb to give away all that merchandise without checking, verifying through me, you should've given him the whole store, not just twenty-four dresses!"

Phil St. James was the only one to officially bear the title "Joe Franklin Talent Coordinator." He didn't get paid, but he was able to get a little clout, go to movie theaters for nothing. Phil always gave out a phone number and told people, "Don't call me until after two o'clock. Important. Don't call until after two." If, out of curiosity, you called at 1:45 and asked, "Is Phil St. James there?" somebody would answer and say, "Who's Phil James?" "Whattya mean, who's Phil St. James. He gave me this number." "Listen, buddy. This is a phone booth." Phil St. James did his business every day at the phone booth at two o'clock.

Phil St. James got me many guests straight from the Apollo Theatre. I'm proud to say I was one of the first to have black guests. I didn't do it intentionally; I was just seeking out talent. Many years later, I was at an opening of a new Martin Paint store, one of my longtime sponsors. The big black security guard approached me—he was *big*—hovered over me, and growled, "You Joe Franklin?" I started trembling. He said, "We black people, we love you. Anybody in the world can put on Sammy Davis or Harry Belafonte or Bill Cosby, but you put on the black people that nobody knows." That made me cry. That moment was one of the highlights of my entire life.

I was always very, very loose, careless about my talent scouts or bookers using my name. A couple of times it backfired and got me in hot water. If I wasn't attending an opening, I would tell people to use my comp tickets. I couldn't stand to see them go to waste. But a few days later the press agent would call me and say, "Joe, why'd you do that to me?" Giving press tickets away is a real no-no, and I was taken off a few lists.

I was once invited to the preview of a show called *Catskills on Broadway,* starring the comedian Freddy Roman. I couldn't make it and gave my tickets to somebody else. After the curtain went down, Freddy raised his hand, silenced the applause, and said, "Ladies and gentlemen, tonight we are privileged to have my all-time favorite television host, a unique and wonderful man, the talented, the legendary, the dynamic Joe Franklin!" The lights swung through the crowd, searching me out. They swirled and swirled, unable to find me. At last Roman realized I wasn't there and said, "Aw, fuck him. I never liked him, anyway!"

Sometimes I went to premieres even when I was tired or didn't feel like going. You couldn't have an empty seat at a Broadway opening. After the lights dimmed, I would doze off. I would always laugh when I saw the other critics dozing off, too, and wondered how they produced all those great reviews.

Ed Sullivan didn't doze during premieres. But I do remember, during the opening of *Sweet Charity* on Broadway, sitting behind Ed Sullivan and his wife, Sylvia. Ed Sullivan didn't understand what the humor was. Every time there'd be a comic line on the stage, the audience would laugh, and he would nudge Sylvia. She would explain it to him. Then there'd be a delayed reaction, and he'd laugh thirty seconds later. He was a great showman, Ed Sullivan, but he didn't understand simple jokes.

At the start of my Channel 7 program, we didn't have a single sponsor. Since I was working on a percentage basis, I was making nothing. The only time I got anything for those first shows was when I mentioned the words Knickerbocker Beer. Irving Zussman of the Knickerbocker Beer Company would send me a free case of beer. I did my first few weeks on TV for a couple of cases of beer.

My father, who had never before really supported my career,

started to become a big fan. When I went on TV he tried very, very hard to help me get sponsors. Being in the paper and twine business, he did business with paper companies, cleaning companies, and textiles. He wrote letters to all his contacts, and he actually got results. Brillo came on board, and so did Soft-Spun napkins. They were my first sponsors, from my father.

Soft-Spun wanted me to pitch their toilet paper on the show, and I didn't have the nerve to tell them that the network censor—Grace Johnson again—had never permitted a toilet paper commercial before. In continuity clearance, I would clear only copy for their napkins. But we would bend the law and do the toilet paper commercial, anyway. A hostess—played by my fiancée, Lois—would hold rolls of toilet paper and caress them, love them and cuddle them, hug them. Doing something like that was absolutely unheard of. I only prayed that Grace Johnson wasn't watching, and sure enough, I guess she wasn't, because I never had a complaint.

Another early sponsor was Robert Hall Clothing, then *the* name in men's clothing. I owed the account to a young man named Jerry Bess. Robert Hall became a sponsor for many, many years. I was their spokesman, appearing at clothing and department stores along with other celebrity spokespeople, including pioneering rock disk jockey Alan Freed and William B. Williams. Jerry Bess, incidentally, was to follow me to WOR-TV in later years. Early television broadcasting was a small world, a big business but a tight-knit, small community at the same time.

Once the first sponsors fell in line, it became an avalanche. When I first started with Channel 7, my deal was fifty-fifty. I would receive 50 percent of the ad revenue. Not even the biggest stars, the biggest names would get a deal like that. But they figured, who's going to watch? What's 50 percent of nothing? Then I began making $8,000, $10,000, $12,000 a week, so they chopped my percentage down to 35 percent, then 25, 10. It was still an incredible take. Nobody ever thought TV was going to take off the way it did in the daytime.

I began to get big sponsors, national corporations like

☆

Nabisco, Best Foods, Lever Brothers. I had Grossinger's bread for a sponsor, and Shapiro Wine, "so smooth you could cut it with a knife." Necchi Sewing Machines was another major sponsor. The first time I did a Necchi commercial, I was supposed to demonstrate the machine, which was waiting in the wings. When it came time for me to bring out the machine, no one could find it. Someone had stolen the prop. I had to ad-lib the commercial without the sewing machine.

Melmac dishes was an early sponsor, and their claim was that their dishes were unbreakable. We were going to prove this on TV with a live demonstration. I stood in front of a table filled with "indestructible" Melmac dinnerware. I put my hands on the tablecloth and pulled. Piles of plates, cups, and saucers all went flying, with a crash resounding through the whole studio. I stepped back and surveyed the damage while giving careful thought to my next line: "That's what *would've* happened if you hadn't used Melmac dishes!"

As if contending with network censors wasn't enough, the sponsors had their own codes of conduct. They were very concerned about every line, every word, you uttered. The old *Gunsmoke* program was sponsored by L&M cigarettes, manufacturers of Lucky Strikes. In one scene in the script, Chester is shot at and narrowly misses being killed. He was supposed to remark, "This is my lucky day," but they had to cut that because of the connotation. They were alert to every phrase, every nuance.

I was offered a lot of money to do cigarette commercials, and it wasn't that I had any objections because of health reasons. At that time, the health risks of cigarettes were still not well known. I actually did make a test for a cigarette commercial that turned out to be so hilarious that people still look at it and laugh. I had never smoked, and I didn't know how to hold a cigarette, how to light one, much less inhale it.

Another first on my show was the first TV commercial for a motion picture. My radio producer, Ed Gollin, worked for 20th Century-Fox as an assistant PR man to Martin Michel. He said to them one day, "I've got a friend, Joe Franklin. He's got a TV

☆

show, and I think we should buy a commercial on his program for that new Hemingway movie *The Snows of Kilimanjaro*." They said, "You're out of your mind! How can you advertise on a competitive medium?" It was unheard of! He argued with them for a long time, back and forth, and finally he got them to appropriate $200. They gave him the film's press book, and with a scissors we cut out the words "Gregory Peck," "*Snows of Kilimanjaro*," cut out "Ernest Hemingway" and "20th Century-Fox," pasted them all on cards. I spoke while we showed the words on the screen, for a whole minute, "Don't miss the picture, big picture, CinemaScope, matzo balls, prune Danish . . ." That was the first movie commercial *ever*. When they make a movie today, they spend more money on advertising on TV than on the whole cost of the film. After that, little by little, TV advertising for movies got bigger and bigger. But we broke the ice and were so successful with *Snows of Kilimanjaro* that Twentieth immediately followed it up with a second picture, *Park Row*, directed by Samuel Fuller.

One of my longtime sponsors and dearest friends was Bernie Castro from Castro Convertibles. As you might see from many of my photos, he provided me with a cute miniature sofa that used to sit on my desk. I used to go on his yacht every Sunday, with his wife, maybe twenty years ago. Bernie's yacht was a complete business write-off because it was a floating Castro showroom. He took clients on board, along with a crew of forty people, to sell them Castro convertibles. Tragically, his son was accidentally killed by his wife—Bernie's daughter-in-law—with a gun. She heard a noise in the hallway, thought it was a burglar, and shot her own husband instead. Up until that time I'd wanted a gun, but when I heard that, I decided not to keep one around.

Along with their salaries or commissions, hosts and announcers often received freebies from their sponsors. Martin Block had given me my first lesson in receiving perks back when I was at WNEW. He was always inundated with phonograph records from anxious song pluggers and promotion men. He would take the overstock to various camera stores around the city and trade them in for camera equipment, his hobby. It didn't cost him anything, and the store owners were glad to get the latest disks.

One of my sponsors, Dolly Madison ice cream, sent twelve quarts of ice cream a week to my house. Daniel Squillante's Nutrition Center provided me with vitamins and minerals. Another sponsor would send big, big boxes of expensive candy, and Canada Dry ginger ale, for years, would send me soda—every Friday four cases, six cases. After I started putting on a few pounds from all the sweets, I figured I was better off when I was poor and skinny without having all those clients sending samples to my house every week. I always wanted Cadillac for a sponsor, but I never got them, never got a car. A friend of mine, Long John Nebel, had a show on WMCA radio, and he had Frank Campbell's funeral parlor as a sponsor. That was the ultimate barter arrangement.

Some hosts and producers found a new racket by offering prizes to the viewers. When Channel 7 lit up in the daytime, they put on about fourteen brand-new live shows, including the *Joe Franklin Show.* The other thirteen ran contests. They'd get 100 bottles of perfume from the manufacturer. Then they'd announce 100 prizes and give one bottle of perfume to the public and keep ninety-nine for themselves. On Johnny Carson's game show *Do You Trust Your Wife?* a staffer was in love with a girl named Chickie. He gave her the best prizes and forgot to mail out the rest.

For me, my only responsibility, my prime obligation, was always to the sponsor and the viewer. If I ran a contest, I would give every prize to the viewers at home. I was never in business for myself, for better or worse. There was no tight government monitoring the way there is nowadays, or the way it developed after the quiz-show scandals in 1958. It just developed that I was stupidly honest, noncorrupt. I knew people whose salary was $500 a week in those days, but they made $2,000 a week in merchandise prizes that they kept and promoted from the various companies.

It could work the other way around, too. Wooing clients was

an art. I would take them out to dinner, sometimes I bought them theater tickets out of my own pocket. I told them I got the tickets for nothing when I really paid. But most of the schmoozing was wasted, since what it usually came down to was the ratings, anyway.

What kept the sponsors coming back were the ratings. Ratings, as everyone knows, rule the world of broadcasting. Your future isn't controlled by human beings; it's governed by a machine. You're like a product in the supermarket. If it doesn't sell, it's automatically dumped into the ocean. Originally there was the Crosley Survey, then the Hooper Ratings on radio, and today, Arbitron and Neilson, functioning on both radio and TV. Georgie Jessel complained way back in 1943 about the power of the Crosley Survey. "By the way, Mr. and Mrs. America, have you ever met anyone who was called on the phone as to this survey? I haven't, and I've inquired in every part of the country." Today Neilson is controlled by twelve hundred people. I've never believed twelve hundred people could tell what the whole world was watching.

From time to time I've said smart things in the press like "I never look at the ratings, I go by cash register ratings," meaning I deliver sales for my clients. But I now admit that it's just not true. Everybody in the industry knows that can't be true. You depend on the ratings; that's your lifeline. Whether I liked them or not, whether I accepted their validity or not, I studied them avidly. I got away with quips like that because it made good copy from a cute kid.

Once, in the early days on Channel 7, I wanted to find out what the public *really* thought of me, so I dipped into my own pocket and contacted a marketing company called Pulse. I paid them to do a study on my audience ratings, and according to the survey, I came out number one, my rating far and away doubling my nearest competition, the *Bob Crosby Show* and *One Man's Family*. That was a little roundabout insinuation to me that ratings' services could be a little bit bought. I never really examined further whether the ratings' services were prone to be a little corrupt. I wonder what Bob Crosby's results would have shown if *he* had commissioned the study.

Canada Dry proved to be one of my most loyal and enduring early sponsors. They had a restaurant salute, presenting a different restaurant every day. The restaurant would serve Canada Dry. It was a nice tie-in for both sides. They got into thousands of restaurants by virtue of my show; it was tremendous merchandising for them.

I read the copy on big cue cards or from printed sheets on my desk. They moved the camera close to the product, and I read from the paper: "Ladies and gentlemen, we are presented by Canada Dry ginger ale, featured in the world's finest restaurants. Today's restaurant guest is Ismail Kaduchis, from the White Rock Inn."

A restaurant owner then came on and said, "Thank you, Mr. Franklin. It's our great pleasure to serve Canada Dry beverages. I'd like to invite your viewers to sample them at our restaurant. We're at the corners of Avenues X, Y, and Z in Brooklyn. Our restaurant was started by my papa, Vinnie, and we serve the best lasagna in Brooklyn."

Once, however, on live TV, the restaurant owner made a gaffe. "Mr. Franklin, we've been in business 125 years, and our building still has all the original pricks." He meant bricks but said pricks. My camera crew fell on the floor.

The restaurateurs who came on my show had usually never been on TV before, and they tended to be nervous. One came on and got so excited on the show that he had a heart attack, live. I thought he was laughing at one of my bad jokes; he moaned, "*Huhh, huhh, huhh . . .*" like that. The death rattle: "*Ugggghhhh . . .*" I think we cut away to a commercial. He slipped under the table, the camera got off him, and we called for help. We did have a doctor at ABC, but he was busy reading the racing form. Nixon and Kennedy were in the next room rehearsing for their debate, and they ran in to help revive the guy. I had no choice but to keep on going, to talk to another guest, the camera in close, while they worked on the restaurant owner. It was already too late; he was dead. Somehow we finished the show.

I went up to the projection room at four o'clock, when the studio was totally empty. The restaurant owner's body was still sprawled on the floor. Hans Dudelheim came back at seven and told me the body was still there. Since he had died at the scene, they had to call for a coroner. The coroner had had a busy day and couldn't come until 8:00 P.M.

By mid-decade, *Joe Franklin's Memory Lane* had taken off and was a fixture on daytime TV. My face was all over the city, appearances at charity events, the opening of Palisades City Amusement Park, at Gimbel's, Roseland Dance judging mambo contests, showing Chaplin movies at Coney Island, featured at the United Auto Workers Christmas party, host of National Pharmacy Week, live in person at Long Island's Club Safari. I was so successful that, as in radio, I got requests to do other shows. I hosted *Romantic Interlude,* featuring half-hour clips of movies, full-length movies cut down to half an hour, sloppily chopped and crudely edited. *Memory Lane Cavalcade* featured vaudeville and old-time stars. I was the emcee of *Spotlight to Stardom*, a talent show airing on Monday nights and featuring new talent. Diahann Carroll was one of the performers we introduced. We only lasted four to six weeks; we were taken off the air because Dennis James had a similar show called *Chance of a Lifetime.* Even though mine was only local and his was national, they made us discontinue. Although we were getting high ratings, the show was very popular, the network said, "You gotta remove that show."

Joe Franklin Junior was possibly my most offbeat entry. I showed cartoons to an audience of kids and played games with them. It ran for two full seasons, sponsored by Flav-r-Straws. Flav-r-Straws always amazed me: Put the straw in the milk, it comes out strawberry. Chocolate, vanilla. They were a big sensation; then they just vanished after a while. With a show like that and with my other commitments—personal appearances for the

sponsors, emceeing charity and community events—I was just
going through the motions. I had one other kids' show at the
same time, *Memory Lane Jr.*, which was kind of an asinine concept. Kids who are five, six years old can't have long memories.

Though I enjoy children, I never had a yen to follow in the
footsteps of Uncle Don, my childhood idol. By the 1950s, I was
far more interested in adult oriented entertainment. Like millions of other Americans, I developed a strange fascination for a
blonde actress I first met when she was being interviewed on
Luncheon at Sardi's. Her name was Marilyn Monroe.

Georgie Jessel

Georgie Jessel was on my show the same day as Eddie Fisher
and Debbie Reynolds, when Eddie Fisher had just married her.
I'll never forget one line, when Georgie said, "I hope you two
can be as happy as I could've been on many an occasion."

Greta Garbo

I was on a side street, Fiftieth between Second and Third, eating at the Nutrition Center, one of the city's first health-food
restaurants, owned by my friend Daniel Squillante. Greta Garbo
came in and sat at the lunch counter. I watched her take off her
shoes, put on a pair of slippers, and when she was done eating,
leave the restaurant without the shoes. I picked up the shoes and
took them home. I could probably get $300,000 for those shoes
at an auction today.

☆

The Happiness Boys

Nobody was more popular in the early days of radio than the Happiness Boys, Billy Jones and Ernie Hare. In those days, comedy teams were called after their show's sponsors, and they were named after their first sponsor, Happiness Candy. Their second sponsor was Interwoven Socks Company, and they became known as "the Interwoven Pair."

Harry Gribbon

When I look at the stars of yesteryear, many, many years after their prime, I still envision them as young and at their peak. The hands of time turned back.

I was on ABC radio in the morning, and every afternoon I would see this man, Harry Gribbon. His room was filthy, but I would look at him, and think of him when he was so young and making pie-in-the-face movies for Mack Sennett and Hal Roach. I said to myself, How sad the industry neglected the ones who built up the business.

He was almost too drunk to know what the hell was going on. I would bring him coffee and leave twenty-five dollars on the table. The hotel room in those days was three dollars a day. I spent a lot of time with those people when I was young.

Mary Pickford

Mary Pickford once called me on the phone. You've got to remember how popular she was; she was the most celebrated woman ever in movies. She called me up and said, "Mr. Franklin, could you help me to buy up all of my films, because I want to take them out of circulation?"

I said, "Miss Pickford, how could you do that? There are millions of copies made all over the world."

Henry Burr

There was an old-time singer who made more records than anybody else. His name was Henry Burr. In making the rounds of junk shops, I ran across a Henry Burr record, and when I played it, his voice just did something to me. I became a fanatic of old songs and corny old tenors. They touched me emotionally. They gave me goose pimples. They still do.

Usually I feel closer to records and old songs than real people. That's my escape. Most nights I go home, even now, and play my old 78s. Ballads move me. "I Wish I Had My Old Gal Back Again," "I Wonder Where My Baby Is Tonight." Ballads from the 1920s. "Am I Wasting My Time on You?" "Are You Lonesome Tonight?" Old, old songs. I gave Tony Bennett ideas for old songs, Connie Francis—I gave her a lot of old-time songs.

Luise Rainer

Joseph Cornell was a box maker and he had a fixation on a lady who was on my show. Her name was Luise Rainer, a brilliant actress who didn't appear in many films but won two Academy Awards in consecutive years, for *The Great Ziegfeld* and *The Good Earth*. Briefly married to the playwright Clifford Odets, she retired in later years to Switzerland.

☆

Every year, a fan of hers sent her a small decorative box, with a little Christmas card. And she put them in the closet. The boxes continued piling up and piling up. She sold her house about a year and a half ago and threw out all kinds of stuff, including the little boxes. Luise never even answered him, she had never heard the name "Joseph Cornell," and when she saw the postmark, "Astoria"—Queens—she dismissed him, possibly assuming he wasn't to the manor born.

She sold her house in Switzerland and returned to New York. Not long ago she was walking down Park Avenue and looked into a store window: boxes by Joseph Cornell. She had thrown away about twenty of them! The store was closed, but she called up a museum the next day and asked the approximate worth of a box by Joseph Cornell. She had thrown away about $20 million in boxes.

Shannon Day

One of my first friends ever was an old-time Cecil B. DeMille contract player who was on my show several times, totally forgotten now, Shannon Day. She told me that she could have gone further in the movies if she had been "nicer" to Cecil B. DeMille. That was one of the first times we got something juicy on my TV show. For the period, it was steaming, seamy, shocking, sexy!

Frankly, I never believed her. Many actresses who never quite made it will say thay would have gone farther if thay had "made it" with directors. I've found it to be sour grapes in most cases.

☆

Harry Richman

Harry Richman, Georgie Jessel, Georgie Price—the audience will know when I'm bored or when I'm really bouncing. The old-timers spark my interest. They're going fast. One of my saddest recollections of Harry Richman is when I saw him at the Latin Quarter and he couldn't sing. It was a major, major Broadway nightclub, and they had to play records while he pantomimed to the sound of his voice. It was so sad.

Shirley Temple Black

Shirley Temple Black came on and said, "I don't want to talk about the old days." I agreed, for it was such an honor having her on under any conditions. As the interview began, she quickly said she was involved in this, doing this and that, what it was like to be an ambassador. Suddenly, we were right into every movie she ever made and how Hollywood was at the time and how she felt as a child star. She didn't want to leave. She called me a charmer.

Johnny Marks and Gene Autry

Somebody I really miss around holiday time is Johnny Marks. He wrote a song called "Rudolph the Red-Nosed Reindeer," made a home demo of it. He told me many times how he sent that to every singer in the world and never got any response. Then somebody said, "Why don't you send one to Gene Autry?" Gene once had a hit called "Here Comes Santa Claus" and he

★

might be in the market for a follow-up. Figuring he had nothing to lose, Johnny sent it to Gene Autry, and the timing was pretty good. Gene was at that time about to make two records—four sides—and he had already chosen the first three songs.

After Johnny played the demo, Gene Autry said he just didn't like it, too much about reindeer; reindeer songs are just too silly. But his wife liked the idea about the world's greatest reindeer and how the other reindeer wouldn't let him play in their game. She said to Gene, "Bear it in mind." They had ten minutes left at the end of the recording studio, and he said, "All right, throw it in," and he threw it in, and by now it's sold 15 million copies. When Johnny Marks died, he left one of songdom's largest fortunes.

Johnny Marks was my guest every holiday time, on my TV show and on my radio show, for about thirty-five years. We'd reminisce about his songs. He wrote one during the Second World War, "I'd Rather Be Asleep in a Jeep with a Creep than in the Back of a Hack with a WAC." I really miss him. I really get the blues around holiday time for Johnny Marks.

Mitchell Parrish

Mitchell Parrish wrote "Stardust," probably the best-selling song of the century. He was a great jazz composer, but he was known as the nastiest man in the music world. The word was that Mitchell put up with nobody. After a fall, Mitchell came on the show in a wheelchair. We took away the regular chair and made room for the wheelchair. I expected the worst. But Mitchell was just a sweetheart.

George Murphy and George M. Cohan

I would say that actors and entertainers became more openly political when George Murphy became a senator from California. George Murphy was a great song-and-dance man. He came on my show both as an actor and as a politician. I used to tell him that he should've had the part in *Yankee Doodle Dandy* that Jimmy Cagney played. George was very flattered. He told me he was always a great fan of George M. Cohan's. Any time Cohan's show got boring in the middle, Cohan would come out with an American flag, and that was a surefire audience getter, a Broadway showstopper.

Duke Ellington

One famous musician who was on my show used to tell Hal Stone, my right-hand man, "Hold my pot till the show's over." That was Duke Ellington. I loved Duke. I had dinner with him about six times. At dinner, he'd always have his dessert first, because he said he knew he wouldn't have room for it at the end.

Benny Goodman

Did you know, long ago, that Barbra Streisand used to be a waitress in a restaurant I dined at, Oscar's Salt of the Sea? Oscar was a very good friend of mine. One day I had Benny Goodman on my show for an entire hour. One hour, nose-to-nose, a great show. He was my only guest. Later that day I ran into him at Oscar's Salt of the Sea, and he didn't know me. He had been face-

★

to-face with me six hours before. In other words, he was really absentminded. He was in a blur. A whole hour of live TV, I say hello to him in a restaurant a few hours later, and he didn't know who I was.

Johnny Ray and Dorothy Kilgallen

Johnny Ray was a very dear friend of mine. I loved him. People always overlook how important he was. He was gigantic. In one fell swoop he pushed Bing Crosby off the best-seller list. The song was "Cry." He wiggled and gyrated; the audiences went crazy. They shrieked. They couldn't press his records fast enough.

Ray was a victim of changing vogues, changing styles, plus the gay thing. They entrapped him. Which was cruel. But he was enormous. He was the Beatles of his day. I met him at the junket for *The Great Race* in Hollywood. He was with Dorothy Kilgallen, the famous columnist. That was an open fact. I think they were just good friends. She was married to Richard Kollmar, the famous Broadway producer and actor. It was a strange kind of union, a marriage of convenience. They were very seldom together. She was always traveling with Johnny Ray.

Some people have a meteoric downfall. He had a cyclonic downfall. Johnny Ray was virtually stone deaf. It was amazing he could have that great tone, great sound, keep on an even keel. He was not only deaf, he was also in pain because of his hearing affliction. I miss him. He was a big name.

Sal Mineo and James Dean

Sal Mineo was a good friend of mine. He gave me some record albums, which I still play on the radio. I had him on once with Tony Curtis when they were in a movie called *Six Bridges to Cross*. Yes, Sal was a fine singer.

I always imagine how these people would've looked had they lived until they were sixty. Sal Mineo, Marilyn, James Dean, who died when he was twenty-four.

James Dean was very, very nice, polite, but even then I could spot that inner fire. I knew he had that inner smolder, but I didn't think he'd get that big, as big as he was.

Robert Q. Lewis and Wally Cox

I loved Robert Q. Lewis. I had dinner with him many times with Georgie Price, the old-time entertainer. He had a marvelous speaking voice. He was a great disk jockey, an actor, and began on TV as a substitute for Arthur Godfrey.

Robert Q. Lewis would've been big today. He toured with Don Ameche in *The Odd Couple*. I loved him; he was pretty popular there for a while. He made a lot of record albums, singing. I play him on the radio very often. He had his own TV shows, like *Songs for Sale* and the *Robert Q. Lewis Show*. He just missed by a little bit. But he was there, reliable.

Wally Cox used to come on my program with a fella named Robert Price, "the Doodler." We would do a segment called "Daffy-nitions" or "Definition-itis." We'd have fun with words. I have a list of them somewhere. Here's an example: "The definition of 'efficiency expert': A man who is smart enough to run your business but too smart to start his own."

Wally Cox was Marlon Brando's roommate! Very nice. His

personality was just the way he acted on the screen. Very meek and kind and humble and gentle.

The Wally Coxes, the Robert Q. Lewises were so different from today's performers, so real, not smirky, not wise-guyish, not brash. I really miss that era. I really miss people who were nice. Sadly, I don't think they will be remembered. There are kinescopes; there are shows that make the rounds. But who's immortal? Nobody.

☆

Women

Love, like spinach, is highly overrated.

—Georgie Jessel

I dreamed about Marilyn Monroe the other night. We were talking, and she said, "Joe, why don't you go back on TV?" I told her I'd rather rest. Then she told me she was always sorry our book hadn't come out as planned. She and I had worked hard on her biography. It was the first book about her life, written and published in 1953. She was called back to California early in the interview sessions, and the book ended up being mostly a collection of press releases and blurbs, ghostwritten by a woman named Laurie Palmer. Marilyn said to me in my dream, "Joe, I want to come back now and finish the book as we originally planned." I didn't know what to say to her. Isn't that an odd dream? Maybe it ties into my thoughts now, as I am writing my own story.

I met Marilyn after a press agent from United Artists called me at the office one day wanting a favor. He wanted to get a starlet on *Luncheon at Sardi's*. She had been in a few films, and now her career was beginning to take off. He knew I could introduce her to the show's producers, Gary Stevens and Irving Cahn, and the host, Bill Slater. He told me the starlet's name: Marilyn Monroe. I said I'd see what I could do.

We rendezvoused in Sardi's, and she was very beautiful yet very meek. Her hair was not blond then, as it was later; it was a very light brown. "Mr. Franklin?" she whispered in her breathy voice. She seemed uncomfortable in the crowd of people, amid the microphones and the activity, the eyes that gazed at her from all corners. "Will you sit down with me?" she invited. "I'm all alone." I felt my knees weaken, and I took a seat beside her. From that first meeting, I knew right away she'd become a star. She stole the interview and had photographers shoving to get position. When she walked into a restaurant, it was electric; she had a great wiggle.

I suggested to a friend, the small publisher Rudolph Field, that Marilyn and I write a book together. Field thought it was sure-fire, and we were able to work a deal. Marilyn and I spent many hours working together. She was very relaxed with me, very open. We established a rapport in the first minute. She found me funny, liked my jokes. She told jokes. We watched the quiz shows. Her favorite was *What's My Line?*

In the course of my interviews with her, she spoke of her early marriage, at sixteen, seventeen. Before she was twenty she had already become a national sex symbol, featured first in pulp magazines, then in the slicks and daily press. She was soon the hottest model in Hollywood. She laughed with some bitterness about her calendar, how somebody made millions of dollars from that calendar and she got paid fifty dollars. I found her a good conversationalist, the exact opposite of what people would think. The exact opposite of a "dumb blonde." We worked late hours on the book, sending for Chinese food every once in a while. She didn't seem to care about her diet or her figure; she ate what she wanted.

One night we were working late on the manuscript. I was astonished to feel her hand on my knee. I stammered a weak protest. The rest is a fog of Chinese food and Garry Moore. She

☆

had a very severe biological need, a strong biological urge. I would characterize her as straight-ahead, unemotional, businesslike. Not kinky. Neither dominant nor submissive—neuter. A man could get her in the sack, and he would think he was the conqueror when actually *she* made the conquest. Not that she was as active as people were later to claim she was. She used to tell me that if she went with as many men as the press claimed she did, she never would have had time to make movies.

Because of contractual obligations in Hollywood, Marilyn was called back to the coast before we could complete the manuscript. The book was finally released in 1953 as *The Marilyn Monroe Story* by Joe Franklin and Laurie Palmer and is universally recognized as the first of hundreds of books on her life. The book was wholesome, nothing salacious. It's all-American, a Nancy Drew book, almost.

Tragically, the publisher, Rudolph Field, died the same day the book was released, so very few copies ever saw the light of day. They've become very, very scarce. I only had one copy, and it was stolen. It is selling now, I heard, for $3,000, if you can find it. I've been trying to get copies, both hardcover and softcover. I don't know how many leaked out, maybe five hundred copies, who knows.

I'll tell you one funny thing: When I was young, I was one of the tallest kids in my class. Then one day I had an operation. I had what they call a thyroglossal cyst, which I believe affected my growth. I think I stopped growing at the age of thirteen or fourteen. It affects the thyroid gland. But I wouldn't want to be any other way. I was walking on the street the other day with a woman who was six feet two and a half, without shoes! She said to me, "Joe, I want to tell you something. You're the first man in my entire life, or the last twelve years, when you walked with me, you didn't subliminally walk a tiny bit ahead or a tiny bit behind. You walked even with me." So that made me feel secure.

I always liked tall blondes. "Gentlemen prefer blondes," that was me.

★

Another blonde I developed a big, big crush on was Jayne Mansfield. Jayne Mansfield was a big star, appearing in the late 1950s in a Broadway show called *Will Success Spoil Rock Hunter?* with Tony Randall. She was on my show at least twenty times. Everyone remembers her as a voluptuous blonde, but she was also a brilliant violinist. She played the violin on my show many times, and she had a genius IQ.

One night she was scheduled for an eight o'clock curtain on Broadway. She and I were having a drink alone together near my office when I felt her smoldering touch, sensed her eyes filling with longing. I let the alcoholic glow silence my resistance. What happened next is a blaze of Toscanini—as I say, Jayne Mansfield was a brilliant violinist. At about seven forty-five, at eight o'-clock, there were frantic calls all over town from the theater, from the stagehands, director, the producer, until Jayne showed up, a half hour late for her curtain. If someone asks, I didn't tell you this. You heard it from somebody else.

Marilyn and Jayne Mansfield both met tragic ends, both dying when they were still young, vital, beautiful. But sex goddesses do not always age well. One of my closest friends was the actress Veronica Lake, described in her heyday as "the essence of hauteur," a "sex siren." Her famous hairdo, with strands sweeping over one eye, created a national style. Preston Sturges, the great director, said with admiration, "The screen transforms her, electrifies her, brings her to life." She starred in big, big movies, *I Married a Witch, I Wanted Wings, This Gun for Hire,* and *The Glass Key.*

But Veronica Lake was never popular with the press, and after the war, her popularity waned. It got to be a bad joke: what *isn't* the press saying about Veronica Lake? During the war, she once told me, she raised about $40 million selling war bonds for the government. She made page one headlines when she received a special Congressional Medal of Honor for her efforts. Five years later, they locked her out of her house and threw her into the gutter because she couldn't pay her income tax.

Veronica Lake had nobody to guide her. She was earning ten thousand dollars a week in 1945. When I knew her, she was penniless. At one point, in the 1960s, she was a waitress in the Martha Washington Hotel. As a waitress, she made eight to ten dollars a night. Slim, sleek, slick, smooth, suave—it's a shame how she went downhill. She wasn't bitter; I think she was relieved not to be on display. She was most philosophical about her demise. Stoic. Brave. Matter-of-fact. I used to give her $100 a day to come on my show, enough to pay her rent at the hotel. She insisted that I take some form of collateral and passed me a jewel box. I told her I didn't want it, but she pressed it on me. The jewels had already been hocked at a pawn shop, but it was a beautiful box with the initials "V.L." engraved on it.

Veronica Lake often invited me up to her room, but I never went. She threw herself at me, but I always refrained. I've fantasized how it could've been. Not because of her beauty but because I always liked movie stars. I always respected somebody who had amounted to something. I respected great talent, even if the press had decided that they were "washed up." In my mind, she remained the Veronica Lake of *The Blue Dahlia,* not of the Martha Washington. I like this description of her: "A tough broad who saw life realistically."

Though her demise was sad, at least Veronica Lake had her memories, her fling with fame. Many never do. I've seen so many over the years. The ones who want to be "Movie Stars"— the glamour girls—go directly to Hollywood. But the serious actresses still head for New York. Mostly they find work as waitresses or office temps, jobs that won't interfere with the business of going on auditions, open calls, or taking classes in acting, singing, or dance to enhance their hireability.

They live in walk-ups in funky neighborhoods or double up with one or more girls in a "nice" doorman building on the East Side, someplace deemed relatively safe and okay to show their parents. The names and faces of the roommates are ever changing as girls drop their dreams of becoming great actresses to get a steady job or move in with a boyfriend. The luckiest ones of

this group wind up marrying somebody who is wealthy enough
to pay for their acting, singing, dancing, or elocution lessons.

Occasionally something exciting will happen, a part in an off-
Broadway show, a voice-over, or a role on a TV commercial. The
smallest theatrical job or break is cause for at least six more
months of perseverance, the confidence that this may be the one
big break that gets them a great agent or an "in" with a big producer.

Some of them set dates, time limits, for when they plan to give
it up. Others refuse to admit that the clock is ticking. That's why
you see women with wrinkles around their eyes going out for in-
genue roles. When I was in my mid-twenties, I met a middle-
aged woman named Sara Young. She walked into my office on a
Friday and said, "Mr. Franklin, I would like to be on your new
program." I asked what her talent was, and she showed me a
copy of *Look* magazine from the 1940s. Who was on the cover?
She was, a gorgeous young woman! Now, it was ten years later,
and the charms were starting to fade a little bit.

I said, "Sara, you are a very nice lady, very pretty, I like you.
But what do you want to talk about on my show?"

"Christian Science."

She's now a Christian Scientist! I wasn't sure how that would
play. I led her to the door. "Look, I'm very tense, I've been on
the air for five, six years in a row, not one day off, and now I've
got a TV show. I'm going to Atlantic City all by myself to take a
little rest. I'll be back in town Monday. We'll talk then. If you
need me, I'll be at the Hotel Ambassador in Atlantic City." I
didn't give Sara a second thought.

That night, as I was getting ready to go out for dinner in Atlantic City, I got a call from the lobby of the Hotel Ambassador.
Sara Young was in the lobby. I got her a room. I'm very proper; I
always was. She leveled with me. "Joe, I need someone to finance my acting career." Maybe somebody would subsidize a
rock-and-roll group, but nobody's going to subsidize an actress.
Her voice was urgent as she continued, "I haven't paid my rent
on my apartment on Fifty-seventh Street. Could you help me?"

☆

So I took a jitney bus to Western Union, and we sent back her rent, which was $300 a month, a lot of money in those days. She wasn't done yet. She said to me, "I feel like I'm at a banquet but I can only eat the rolls." She's got more expenses! I gave her more money. But as I was passing her the check, I looked at her hands. I saw that they were beautiful hands. Long fingers, sensuous, tapered. I was making commercials at the time for a company named Bertolli olive oil. When we got back to New York, I got her a a job pointing to the bottles on the commercial. She made $1,500. Back in the city we used to meet on an occasional Saturday night to go to a show, or to a movie. She was beautiful, dark hair, a few years older than me, about five feet seven, very attractive.

One night she didn't show up. I called her once or twice but couldn't reach her. A few days later, I met a friend of hers and asked what had happened to Sara. The friend explained to me, "You represent the time to her when she was broke." The $1,500 made her rich? An olive oil commercial? *Sheesh.* She called me a couple years ago; I didn't take the call.

My romantic period began when I was a fourteen-year-old kid in summer camp. The boys and girls paired off, matched up, and spent the entire eight or nine weeks with their partner. There was a girl that I went to socials with and danced with named Lola Reider. Camp ended, and all the boys and girls kept in touch. Some of them made dates to meet in the city. She was my first infatuation.

Lola and I made our tearful good-byes, but since we both lived in the New York area, we promised to meet again. We talked, and we made a date to meet on a certain Sunday in front of the Astor. Come the appointed Sunday and I stood in front of the Astor. And waited. And waited. No sign of Lola Reider. The hours passed, and I was sure that I had been stood up. I was too embarrassed to call her and find out what happened. We lost contact.

Cut to about twenty years later. I'm lying in bed about to fall asleep when I suddenly get this wild mental flash. I had waited

☆

in front of the Astor *Theatre*. And I suddenly realized she must have waited in front of the *Astor Hotel*. Because anybody with any brains would know when you say, "Meet me at the Astor," you mean the Astor Hotel. But I was so dumb, so enamored of the movies, I was a block away at the Astor Theatre. She must've thought *she* had been stood up.

I recovered from the disappointment of missing Lola with my second girlfriend, Shirley Kleinsinger. Her father was a dentist, and we went out for a year. We had a lot of laughs, a lot in common. Amazingly, she seemed to share my passion for radio shows like *Stoopnagel and Budd* and the *Happiness Boys*. Maybe Shirley was just pretending—I don't see how any girl of fourteen could've liked those great cornball comics. But I didn't care. I was bitten, smitten. I wrote in my diary on July 5, "The fireworks were great last night, but nothing compared to Shirley." I was hooked. I looked forward to every Saturday night. We went to movies together like *Strike Up the Band* with Mickey Rooney and Judy Garland and *We Who Are Young* with Lana Turner and John Shelton. The films flamed our budding ardor. Our moments together were smoldering with pent-up adolescent desire. We shared popcorn, held hands. Once I gathered the nerve to put my arm around her. (I was too shy to do anything more than that.) The relationship died of natural causes, but that was the first year I played an indoor game called spin the bottle.

A few years later, after I started working in radio, I got a phone call from Shirley. She asked if I'd have lunch with her. We had a strange kind of forced lunch. She just stared at me a lot. We didn't talk much. I felt a little bit uncomfortable. We ate our lunches; I said good-bye and then went back to the studio. I looked in the *Sunday Times* about four to six weeks later and saw a picture of Shirley, engaged to be married. Had she called all her former boyfriends before she decided to tie the knot? Did she want to take a last look at the competition? I said to myself, I'll bet that marriage is doomed.

Many years later, I was at Grossinger's Hotel, introducing the

⭐

Ritz Brothers on the stage. Whom do I see in the audience after the show? Shirley! I said, "Shirley, how do you feel?"

She said, "Joe, everything is great."

"Shirley, how's married life?"

She answered, "Oh, we got divorced a long time ago."

I knew the first marriage was doomed because of the way she was looking at me that day. If she had been that sure about her decision, she wouldn't want to see her old boyfriends. I said to Shirley, "Is there anything you need?"

She said, "No, Joe, I made a brilliant divorce." I never forgot the line: "a brilliant divorce."

Lois Meriden, née Knobloch, was the daughter of a businessman who went broke during the Great Depression. He tried to recover, opening a ladies' clothing store, a bar, and about twenty-two other businesses. Her uncle, a rich bootlegger, left $7 million to her cousin, but her father died poor, a bitter man. Her mother, Marion, worked for the welfare department in the city of Passaic. A tall, beautiful blonde, early in life Lois decided she wanted to be in show business, a singer or a model, and her big break came when she was offered a chance to tour with Sally Rand's Fan Dancers.

Sally Rand became a sensation at the Chicago World's Fair in 1933, leading a troupe of nude chorus girls who covered themselves with hand-held fans. Sally, who had been busted a few times for lewdness, became a fixture in vaudeville and put together a touring company. One of her groups was called Sally Rand's "Rancherettes," in which forty-two young women, clad in G-strings, bandannas, cowboy boots, and cowboy hats, frolicked and played outdoor sports. Sally Rand was years ahead of her time, and her act retained its vitality and popularity until her last days on this earth.

When Lois was touring with Sally Rand in the late 1940s, the ensemble played small towns, fairgrounds, and clubs throughout the country. A comedian warmed up the crowd; then a singer crooned to such lyrics as "Omar knew . . . the thrills of baseball / he knew his way around the village green . . ." The lights dimmed as the singer stepped off the stage. The real show began. The women, dressed in harem costumes, Lois among them, came on one by one to the strains of Debussy's *Afternoon of a Faun*. During the dance, the girls occasionally flashed their fans to reveal glimpses of their anatomy. The "bally" was greeted with thunderous, overwhelming applause. (Sally always insisted that she was a ballet dancer, not a stripper. And she hated the term "exotic dancer." She said, "There's nothing exotic about me. I am not strange. I was born and raised in Hickory County, Missouri.") In the course of their grueling tour, Sally's girls performed in dozens of cities and towns, up to eighteen shows a day.

After touring with Sally Rand, Lois returned to New York to model, appearing in full-page ads in the *Sunday Times* for fashion companies like Judy Bond Blouses. I was on three radio stations at the time, and my television career was just under way. I needed a secretary. I advertised in the *New York Times*, and Lois answered the ad. When she came into my office, she looked around and asked, "Where's the boss?"

I said, "I'm the boss."

She said, "You're kidding."

I don't know what she expected, a suited giant, I suppose, but I had to prove that I was Joe Franklin, doing impersonations of myself on the air. She thought I was a sixteen-year-old kid. I offered her the job. Once she was convinced that I was indeed the radio disk jockey Joe Franklin, she accepted.

I was then, as I am now, a theater and movie critic. And I've got to tell you, then, the same as now, when I go to a theater or a movie, I fall asleep right away. I soon began to lean on Lois to tell me what to say. She helped me write reviews, put together my shows. She became a very important part of my professional life. She told me what to say.

I admired her intelligence and was infatuated with her looks. She was the tall beauty that I'd always dreamed about. Soon we were beginning to be seen around town together. In her column,

Dorothy Kilgallen wrote that we were "waxing amorous." Walter Winchell queried in his column, "What radio voice with initials J.F. seen 'round town with model Lois Meriden?" Every morning when I did my radio show, Lois and I went to the radio studio for my live broadcast at six-thirty in the morning. Lois made faces at me through the control room window, wiggling her ears and her nose, particularly when I was doing commercials like Rat-Rid and Crotch-Itch. I had funny commercials. She'd break me up. I took her on dates to the flea circus in Times Square. We'd go to Coney Island to ride the Cyclone. She accused me of having notoriously bad taste. She laughed at me because I'd go into a Chinese restaurant and order American food. We went to an astrologer together, and the astrologer told her to marry someone else; she could find someone better.

Though we spent our days and evenings together, we continued to live apart. It wasn't proper to live together in those days. I was still staying with my parents, and she was sharing a furnished room on the West Side with a girlfriend. It was about three dollars a week then, so I didn't mind pitching in.

Then she started putting pressure on me. She was dating other men, the older, elegant silent film actor Conrad Nagel, and Red Buttons wanted to go out with her. She wanted commitment. Nelson Rockefeller asked her out several times. One night I was broadcasting from Jack Starks' restaurant on Forty-third Street. I told Lois not to come because my mother would be there. What I really didn't want to tell her was that I had a date with another woman. But Lois showed up, anyway, with a date herself—Conrad Nagel. She saw me with my date, Eleanor Appleton, a pretty debutante. I spent most of the night at Lois's table, and Lois ignored Conrad Nagel. At last, she gave me the ultimatum: "Joe, if we're not going to be engaged, I don't want to go out with you."

Even though I was making money, I was spending it all on my press agent, on memorabilia, movies, and old records. Every weekend I'd go to Nyack, to garage sales, flea markets, everywhere, so I truthfully told her I didn't have any money to get married. I told her I wasn't prepared to take on the financial

★

The young platter spinner

I got my first break on Kate Smith's show.

Me, the Missus, and my idol, Eddie Cantor

Jimmy Durante with me on Al Jolson Remembrance Night, 1951

I enter the world of television!

5

6

Bandleader Paul
Whiteman usually
preferred something
harder than breakfast
cereal.

7

The Defiant Ones: Sidney Poitier
and me. Dig those blazers.

8

Paul Newman and me. I'm the handsome one.

The great blues singer, Ethel Waters.

9

I explain the finer points of
comedy to Buster Keaton.

They love him in France. Jerry
Lewis turns up his nose at one
of my stinkers.

Mike Douglas was a
great pioneer TV talk
show host. He started
in insurance.

13

Mr. New Year's Eve,
Guy Lombardo

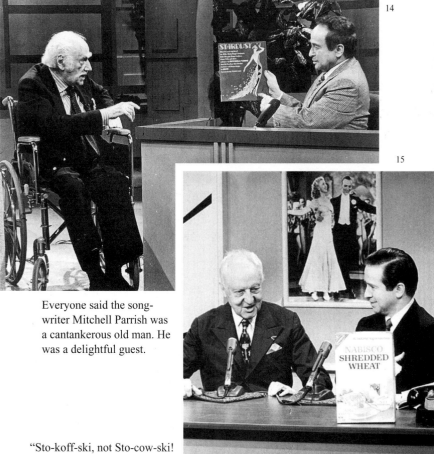

14

15

Everyone said the song-
writer Mitchell Parrish was
a cantankerous old man. He
was a delightful guest.

"Sto-koff-ski, not Sto-cow-ski!
I am not a cow!"

Dangerfield and Georgie Jessel: these guys could tear me to shreads.

What else can you say about John Houseman and Myrna Loy? She was a great director as well as an actress.

18

19

20

21

Stella D'oro

22

23

24

25

26

7

28

29

30

32

31

33

34

Tony Curtis and I have been friends since childhood. I interviewed him before the premiere of *The Great Race.*

Joan Rivers was one of the many comediennes to start out on my show.

A surreal moment with Salvador Dali 37

The Happy Family: Lois, Brad, and me.

38

Rudy Vallee, Barbra Streisand, and Jack Lalanne. Rudy thought she'd never make it. 39

Not your everyday
Joes. With Joe Louis.

40

41

Lamb Chop Meets Tiny Tim.

42

Howard Stern tells me his sex secrets . . . but he didn't show me his private parts.

One of my great all-time thrills: Mr. and Mrs. Bing Crosby.

J. Geils was number one, and I was the only show to have them.

Garth Brooks was a boot salesman when he made his first appearance on my show.

45

47

Cosby stuck with me through thick and thin.

Like Georgie Jessel, I like having a woman on each arm. These are, of course, Elizabeth Ashley and Sally Kirkland.

The world's fastest painter, Morris Katz

Did you ever see *Ghostbusters?* Dan Akroyd did the show for real.

50

Note the careful filing system.

51

The big three of WOR's *Joe Franklin Show:* host, director Bob Diamond, and producer Richie Ornstein

commitment. I was making probably about $6,000 a week then, $8,000 a week, but I spent it all. I didn't save a penny. Lois refused to take no for an answer. She promptly went to a loan company and borrowed $500. She cosigned a loan for me, enough for us to get an apartment together. I guess I've been paying off now for about forty years.

We were married on a TV show called *Bride and Groom,* a national show sponsored by General Mills, hosted by a fellow named John Nelson. It was described by one of its writers, John Reddy, as a show in which "bedazzled couples committed matrimony before the cameras while several million housewives sighed from coast to coast." They married somebody every single day on that show, five days a week. They sang your favorite song, gave you wedding prizes, dining-room sets, silver service, honeymoon suites, vacations, provided the minister, the priest, rabbi, witch doctor, whatever you wanted. I mentioned to ABC that I was getting married, so they said, "Would you do us a favor and get married on *Bride and Groom*? We'll give you double the prizes." Lois thought it would be fun, so that's where we tied the knot, appropriately, considering my career, before the cameras, in front of 15 million people. Fred Allen said to me in a restaurant one time, "Joe, you won't be able to have relations in twenty states until they show the kinescopes."

The honeymoon was at Grossinger's in the Catskills. That week, Jackie Mason was the comic. I asked Lois if we could go to the stage show before we went up to the bedroom. I'll never forget his routine that night. He impersonated non-Jewish performers in a synagogue, davening, people like James Cagney, John Wayne, Jimmy Stewart in his Western drawl: "Wellll, yishmael v'yishmael . . . yishvadov . . . yup!" I fell to the floor laughing; I've never laughed that hard in my life. I had to leave the room; my back hurt, he was so funny.

When we returned to our hotel room, a phone message was waiting. My mother had called for Lois. Lois called her back to find out what she wanted. My mother wanted to know if Lois was still a virgin.

☆

There was a time during my marriage when things weren't going right—it's been like that for forty years—but if we divorced, it would cost me a lot of money. Lois is happy, I'm happy, I live in New York, she lives in Florida. She's happier there, dabbling in real estate and asking me for more allowance.

I always claimed there was no such thing as love. Love to me is an obsolete emotion. Love to me is a habit; it's a habit. I've never been madly in love. The bells never rang. Whom do you marry? You marry the woman you travel with. Poor people marry poor people; rich people marry rich people. They travel in those circles; you marry whom you formed habits with. I got married to Lois after I got to lean on her. I admit, I didn't really want to be married. But I'm fiercely a creature of habit.

Believe it or not, I've met a few women since I've been married, and I started to like them, started to love them. You know what I did? I chopped it off fast. I don't want to get involved. I've got great discipline, great willpower. I'd rather not have a little romance while I'm married. A lot of men do, and it's very hard to fall out of love. I've got a lot of friends who come to me with their problems. They're in love; they're married. It affects their work, their lives, their children. But I guess I'm a masochist, because I know at least three or four different women whom I *know* I would like to have an affair with, I'd like to get closer to, but I cut it off because I'm married.

I still call Lois every day. She was recently here for a visit, and we visit our son in Pennsylvania. I'm just a creature of habit. I could never, ever get divorced. I'd be too sad.

Mae West

I had Mae West on my radio show once. She was in town to plug one of her movies. I asked her what was the secret of her good health. She announced to the world, "Five enemas a day."

She was serious—and those were the days when that kind of remark was shocking on radio. Today, in this era, it's common-
place, but in those days, everybody was stunned. Radio was so
sterile then.

Gloria Swanson

Gloria Swanson was on many times. She really liked me. She
would come on between her matinee and evening performances
of a show called *Butterflies Are Free* on Broadway. She was a
health food lady. Always antisugar. Wrote a big book called
Sugar Blues.

I didn't talk about her romance with Joe Kennedy. In those
days, I guess I was too shy, or the code of decorum demanded
that you didn't ask those questions. I loved Gloria. She played in
the first movie to ever appear in the Roxy Theatre, a picture
house which is no longer there. It was called the *Loves of Sonja,*
1926.

Betty Hutton

Nobody ever writes about the old-timers; call them has-beens,
past their heyday. The ones who never had the right management, never had the right agent.

I met Betty Hutton one time at a banquet. She told me Marlene Dietrich, Greta Garbo, and many other actresses had en-
listed managers or finance men or accountants who guided their
living expenses. She'd had nobody, and somehow she blew all
her money.

☆

Shirley Temple and Deanna Durbin

I had a panel once with two men who virtually knocked World War II off the front pages when they kissed their leading ladies on-screen. The first kissed Deanna Durbin: Robert Stack. The second, Dickie Moore, kissed Shirley Temple. Remember Little Dickie Moore? He is married now to gorgeous Jane Powell of MGM fame.

Joan Crawford

I loved Joan Crawford. One time Oscar Levant told me that he made a movie with her. He said she was always knitting when she wasn't filming, knitting, knitting, knitting, maybe for therapeutic reasons. Even when she would talk to him, she was knitting. That bugged him, so he said to her, "Do you knit when you fuck?"

Bette Davis

I just felt so sad when I saw Bette Davis on TV after her stroke. She looked pathetic. I said to myself, I wished she had quit the way Greta Garbo did, remaining an untarnished image in our minds.

There used to be a song "Laugh and the World Laughs with You, Weep and You Weep Alone." There was a takeoff on it: "Laugh and the World Laughs with You, Weep and You End Up in a Bette Davis Movie." Bette was in dozens of sad movies where she had to cry, but she was never able to actually do so. They would try onions, glycerine; nothing could make her cry.

★

So one day her director had to pull a hair out of her nostrils. It was the only way that she could truly cry.

Merle Oberon

I always had a fixation on an actress I wanted to meet named Merle Oberon. I was in love with her; she could do any part. I always wanted to meet her. I did, once, and I was amazed, for she had very bad skin. She told me it was from the makeup that she used when she was younger. They gave her the wrong kind. She was exotic; she could play a slut or a countess. I always thought she should have been in *Gone With the Wind*.

Weathergirls

The early 1950s was the era of the "weathergirls." They wore sexy clothes and nice makeup; they were pretty girls. Sandy Scott was the first, the very first weathergirl, a beautiful little blonde. She talked as if she had mashed potatoes in her mouth. In those days most of the emcees were men. They didn't have any Oprahs or Sally Jessy Raphaels in those days; there were mostly male hosts, so it was tokenism to make a woman into a weathergirl—pretty girls doing the weather reports.

It wasn't important for them to talk. The main thing was for them to look pretty and decorative and give the weather. They were close to the people at the top—that's how they usually got their jobs. They didn't get them on merit. There are no more weathergirls; now it's bonded, bona fide, certified meteorologists. Now we have ugly men doing the weather, usually fat men and bald men. Ugly men with college degrees.

☆

Lucille Ball

Lucille Ball was one who told me on my show that she never wanted a man under her feet. She was always married, but the man was always in the next room. When she wanted him, she would push the button. He would come in, provide his services, and then out. Strictly the biological urge.

Judy Garland

Judy Garland said something on my show first that was picked up by all the papers.

She said, "Joe, if I'm a legend, how come I sat for so many years at home waiting for the phone to ring, staring at the phone?" I never forgot that. She told me, "When I was pregnant, I called the operator to ask if the phone was out of order. She said it was, but it wasn't. She was just being kind."

Joseph E. Levine and Carroll Baker

I've been to a lot of banquets in my day. One time I was at a banquet, and I was the host. I said, "Ladies and gentlemen, in the audience is the noted impresario and film producer Joseph E. Levine." He got up and took a bow. Then I said, "At this table is a fine actress, a young lady named Carroll Baker, who's going to star in Joseph Levine's latest epic." And he walked over to her and said, "If that's what Joe Franklin says . . . would you be in my next movie?" She said yes, and it was called *Baby Doll.* No—*The Carpetbaggers.* So that's how that happened, from my making a funny, chance, dopey remark at a banquet.

Big Bandleaders

I was a big fan of the big-band era, the excitement of Benny Goodman, Louis Prima, Charlie Spivak, Glenn Miller, Artie Shaw, Charlie Barnet, and I used to always notice how all these bandleaders had beautiful wives. Harry James married Betty Grable; Phil Harris married Alice Faye; Ozzie Nelson married Harriet Hilliard. I wanted to be a bandleader once; maybe subliminally I was looking for a wife like that.

Sally Kirkland

Sally Kirkland has been my guest many, many times. I was the first to put her on the air with clothes on. Previous to that, she had only appeared in a nude role in *Oh, Calcutta!* Sally and I talk on the phone constantly; we've sung duets together, on a record label somewhere.

There's no secret I've always lent her my car, my limousine. Sally is a dynamic woman, gorgeous, gorgeous, and always working, but for some reason, which she will not deny, she used to always be cash poor. She's financially fine, always working, but for some reason she always needs a little extra cash, and I have never turned her down. She's gotten me my highest ratings. If I had to choose the people who got me my highest ratings of all time, she'd be in the golden dozen. She's been on my show at least seventy-five times.

Sally Kirkland would come on the show with her dress up to her waist, to her crotch sometimes. She had one smoldering ambition: to be a talk-show lady. I threatened to package her but just never did.

Sally was quite upset with me once because I hadn't gone to see her movie *Anna,* for which she was nominated for an Acad-

☆

emy Award. It's no secret that if she had had more time and money at that time to publicize and promote her potential for winning that award, she would've won it that year, but there were studios that had more money to invest. They showed Sally on TV at the show biting her lip until they announced that Cher won it. But she was a hot contender.

Even after the awards, I hadn't seen *Anna.* She said, "Joe, if you don't go and see *Anna,* I'll be very upset."

We went to see the picture together at a Greenwich Village theater, and I must confess I was very tired that day, having taped three or four shows. I dozed off and on during the picture, which of course was in bad taste. But I did recall waking up during one scene where she is standing in the rain with her boyfriend. She says to the boyfriend, "I want you to get down on your knees." He says, "No, no, no!" She says, *"I want you to get down on your knees! I insist."* Very dominatrix type, strong, pushy, commanding, aggressive. After about a few minutes of that, he reluctantly gets down on his knees in the pouring, pouring rain. Now she says, "I want you to get on your hands and knees, on all fours!" He says, "No, no, no, no!" Finally, he gets on his knees *and* hands in the drenching, pouring rain. They are totally soaked, both of them. Then she makes him bark like a dog.

Sally is a lady who teaches acting. She's one of the experts on the Strassberg method, the Stanislavski method, the inner smolder, the fire, the various shadings, the interpretations, the meanings, the hidden subtleties. As we were leaving the theater, walking up the block to get a cup of coffee, I said, "Sally, that one scene in the rain where you tell your boyfriend, 'Get down on your hands and knees . . . and bark in the rain.' Do me a favor; give me the inner meaning. Give me the reasoning, the symbolism, of that kind of sequence."

She said to me, "Joe, I've got no idea what that was all about! My director told me to do it—and I did it."

I had the greatest laugh over that response.

Once Richie Ornstein was driving us all out to the studio in

⭐

New Jersey. We had just entered the Lincoln Tunnel when Sally suddenly yelled, *"Stop! Stop! Back up! Back up!"* She was frantic. Richie began backing the car through the tunnel until he finally got out, car horns blasting all around. "Look!" she said, pointing to a billboard overhead. "A poster for my new movie!"

☆

PART III
The Joe Franklin Show

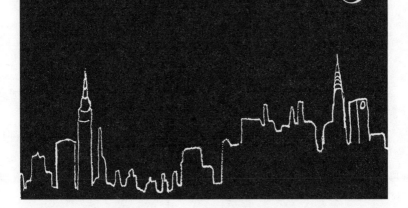

Life in Times Square

I was on jury duty one time and this man, sixty-six years old, said Joe's show was boring. He called Joe boring, and I said that's the stupidest thing I ever heard.
— Johnny De Maria

One of the most notorious, the most immediately recognizable, the most enduring elements of my years on-screen is my office. My office has been immortalized in countless documentaries, profiles, and write-ups, from *The New Yorker* to *Spin* magazine. It's been shown on Conan O'Brien, MTV, the Comedy Channel, the Matzo Ball Channel. Outsiders gawk and gape at my office quarters, my home away from home. I am a person who does not like change, and my offices have reflected that. They are loaded from floor to ceiling—every crevice, every cranny—with souvenirs, memorabilia, newspapers, records, compact disks, books, empty coffee cups, and about 350,000 other things you could probably think of. *Newsday* wrote that my office "combines Chancery Court in Bleak House and Bob Dylan's 115th Dream. This is an office that makes the stateroom scene in *A Night at the Opera* look like a lawn party at the Duchess of Kent's."

Into this office, every day of the year, 365 days a year, comes an assortment of characters, from princes to paupers, the royalty of show business and the down-and-outers, politicians, stars, starlets, and bums, the old-timers, the new-timers, the no-timers. My door is always open, and anyone can see me anytime. This makes for a bizarre mix, and at any hour of the day or night, you may find a party going on in a room eight feet by twelve feet.

People ask me, "Is your office really like that? Is it really that chaotic?" I nod my head yes. Stacks of paper from floor to ceiling. Record jackets without records. Newspapers from years past. Photos without labels, names, credits. Unanswered, unopened mail from years past. Vital documents strewn next to the crumbs of a prune Danish. It's a jungle. But I constantly amaze people, for I can dive through any stack of paper, any mound of material, and find exactly what I'm looking for in two minutes flat. I can have facts, figures, reports, synopses, and bios at my fingertips, because although there is no system that I could ever explain to anyone else, I know exactly where everything is.

There was a camera crew in here not long ago, shooting a segment for a cable TV show. About three or four people, sound man, lighting man, cameraman, and the show's host. They were climbing over chairs and hanging from the ceilings. As they were packing up, I noticed that the cameraman was browsing through a book, a book that's very important to me. I use it to research my radio shows. The crew left, and in the commotion, I didn't notice, but the book had disappeared. I put in a call to the host and asked him—very kindly—if he could please gently ask the cameraman if he had accidentally taken the book. I didn't want to hurt any feelings, ruffle any feathers. Within five minutes the cameraman called back. Yes, he had the book; he was so apologetic you could cry. He returned the book the next morning. But that's how acute my memory is, my sense of order. Even though it seems like chaos, I know every speck of dirt and why it's there.

I amazed my old friend Mimi Dua, an octogenarian I met waiting for a bus twenty years ago. She came up to my office regularly and answered my phones. She received a call from the editor of a national women's magazine. The editor wanted to

★

know the date of an article printed eight years before. Mimi said, "Well, Joe can answer many questions, but I don't know if he can answer that one. He'll call you back."

As soon as she hung up, I said, "Why'd you hang up?" I told her the date of the article, the name of the piece, the article, and the column.

Recently, I surprised another office regular, Prof. Bill Brooks, possibly the foremost expert on the World War II era of radio in America. His archives are a prominent part of the University of Georgia's School of Broadcasting library. We got to talking about the great singer Henry Burr, a giant in his day but nearly forgotten today by the general masses, the balladeer who sang "Just a Girl That Men Forget" and "I'm Sorry I Made You Cry." Someone asked when Henry Burr died, and Professor Bill proudly answered that it was 1941—not an easy trivia answer. Then he added, to impress the audience, "April 1941."

I let him savor his achievement for a moment, then added, "Bill, I believe the precise date was April 6, 1941. Burr was fifty-six years old." Bill was dumbfounded.

One of the great thrills for me is the string of old-timers and greats who come through my doors. People whom the general public doesn't immediately recognize but who were great stars, great talents in their time. For example, a black gentleman, ninety years young, came through my doors recently. Slightly hunched, probably the type of fellow you might pass on the street and never give a second thought to. But after you talk to him, you find out who he is and what he has accomplished.

His name was Charles Linton, and if the name still isn't familiar to you, Charles Linton was a much-recorded, talented big-band singer and the man who introduced an eighteen-year-old Ella Fitzgerald to bandleader Chick Webb in the mid-1930s. He made the introduction after she had just won first prize at the Apollo Theatre. Chick Webb wasn't interested, saying, "Winning first prize don't mean nothing, nobody's looking for a singer or a dancer with ribbons. They want 'em to sing!"

Charles Linton said, "If you don't listen to her, I'll quit."

And Chick Webb replied, "Okay, okay, bring her to the Savoy Ballroom, and I'll let her sing with the band. If the public likes her, we'll keep her. If not, out. No pay."

As Charles tells it, "He ended on 'No pay,' and I said, 'Okay!'" She sang one tune for the band, "Judy," and that was the beginning of a music great.

Howard Extract is yet another character who goes back with me many, many years. He was my counselor at summer camp! He comes to my office every other day, a sturdily built, striking man in his seventies, with a full head of blond hair. Today he is in real estate, but in his day he was an all-American football player and later a pro in the National Football League with the Philadelphia Eagles. Still a tower of raw strength, he gave me a fitness tip. He keeps his boyish figure by bumping his buttocks against a stone wall 100 times a day.

These guests are important to me. They're my lifeline. They keep me in touch with what I truly love. A man named Al Adamson is a visitor whenever he comes to New York. He is the director of films like *Satan's Sadists, Dracula vs. Frankenstein,* and 150 others. While I'm a horror-film fan, what fascinates me is the saga of Al Adamson's father, an old-time cowboy star named Art Mix. Art Mix was discovered in Australia by William Morris, the famous agent, the man who started the agency. William Morris put Albert Victor Adamson, Sr., on the stage twirling a rope and snapping a whip. He dubbed him "Denver Dixon" and, later, "Art Mix," hoping to cash in on the other great cowboy star at the time, Tom Mix. Art Mix's first movie was called *Stockman Joe,* one of the first Australian films ever, before he worked his way over to the States and made westerns here.

Eddie Cantor used to entertain a constant string of friends, acquaintances, and hangers-on from his suite in the Sherry Netherland. I like to think I've modeled my office after his style. Like Cantor, whose generosity and charity were unbounded, who would perform two or three benefits a night, when I see the one-time stars who have fallen on hard times, I try to help. Georgie Jessel, though he always lived in style, was constantly in need of money. I always paid Georgie Jessel $100 an appearance, although my show never paid a fee. I always gave Veronica Lake a fee. An old vaudeville performer once came to say hello to me. He had once been at the top of his profession, played the Palace with the best of them. But now, I could tell, his clothes were a little ragged, he had a two-day growth, and he seemed saddened, downtrodden. Without his asking, I shook his hand, discreetly passing a folded hundred-dollar bill in my palm.

He looked at me in amazement. "What's this for?" he asked, almost offended. "I didn't come up here looking for charity."

"Keep it," I said. "Consider it payment deferred."

"Payment deferred?"

"If I had been alive to see you at the height of your stardom, I would have spent at least this amount going to your shows. Consider this what I *would have* paid if I'd had the chance."

I left him shaking his head, but he kept the money. And it is true. It was a privilege for me to help him. What I'm paying now is for the tickets I would have purchased had I been around fifty or sixty years ago. I got that idea from Fred Allen, who, even when he was a great radio star, never forgot the people who worked with him in the early days. I remember Fred Allen walking from his apartment at Alwyn Court, on Fifty-seventh Street, down to Forty-second Street. Though the Palace Theatre had closed many years before, the vaudevillians were still hanging around; they thought the talkies and radio were just a fad and that vaudeville would come back. Fred Allen would see the guys, shake hands with them, and always chat with them, help them any way he could. I was influenced by that.

I make pitches for hundreds of charities, from WNET Channel 13 to City Harvest, a nonprofit organization to feed the homeless. I first learned the power of the media in raising money early in my career. Just prior to an Eddie Cantor appearance on my show, a synagogue in the Bronx was firebombed. Eddie Cantor spent ten minutes of his guest spot begging—pleading with—the audience to help rebuild the synagogue. I figured that he would collect maybe $100, $200. After all, this was the early,

early days of TV. Only a few hundred thousand people owned sets. But from that one appeal on my show he got $10,000 cash. That's when I first realized how potent TV could be as a source of good. So often, sadly, I feel that television has failed in its responsibility.

I do go on telethons, but I don't especially believe in them. I want to know, with all the money being exchanged, where's the cure? The people in charge make very big money, and I'm sure they're worthy of it, they've earned it, but I'd like to see them take less money and put it into research, finding a breakthrough.

I used to travel with Paddy Chayefsky, who wrote not only *Marty* but the great movies, the revealing, devastating exposés *Hospital* and *Network*. The last film he was working on before his death was to be titled *Telethon*. Who knows what that would've done! For research, Paddy used to sit in the back row and watch telethons all the time. Had that movie ever been made, it would've perhaps been an eye-opener.

My office, since leaving the Hotel Wentworth in the early 1950s, has always been in the Times Square area of Manhattan. My first Times Square office was at 152 West Forty-second Street. Then I moved to an office on the fourth floor of 147 West Forty-second, at the northeast corner of Forty-second Street and Seventh Avenue. I worked there for many years, in a tiny room. You would go past my neighbors, a Chinese acupuncturist and then the "Escuela Publica de Musica," before arriving at the hand-painted sign that read MEMORY LANE. People auditioned in the halls, danced on the desks, sang opera up from the street, anything to get on the show.

There were swarms of people in the office, people hanging out in the hall, hoping they would be discovered, that I could make the marriage with a big casting agent or producer. You'd find Jack Walsh, a.k.a. Herculo, the World's Strongest Man, bending railroad spikes with his teeth. Jack Walsh played Superman for thirteen episodes after George Reeves died. The singing fat lady from vaudeville would be filling the couch; she was like four or five people in one. There were ventriloquists, always ventriloquists. One by the name of Otto Peterson prayed that I would put him on the show. He had an X-rated ventriloquist act. He worked at the Ripley's Believe It or Not museum in Times Square and had a couple of gigs at the Playboy Club.

Consider the performers of genius who have come to my office over the years, greats, superstars like Jimmy Durante, a man with a brilliant mind and memory. He would sit and tell anecdotes hour after hour. I often welcomed Alan Reed, an actor with a booming baritone voice that soon became famous to the world as the voice of a cartoon character named Fred Flintstone. Bill Cosby came in to plug where he was working. Barbra Streisand used to frequent the office. Tony Randall, Sally Kirkland. Woody Allen dropped by to chat, he was intrigued by my nostalgia collection. He would talk about show business and his latest projects. Steven Spielberg came by, wanting to study my film libraries and talk about the great silents. He was a brilliant young cinephile, dedicated to finding every nugget, every treasure of knowledge he could about the film heritage. Sid Caesar would come in, accompanied by Imogene Coca. Davey Burns, the best straight man in the history of show business, was there. There were TV pioneers who had enjoyed great success in the early days, men like Bill Russell or Al Hodge, best known as *Captain Video*.

We've had in my offices a diverse cast of characters that no one in the world could ever imagine. Linda Georgian, of the phenomenally successful *Psychic Friends Network,* might drop by. Richard Selkowitz, former New York City police captain turned collectibles dealer. My barber, Roger deAnfrasio ("Joe does not wear a toupée! I don't get it; why do people always ask me that question?"), author of *The History of Hair* and, incidentally, also Frank Perdue's and Tony Bennett's barber. Kamarr the Magician, "the only Greek who didn't open a diner," "Greece's answer to Houdini," a regular on *David Letterman*. Watch him make a quarter disappear. Suzy Chaffee told Kamarr, "I've seen magicians all my life, but you've got personality!" Morris Katz, "the

World's Fastest Painter," might be sitting with his sketchbook on the couch. Before he appeared on my show, he'd get fifteen dollars a painting. After, he'd get ten dollars. In truth, he makes $800–$1,000 a painting. It takes him five minutes, eight minutes, to produce a masterpiece.

This is the office scene for the past thirty to forty years. Only the names, the faces, change. My son Brad grew up in this office. My lawyer and friend Leon Charney, a multimillionaire, calls it "like going to Disneyland." Every type of person, every line, and they all add color to the place.

When she was alive, my mother, Annie, came up to the office every single day. She carried little bags of carrots and celery, peeled and cut perfectly, just as if I were a little boy. As soon as she went to the ladies' room, I sneaked my hand under the desk and reached for my Danish and coffee. I had ninety seconds to choke them down.

I once had a chauffeur, Leroy Allen, to drive me around, but he was usually drunk and weaved all over the road. I always had gofers in the office to run my errands, to fetch coffee, to answer the phones. Some of them were sorrowful characters looking for a chance in life, just hanging on. In some ways they were comic, in other ways pathetic, but in nine cases out of ten, they won my heart.

Happy the Clown was a fixture at the office, a circus clown who didn't work much anymore. Happy (born John Kuhley) had about 50 percent of his brain eaten away as a result of a mastoid operation he'd undergone when he was young, but his mind was basically all there. He had long, funny hair that he was, for some reason, proud of. One time he got a haircut that he wasn't very happy with. He came to the office and said, in his Tennessee southern drawl, "I'm gonna keel that sumbitch. I swear, I'm gonna keel him!" He was fiercely loyal, carrying my valise, fetching my coffee. He would do anything I asked. One time when I was going on vacation, I paid him in advance for the whole two weeks. "Here's your two weeks' salary, and do me a favor and come in and pick up the mail from the floor."

☆

He asked, "How often?"
I said, "Every day."
He said, "E-ver day?"
Happy was under contract to an agent named Saxi Holtsworth, an agent for clowns and fiddlers. Saxi's building had been condemned, and as the bulldozers moved into position for the demolition, Happy was on the roof playing the fiddle. He didn't want to see the building come down.

Happy had always wanted to be a singer and never stopped pursuing that dream. One day he slipped on a pothole in the street and chipped his elbow. With the help of some of my acquaintances, I was able to get him a lawyer who was able to win him a fast $1,800. No sooner did Happy get the check than he ran out to a recording studio and made a demo. He hired an orchestra and blew the entire $1,800 in one hour. He recorded the song "Let's All Sing Like the Birdies Sing," a parody of—or more likely, in homage to—Tiny Tim on *Rowan and Martin's Laugh-In*. He figured if Tiny Tim could make it in show business, so could he.

He came into the office waving the demo. "I'm ready, Mr. Franklin! Kin I come on yer show?" I tried everything to discourage him, but he had just sunk a veritable life savings into the demo, and I couldn't say no, I wouldn't be able to face Happy ever again. It would have been crushing, devastating, to him. He would have felt betrayed. I finally broke down and told him he could make an appearance. For days, weeks, he groomed himself, rehearsed his act, playing the violin and singing "Let's All Sing Like the Birdies Sing" in a Tiny Tim falsetto. I tried every way possible to discourage him, but nothing worked. At last it was the big day.

His appearance was painful. The director was crying, it was so pathetic. The cameramen were writhing in discomfort. I had to close my eyes. We had to break into a commercial just to stop it. The only time I was ever in my life really criticized by the station was after Happy's pitiful performance. They put me on the carpet. "Joe, have you lost your mind?" They read me the riot act, and I could only hang my head in shame.

He was a funny guy, pathetic, but I loved him. He died recently. He stayed with me at least ten years. Happy the Clown and Joe Franklin were inseparable.

Then I had another regular named Pop. Pop, a.k.a. Frank Ransky, had been a Polish watchmaker. Every time I got annoyed or upset, Pop had a surefire way to relax me. He would make lamb chops on a portable stove in the office, which never failed to calm me down, although the office always smelled like a kitchen. Pop's whole life would've been changed if he'd had teeth. He didn't have a tooth in his mouth. We could never understand a word he said, but he was clever, loyal to me, like a soldier in the army. He was about forty-eight years old; he looked ninety.

Pop made a bizarre claim to fame. In the office, in between all the coffee cups and pictures of movie stars—Clark Gable, Eddie Cantor—there was a big picture from the *Daily News*. I think it was from 1931, and it was just a shot of about thirty nondescript men in the street. Pop claimed that all the way in the back of the photo, one of the unrecognizable men was him. Pop brought everybody who came into that office over to admire that picture—of a crowd.

He hung around for years, coming in every day, and then, suddenly, he disappeared. I knew something was wrong. I put together a search party, and we drove out to an address deep in rural New Jersey. We drove for hours to find Pop lying on a dirty mattress, dead drunk. At his side was some stale food that even the cats wouldn't eat. We revived him, called his long-lost sister, and gave her twenty dollars to get him a good meal.

Phil Schindler was not a popular character in my office. He looked like the Frankenstein monster. He was about six feet six, and he rarely bathed. I sprayed the office with Lysol every time he came in. He smelled so bad it was unbearable. He had been a rabbinical student and a true religious believer. Then he had suddenly cracked. He decided that all religion was hypocrisy. He turned a little bit screwy. He would talk to himself in the streets and wave his arms late at night as he expounded on the metaphysical at the top of his lungs. Many's the time that I'd get a phone call at four in the morning from the police and they'd say, "There's a man who fell asleep on the subway train; he says he works for you, Mr. Franklin. Is that true?"

I always answered, "Yeah, he works for me. Let him go."

Today I've got two wonderful assistants, Wally Banks and Johnny De Maria. Both of them are fiercely loyal. Wally is a tall, young black man with a big mouthful of teeth. He runs errands, cleans my office, warns visitors not to spill crumbs on the floor because of roaches, and answers my phone loyally on the first ring: "Mr. Franklin's office!"

Wally is not known as a conversationalist. Ask him the strangest thing he ever saw in the office and he replies, "Different things." Press the issue and ask him, "Like what?" and he answers, "Quite a few things. I don't know, there's so many interesting things that happen here, it's hard to put a finger on it." Ask him about himself and he'll reveal the in-depth story: "Me, I'm originally from Brooklyn, Brooklyn, New York, and now, Manhattan."

Johnny De Maria works on Wally's off-hours, usually evenings. A short, likable, heavyset fellow who wears thick black-framed glasses and a cap with a wool tassel all year round, Johnny describes how he and I met: "I met Mr. Franklin at St. Francis Xavier. You know, there's a memorabilia convention they put on on Saturdays, only on Saturdays, in Manhattan. It was in the afternoon, I was with two friends; I used to work with them doing photostats. I went in there, I was lookin' around, and one of my friends pointed out Joe, and I went up to him and said hello and introduced myself. I've been workin' for him about two years."

Johnny's seen it all in my office, and likes to talk about it. "Anything can happen. People pop around, you name it, anything crazy, we got it." About Johnny's background: "I live with my brother. I'm the same as Joe, we're both nostalgia buffs. We like the o'de stuff, o'de movies, o'de books.

"I knew about the o'de movies since Newtown High School. I met a teacher named Lance Lester, he got me to see the Marx

Brothers, *A Night at the Opera;* Charlie Chaplin, *The Great Dictator;* Buster Keaton . . . O'de movies, o'de books . . . anything o'de, it don't make a difference."

I've had people working for me, and I've sent them to the bank with $1,500, $2,000 in cash, and they've come back and said they got mugged. I had no recourse; I had to believe them—and you know they didn't get mugged. What could I do? I think it all goes back to something I got from my father. He used to bring those bums home I told you about. But when I found an honest man like Happy, like Pop, like Johnny or Wally—these guys will come back with a penny. If Wally or Johnny finds a penny in his pocket, he'll come back with the penny from 195th Street.

Grandma Rosie, a Ms. Senior America New York State of 1989, and a singer-performer whose stage name is Contessa Rose, is a frequent visitor to the office. She has extended an open invitation to her home on the Long Island Sound. I often go out for Sunday brunch. I gorge myself on lox and deli food at her home and end up falling asleep in her bedroom. She laughs. "Joe, you may take a nap, but don't tell anyone you've been in my bed."

I never had a secretary until a few years ago, when my friend Mike the Greek asked if I could help a Greek friend of his. He knew the father, who owned a diner; the daughter wanted to be an actress. But I never had a secretary before or since. I didn't need one. I always answered my own phone. I'm an accessible person. You can't call up any other celebrity on the phone and reach them directly, they have 100 secretaries, PR people, agents, managers, lawyers. I'm now doing some work for a man named Michael Bloomberg, who runs a gigantic multimillion-dollar empire, and he's got no secretary, either. The only difference is about $400 million. But there are so many women who have become a part of the office scene.

Many of the women who have come through my office are young, aspiring performers looking for that big break. I listen to

their love problems, their trials and tribulations. As Sophia Orculas Robbins, a former receptionist and actress, now star of
Class of Nuke 'Em High 2 puts it, "It's like a soap opera in Joe's
office. You could just tape it and it would be better than *All My
Children*—guy problems, girl problems, they'd ask Joe's advice,
or anyone's advice who happened to be handy."

There's Katerina, a dancer from Sweden, studying theater in
New York. Carol Lee is now living in Texas writing a book on
how to prepare your own motivational tapes. Alexandra, a former secretary, did a commercial recently with Charlie Sheen for
Parliament cigarettes for the Japanese market. She tells me she
can't remember a thing about her time with me. "At twenty-five,
my memory is shot." Kerann, a blonde, who was once Sharon
Stone's body double and is today a leg model. Her legs are pho-
tographed for movie posters; she's the girl in the *Fatal Instinct*
poster, which shows a body without a face. "That's me," she an-
nounces, "from the neck down!"

Pam Chiti, who is now a physical therapist, was described by
my producer, Richie Ornstein, as "so beautiful cars would crash
into buildings." Pam told me that the first time she saw my office, she walked in backward. "I was afraid something would fall
on me!"

I often get involved with the life and loves of my crew. I
played matchmaker with Pam and her husband, Morrow Chiti.
He was not a rich man, but I liked him and sensed that he truly
loved her. Rich men, multimillionaires, would call for dates with
Pam, but I would not let her talk to them. She used to say, "But
Joe! I'd like to go out with rich guys!"

I said, "Nope, they're not going to get your number. Stick with
Morrow. He loves you."

Another of my favorites was Sophia. I tried to play matchmaker with her and a rock and roller named Billy. "Drive her
home, Billy, do me a favor. She lives up in Rockland County."

"No, Joe, I can't. I'm busy."

I'd beg him. This went on for a year and a half. "No, Joe, I
can't, I'm busy." Then I found out the two of them were meet-

★

ing at *his* house every night. They were making a fool out of me.

Sophia learned my habits quicker than anyone: my lines on the telephone to people I don't want to talk to ("God bless you, you're a great American"), what I say when I belch ("Tight shoes!" "What'd you say?" "Static on the line?"), my dental problems (implants that didn't take), how I drink my coffee. She describes the ritual: "Joe only sips at it. By midday, he has at least fifteen cups of half-filled coffee sitting on his desk or on shelves. At least once a day or twice a day—it never fails—a cup spills on the floor. That's the rule, we always spill at least one cup a day. It just has to happen.

"Like the coffee, eating is a ritual at Joe's office," Sophia continues. "He likes to order sandwiches, corned beef from Smith's deli on the corner of Forty-fourth Street. He has half himself, and then he gives you the other half. If he gives you the whole sandwich, you're privileged, you're honored! Believe me, not a lot of people get a whole sandwich! A lot of people only get half, and some only get *half* of a half. And Wally gets the pickle.

"One day we ordered something, and Joe was upset because he didn't like his food, and I'd put Wally's order to the side. Wally stepped out for a second, and Joe ate his food. I felt really bad. Wally always gets the end of the stick, if there's anything there. He puts up with it; he gets a dry piece of rice or something. But while Wally suffers, Johnny De Maria eats better than everybody else. Joe feeds him the best!"

I would never have found my newest office without the help of Arnold Wachtel, proprietor of the Fun Emporium, a magic shop next to Show World Center on Eighth Avenue. Arnold has looked out for my best interests for years, and when my office at 147 West Forty-second Street was condemned by the Urban Development Corporation as part of the Times Square "revitalization," I needed to find a place in a hurry. I wanted to be in the immediate area because I do my radio show every week on WOR. He knew I wanted something cozy, where everybody can come, feel comfortable. I don't need a receptionist and a lobby. I wanted a place where I could come and talk nostalgia, schmooze. I still have a rotary phone, still have a manual typewriter, still have a black-and-white TV. I didn't need a fancy office.

Arnold found me a place off Eighth Avenue, twice, three times the space I'd had on Forty-second. Not that you could call it roomy, but after thirty years in a closet, it felt palatial. Moving took days and days. I had archives of nostalgia, among them priceless souvenirs like Rudy Vallee's megaphone, Charlie Chaplin's bowler hat, the Greta Garbo slippers, old kinescopes, lobby cards, 35-millimeter films. I found a lot of old pictures I didn't even know I had, with Elvis, Liberace, Barbra Streisand before anyone but her mother knew her. One record I remember coming across when we were moving was *The Caine Mutiny*. At the Collectors' Record Shop I saw it priced recently at over $2,000. And that was lying around my office like a piece of junk. I had two guys, two small guys, move every single thing, but not with a truck; they walked from Forty-second Street with handcarts. At least forty boxes of records.

It took about ten minutes after everything had been moved before the new office looked every bit as cluttered and confused as the old one. But I could locate anything at a moment's notice. People still walk in from the street unannounced, unrehearsed, carrying their 8 x 10s, their press material, their reviews, looking for the big breaks. They know I'll always lend them an ear. It is the office that gives me security, that gives me access to the world and introduces me to the great characters of my life.

☆

☆

Intermission:
The Joe Franklin Guide
to Phone Etiquette

Joe has really bad habits. I used to hate to have to do this, but it was part of my job to say "Call back in ten minutes," or "Call back in twenty minutes," and he would have the same person call back at least ten times a day. I'm not lying to you. And they would keep calling, because he would say, "Oh, I have good news for you, I have good news, call back, something great's going to happen," and they would continuously call thinking that something will. The worst part of it is that, say, we close the office at eight, he'll say, "Call back at eight-ten," and we'll leave, and they'll call. The phones will be ringing all night. If you walk past the office after eight you'll hear the phones.

—Sophia Orculas Robbins

1. "You are *so great.* If you were poor, I'd send you to college."
2. "Tell you tomorrow, my word of honor . . ."
3. "I'm talking about you on the other phone, I swear, I swear."
4. "Call me tomorrow, ten, very important, you promise? Ah, you're a great man."
5. "I was just thinking about you! Good news! Good news!"

6. "Tell her I've got very good news. What time can she call me tomorrow morning?"
7. "They hung up?"
8. "I've got a dozen people in the office."
9. "They're filming me for *60 Minutes* right now. Call back in an hour. Very important."
10. "I've got a roomful of lawyers; they're all charging by the hour."
11. "My lawyer's here, he's charging $150 an hour."
12. "My writer's here . . . we've got a big book . . . I'm paying him by the hour."
13. "My writer's here . . . we've got a big book . . . you're in it! Yeah, you're in it!"
14. "Honey, I'm talking about you on the other phone! Right now! Right now!"
15. "Call me tomorrow at ten. Very important. Crucial. Vital. Talk to you then?"
16. "Hello?"
17. "Sure I know Pacino. . . . I'll have to talk to him for you when his girlfriend's not there. Will you settle for Pee-Wee Herman? No, he won't play with himself, guaranteed!"
18. "Oh, yeah, we're in good shape."
19. "Make sure we talk July fourth. Very important."
20. "Are we good? Are we healthy?"
21. "The meeting's winding down."
22. "Call me Wednesday morning, I've got my doctor here cauterizing my throat."
23. "Andy! I'm being interviewed here by *60 Minutes*. I'm going to give you a big plug. We're doing thirty minutes at a time. Call me tomorrow, ten."
24. "I'll have great news tomorrow, ten. I'm talking to a tape recorder."
25. "Hey, Coach!"
26. "I've got my shareholders' meeting. There are about twelve men here. Tell him how many people are here. Tell her talk tomorrow about six."

☆

27. "Good news Tuesday, a meeting on Wednesday."
28. "Call me Friday. It's mandatory—obligatory—essential—
crucial—critical—basic—fundamental—obvious—recalci-
trant—lugubrious—salubrious—meretricious—and it would
be nice. Please put it on the critical list. Thank you, good-
bye."
29. "Don't drop that camera. . . . We have two cameras
here. . . ."
30. "You're a wonderful man!"
31. "Call back in fifteen minutes! I've got Israel on the other
line!"
32. "I'm talking about you on the other phone, and I'll give you
the word Friday about noon. Don't forget."
33. "Your friendship is worth over a hundred dollars to me."
34. "I've got so many great things to tell you. Can you handle
good news? Do you want it in bunches or in little sprin-
klings?"
35. "Yeah. Yeah? Yeah. Yeah. Yeah . . . Uh-huh."
36. "Wrong number? Better than nothin'. At least somebody's
thinking of us."
37. "I'm speaking to the man who's writing the book about my
life. I'll give you a big plug in the book. You are the greatest!"
38. "I'm going out to Jersey now, and I'll give you two dates tomorrow. Guaranteed. Certified. Notarized. Bonded. Lock,
stock, and barrel. Signed, sealed, and delivered. It's critical."
39. "Today's Chopin's birthday? Tell him I'm coming to his
party."

☆

The Mets,
the *Million Dollar Movie*,
and Joe Franklin

The programs hereunder are the series of one (1) hour tele-vision programs entitled "THE JOE FRANKLIN SHOW." The programs will be produced at the studios of Station WOR-TV in New York City and will be furnished to RKO either live or on videotape recording. PRODUCER *shall furnish* JOE FRANKLIN *as feature artist on the programs. It is understood that the programs consist primarily of* JOE FRANKLIN *deliv-ering his commentary, conducting interviews with guests, and exhibiting and commenting on various films. The pro-grams will be broadcast on WOR-TV on Monday through Friday of each week during the term hereof; however, RKO reserves its right from time to time to change the time of broadcasting of the program.*

—Excerpt from contract,
RKO General Inc. and Joe Franklin

Towards the end of the 1950s, the networks began to discover a hidden cash cow: daytime programming. The smaller shows, the old movies, local variety shows, news discussion, travel-ogues, classical music, Hopalong Cassidy films being shown for the 350th time, hosted by the Wrangler, had all generated revenues in the early days. But soon the networks began to nudge out this local programming, insisting that all affiliates broadcast a certain number of network shows. This way, they figured to make money three ways: in production, in distribution, and in revenues from sponsors.

The networks ate up daytime with soap operas and hundreds of game shows. Standardization became the rule. Formula programming, mass production created what pioneering TV writer Eric Barnouw called "an efficient, streamlined reality that existed to please the majority." The tide was unstoppable. Affiliates were contractually obligated to sign on to at least twelve hours of network shows. And local broadcasters didn't fight the trend. Who could argue? Network-produced programming often brought in the highest ratings.

By the mid-1950s, *Joe Franklin's Memory Lane* aired at 10:30 A.M., Channel 7, against *Treasure Hunt* and *Play Your Hunch.* I was comfortable with the slot, and I had plenty of freedom. But in 1958, I became a casualty of ABC's "Operation Daybreak," with its "bright, new, big-time look." ABC flooded the airwaves with network shows, endangering the local homegrown product. The newest entries into their schedule included *Chance for Romance;* the *Peter Lind Hayes Show; Day in Court;* the *Liberace Show, Mother's Day*, and *Beat the Clock. Chance for Romance*, typical of the daily fare, was an electronic lonely-hearts club, a precursor to the *Dating Game* and *Love Connection,* where, according to the show's description, "mature unmarried men and women meet, and with arranged and chaperoned dates, nurture the inceptive friendships. The guests are selected by three psychologists, who choose applicants basically compatible." *My Day in Court* dramatized re-creations of actual legal cases in California, with participants improvising instead of using scripts—again, the preview of programming to come many, many years later. Buffeted in among these creative brainchilds was a dusty five-year television veteran, *Joe Franklin's Memory Lane.*

I was one of the lucky ones in the sense that my show sur-

★

vived but shifted around from time slot to time slot as the network bite got greater and greater while it flexed its daytime muscles. I was bumped from midmorning to midafternoon to late afternoon to early in the morning. In 1958, I was on in three different time spots within six months. You needed a compass to find me.

Already I was feeling the pinch, the pressure to modernize, to go network. But I refused to give up the "Mom and Pop" operation that I felt was the secret to my enduring success. I clung to my format in the face of change all around me. I was still playing the old movies, dubbing them with a pianola I kept in my Eighty-sixth Street apartment. I was still broadcast in black and white, still live, and had absolutely no intention or inclination to change.

At last, ABC scheduled me at nine o'clock in the morning. For me, that was unbearable. I detested that hour. It was too early. I had to get up at six, and still I would arrive late for the show, usually roaming into the studio while my opening theme song was being played. I had a harder time getting guests at that hour. The performers I liked to host were usually still asleep. In the rare case when a big star was up at that hour, they were usually cranky, cantankerous. The only people who enjoyed seeing grumpy stars were the Joe Franklin freaks, who enjoyed seeing them as their true, organic selves. My fans liked to see guests in a different light than on the network broadcasts, with every hair in place and coiffed. At nine in the morning they had fallen out of bed and were still in need of their first coffeeing. They were on camera but virtually off camera, hardly at their best.

WOR-TV had begun as a local station, Channel 9, on October 11, 1949. The station signed on at 6:55 A.M. with opening words from radio star John Gambling. Nothing came out of the microphone; it wasn't working. They cured that problem and in a year or so moved their quarters to a tiny office in the Empire State Building, where pioneering television personality Guy Lebow tells me the announcers made their offices in the bathrooms.

By the mid-1950s, WOR had become a movie channel. Owned

☆

by film distribution giant RKO, a full 88 percent of its programming was old movies, most of which they owned outright. WOR had exclusive rights to some of the best films in existence from the RKO library. *Million Dollar Movie* was the station's main offering, shown eight times a week! The same film was played over and over again, once a day and twice on Sundays. I think they called it *Million Dollar Movie* because that's how much they made from it. With *King Kong,* they got a 101 rating, a higher rating than could possibly be! More people were watching than were alive when the movie was first released! It soon became a ritual. Every Thanksgiving they would play *King Kong, Mighty Joe Young,* and *Godzilla.*

The RKO films became so familiar that some of the technical staff had entire films memorized. Unfortunately, most of these film gems were barely recognizable from their original theatrical form because of the way they were edited. A two-hour film would be sliced to an hour and a half, with another half hour lost to commercials. The station wasn't concerned with what parts of the movie were cut out as long as they fit the schedule. Some of the movies had entire plots and key scenes cut out. They made no sense at all. As chopped and mutilated as the films were, the *Million Dollar Movie* put WOR on the map. Today other stations do that, but Channel 9 invented it.

Though movies were their staple, by the 1960s WOR was beginning to branch out, to expand its horizons. Other programs in the lineup included *Romper Room,* hosted by Miss Louise; *Funny Company* with the late Morty Gunty; and *Cooking with the Bontempis*—Pino and Fedora Bontempi. He would sing off-key, and she would cook. His singing range was not quite equal to her cooking range. A clown named Claude Kirschner hosted the cartoon show *Super Circus.* To say he was a clown alone is not quite fair to Claude; he was a great, great commercial announcer. He made loads of commercials. Only one of his delineations was being a clown. Standing at about six feet seven, Claude once appeared on my show with a fellow clown by the

☆

name of Ed McMahon, who had started his career as the star of another kids' show, *Big Top*.

The station was beginning its first newscasts, anchored by Mary Helen McPhillips and John Wingate, with Walter Kiernan doing features. Walter Kiernan once gave me a memorable line relating to TV burnout. He told me, "Joe, I love being in broadcasting, but getting the body to and from the studio gets to be a drag." I recalled his words many times in decades to follow.

In 1962, WOR broadened its horizons by acquiring television rights to a brand new baseball expansion team, the Amazin' Mets. The first year did not bode well, for the Mets lost more games than any other team in history. But even as they lost game after agonizing game, the Mets, with greats like Marv Throneberry and Choo Choo Coleman, won the hearts of the city.

I was getting good ratings from Channel 7 and more than holding my own, but then Channel 9 approached me offering two hours in the daytime. Bob Smith, the program director, was the one to make the initial contact with me. When he heard I was unhappy with Channel 7, he offered me not only the TV spot but a nightly radio show. Bob had known me from WNEW, where he'd been in charge of Martin Block's radio program. Bob Smith is in the history books as the man who created the rock-and-roll format on radio on WINS-AM. At WINS, Bob brought in groundbreaking rock deejays Murray the K and Alan Freed. Bob's next stop was as program director–vice president of WOR, which is when our paths met once again. In pitching the move, he reminded me that the WOR studios were only a block from my office on Forty-second Street. Bob made it clear that I would be able to take the show in any direction I chose. It was a package too appealing to pass up. I felt that it was time to make a change, and I publicly made my announcement. Channel 7 was stunned. Before I left, Leonard Goldenson, president of ABC, took me aside and asked, "Why, Joe? Why?"

I knew I was facing the accusation of moving to "minor league television." But I always felt that was a great fallacy. I saw

the potential for stations like WOR as viable network alterna-
tives long before the days of the superstations would take them
nationwide. I heard all the time people saying how "embarrassing" the show was. It was fashionable to be a critic of the show,
to put the show and Joe Franklin down. What some critics didn't
recognize was that we were spoofing the whole world. The show
is on several levels. We had a level for the ladies in Queens; a
level for the kids who smoke pot; a level for the late-shift workers who just came home and are tired; for the young aspiring
stars of tomorrow looking for a break, a place to be heard. My
audience was always expanding, a demographic enigma, literally
creating a market from eight to eighty.

There was a period of time in the 1960s when the only two
things that kept WOR-TV in the black were New York Mets
baseball and Joe Franklin. Nothing else could get a sponsor.
The revenue to pay the lights, to keep the studio going, came
from the *Joe Franklin Show*. Our budget for a year was less
than most people spend on groceries in a week. Yet our interviews with major names could go up against anything else out
there. Production-wise, we didn't have the facilities, but we
were able to do as much as a network show. A few years later,
there was a big headline when MCA bought Channel 9 from
RKO. Page 1 of the *Post* read "MCA Buys Channel 9, Home of
the Mets, Joe Franklin and Million Dollar Movie." No WOR executive ever told me the show was embarrassing. Many hosts
complained about interference from top management. But
throughout my career I was privileged to be allowed a loose
rein. I was never told how my show should be run.

Only once was I assigned a producer, Madeleine Bloom, to
ostensibly take control and revamp the show. She had many
ideas, a "slicker," more "contemporary" Joe Franklin. She did
her best to make it glossy. I happened to like her, and I appreciated her intentions, but I didn't feel she captured the flavor of
the show. Her attempts to change the direction of the show made
it difficult for all of us. She suggested the kind of guests we
should have, the order of the guests, and how they should be

★

handled. Madeleine wanted to talk to the guests beforehand, preinterview them. The crew, comfortable as we were with our format, inevitably locked horns with her. She had difficulty implementing changes and began to feel she was going crazy. She was with the show less than a year. She went on to a very successful career at NBC until her very premature death of cancer.

At first, the station worked on a rotating basis with its staff directors. They believed this system saved money. It may have in the short run, but in the long run, I felt it was detrimental to the quality of the shows. The system wasn't conducive to loyalty, to a sense of responsibility for the show. I never knew who I was going to see in the control room. There was no sense of affiliation, of partnership. Instead of being a group collaboration, it became a time-clock routine, sensible in a factory but not in a presumably creative endeavor.

The first director I worked with was named Bob Eberle, not the singer. A second staff director, Ralph Giffen, followed. Ralph's primary interest was baseball. The next director to come in was from a whole other world. He had nothing to do with the show. It was obvious to us in the studio, and it was obvious on the picture to the viewers at home. During the show, he would get on the phone and call his wife: "I'll be home for dinner at seven, make arrangements with the Chumskys." He talked to his stockbroker, his insurance agent, as the show played on. Once, he was so involved in a phone conversation that he forgot to switch the cameras. I was talking and telling a joke, and the camera was never on me. I think he thought I was stupid. That director was such a nonfan of mine that he had his name removed from the credits at the end of the show.

I had him taken off the program. I confess I've always been the kind of guy who acted very nice and kind, smiling to everybody, as if I'm a little bit of a softie or a patsy. But when I've had anybody who was on my set—stage managers, cameramen—whom I didn't especially like or if I didn't appreciate their work, I would have them taken off my show. I would do that by going to the big brass, the program director, the vice president. I would

⭐

gently suggest that so-and-so was talking about the station in a negative light. Saying evil things, like a bad seed. It was all a very conniving and cunning way of getting what I wanted. People never knew why or how they were dismissed.

Two of my staffers were having lunch one day at Nathan's and complaining about the day's show. I heard about it within fifteen minutes. Whenever my name was mentioned, I knew about it. I had people who worked for me, privately, reporting back. I was always paranoid, very sensitive about what people would say about me. I had to know. It's like presidents of networks; they have spies who go into men's rooms and stand near urinals to eavesdrop. I'd say to somebody like my office assistant Johnny De Maria, "Go see what you hear." I wanted to know who I should be nice to. I acted as if they could take advantage of me and crap all over me. But nobody ever did.

Many of the directors wanted to be more than simply the director. They wanted to be actors or talk-show hosts. They had to suppress their yearning, not only to play second fiddle but often third fiddle or no fiddle. They would always be thinking that *they* should be doing the show instead of me. But they had no choice if they wanted to keep their jobs.

Ultimately, anyone who went head-to-head with me came out the loser. I have had people at the station over the years try to get me off the air. They were told in meetings, "Mind your business. Don't touch him. I don't care what you do. Joe doesn't go. You'll go before he does." And most of them did go before I did. There were fourteen general managers at the station over the thirty years I was there.

If the first few directors had their minds on other matters, one who never let me down was Bob Diamond. As soon as Bob started working with me at the station, I tried hard to get him assigned solely to the show. At last, after much lobbying with the brass, I was successful. Bob was the first one to break out of the stale WOR directorial rotation and become assigned specifically to my show. He was enthusiastic, enjoyed the show from day one, and best of all, appreciated what I was trying to project. Bob brought out my rhythm, my flavor, my tempo, knew my levels and feelings. He became my pulse and was to stay with me during the entire rest of my engagement on Channel 9, nearly twenty-five years. Our relationship lasted longer than a marriage. When Bob went on vacation, I would take a vacation. I canceled my tapings. Bob said, "Joe, it's up to you, do you want a substitute director?" I said no, I'll take ten days off, too.

Bob kept a camera always fixed on me. I could tell when we had a new cameraman, because Bob would be heard saying, "Excuse me, that's Joe's camera." Bob could anticipate my every move. He knew when I was going to look down and study a guest's bio and when to take the camera off me to allow me to formulate the next question in my alleged mind. Another director would have shown me looking down at the bio or the press book. Bob could intuit when I was going to look down and could shoot away *before* I looked down at the bio. Bob knew if I "liked" something or *really* liked it. I gave a nod, and Bob would say, "Okay, everyone, we'll go to commercial," or, "We're going to get rid of this guest." When I was upset about something, he could tell that, too. The concepts were unsaid. We had meetings without meetings, by telepathy.

The most incredible part of my relationship and collaboration with Bob was that it was all unplanned, unrehearsed. We never sat down formally with a script to lay out the show.

Our communication was just one of those wonderful things, a real partnership. I could walk in and do the show without having to worry about all the petty things that could go wrong. Bob had it all covered.

Bob Diamond came to the station by mistake. He had been stage managing an off-Broadway children's show, and one of the producers asked him, "Are you doing any television these days?"

Bob had *never* done any TV, but he jokingly replied, "Only when they let me."

The producer asked, "Can you A.D.?"

Bob told me he hadn't even known what the term meant but said, "Sure!"

☆

He started in master control, and from there went to stage managing in the studio at WOR. He learned he was to be the director of my show when he received his weekly schedule. It listed him as director of the Joe Franklin Show. Bob went to the studio manager and said, "I think there's been a mistake on the schedule."

The station manager checked the list and said, "No, there's no mistake."

Bob protested, "Somebody else should be here, not me."

The studio manager repeated, "There's no mistake on the schedule." It took Bob at least six months before he realized that I had helped open the door for him.

As archaic as our set had been at WABC, WOR was not much more sophisticated. Singer Jerry Vale and my old friend Rudy Vallee were my Channel 9 opening-day guests, and I had no green room to put them in. Believe it or not, they waited on the *Romper Room* set. My show aired right after *Romper Room,* and there were two minutes for everything to switch over from one show to the other. During the switchover, the stagehands would quietly put in chairs so that my guests could sit while they waited.

Our set was simple enough, consisting of a desk with two chairs behind it, a sort of sofa, and a bookcase behind it, or at least the concept of a bookcase—the books were painted on. For a while I had the miniature Castro convertible sofa sitting on my desk. The crew consisted of two stagehands, two cameramen, a director, and a technical director, Johnny Herbst, who switched the show. His job was to cut from Camera 1 to Camera 2, dissolve to a film or commercial. Johnny ate, slept, lived, and breathed television creating effects that other stations spent millions for using toothpicks and Scotch tape, tissue paper, and Vaseline.

One of the stagehands, Bob Braunstein, had done work in the theater. He would entertain guests while they were waiting to come on to the show. He would talk to them and ask, "How are

☆

you, what're you doing now?" and they would open up to him, because they knew him from Broadway.

The crews worked harder on our show than any other one they worked on because it was totally ad-lib. To me, that was the test of a crew; if you could keep up with us on this show, you were a pro. Whenever someone new came in, I could hear the rest of them warn, "Ohhh, are you in trouble!" There has not been another talk show produced as mine was. Then, and now, they are preproduced, prescripted. Guests come in during this segment, go out there. The music starts here, ends there. The fun of my show, what kept people tuning in, was its spontaneity, which couldn't be achieved on a big network show. The improvisational nature did keep the crew working hard, but it made our show eminently watchable for the next three decades.

Production assistants became a vital new addition to the show. Though seemingly unimportant, the ambience when a guest stepped through the door, when they went into the green room, set the stage for the show. It was an unimportant job from management's standpoint but not from ours. If the guests were relaxed, happy, and comfortable when they came on, it was invaluable to me. I could focus on the performer as opposed to worrying about anything else. A bad assistant could alienate the guests, set a bad tone from the start. Some would look at the guests as if they fell in off the street. They'd ask bluntly, "Who are you?" One didn't know who Jackie Mason was, and he was so offended he walked out. Eventually, we told our production assistants to refrain from asking who a guest was. Instead, if they didn't recognize a face, they were to ask, "I'm sorry, but what is your name?" then check the list and say, "Oh, yes, we're very happy to have you with us!"

Probably the best assistant of all time was our first, Linda Adelman. Linda was a young woman who would wear on her back on any one given day at least $500 worth of clothes. Her total salary for the week couldn't have been more than $85. She went to Kenneth's Salon every week to get her hair done; she had the latest of everything. Her father was head neurosurgeon for the city of San Antonio, and he didn't want his girls to work. But Linda told him, "I'm going to New York, and I'm going to get a job." She acted as if our show were the most important assignment in the world. If we were going to run late, she'd cancel dates for us and reschedule appointments. She was completely devoted to the show and to us, yet she could buy and sell 90 percent of the people who worked in the studio.

Linda had the knack of distracting the guests in the green room by asking, "How do you feel? How's the weather?" She made an art out of small talk. An unskilled assistant would begin her own talk show offstage. "Oh, I read your book, and I was fascinated by it. I'd like to ask you some questions about it." By the time the guest got to me, they had already answered my questions. Instead, Linda would gush. "What a great tie! It really goes well with those shoes!" When she was done prepping a guest, the guest was talking, totally comfortable, but hadn't said a thing about his or her career, movie, or book.

Linda had a way of broaching the most difficult subjects. She once told the highly temperamental director Otto Preminger, "Your fly is open." Anyone else would've paled at the task. She was so up, so bubbly, she could say, "Go fuck yourself," but you'd think she was giving a compliment. Georgie Jessel was appearing on the show at that time a lot to plug the hotel where he was staying in exchange for a free room. One day he teased Linda: "You know, honey, I'm as old as Abraham Lincoln."

She retorted, "I thought you were older than that!" And he loved it, because of her way of saying it. She ultimately left because WOR never gave her a raise.

I hated to lose Linda, but I thought, How important can a production assistant be? I was sure the next one would be as good as she had been. Then I realized within a week that she was one of a kind. No one came close to Linda.

A Typical
Joe Franklin Show,
1977

Jon Hall was our leadoff guest. Not a household name. But he was an idol from my youth and an idol to millions of moviegoers, an elegant leading man who could make women swoon. He played opposite some of the biggest stars of his day, most frequently Maria Montez and Dorothy Lamour, with whom he appeared in the famous film *The Hurricane.* I was fascinated by his recounting of tales on the set, of the great days with the great stars. I could have listened to him all afternoon telling anecdotes about Dorothy Lamour or some of the other classic Universal beauties, about the great "camel" operas—desert movies—he performed in.

But Jon Hall was here not to talk about his glory days but about a new camera process he had developed, "Optivision." Though he had tolerantly humored me as I dredged up memories of his films of the 1930s, his face lit up at the mention of camera lenses. The star of *On the Isle of Samoa* and *South of Pago Pago* began an eager explanation of his technological exploits.

Jon Hall was followed on the panel by Katherine Barker and Mrs. Richard Tucker. Katherine, at the time, was the twenty-three-year-old author of *We Won Today,* her story of a New York Mets season. A former dancer who had discovered baseball at twenty-one, she was the first female ever to write a baseball book. At her side was Mrs. Richard Tucker, a widow after the recent death of her husband, the fine operatic tenor Richard Tucker, who had made the song "You'll Never Walk Alone" a standard years before Jerry Lewis brought it to a telethon. Mrs. Tucker discussed an upcoming benefit in her husband's name, featuring singing tributes from such greats as Placido Domingo and Renata Scotto. All this interspersed with Katherine Barker's comments about New York Mets Wayne Garrett, Joe Torre, Bud Harrelson, and Tom Seaver, "who was a nice man but usually too busy to talk." I predicted that her next book would be a cookbook, and she looked at me in disbelief. Yes, she was writing a cookbook!

The most embarrassing moment of the show came after Mrs. Tucker said, "My sons are such baseball fans. And Richard was such a baseball fan . . ."

Katherine Barker said, "I'll send him a book."

Mrs. Tucker looked at her pityingly and said, "You can't, darling, he's dead."

Katherine stammered. "I meant to your sons."

Before it got out of hand, we brought in a musical number featuring a young singer named Robin Kayser, with Brian Gari as musical accompanist. The crowning moment came as I was named an honorary pearl diver by Michiki Kimbai, "the Pearl Princess," "the Pearl Ambassadress." Did you know I was an honorary pearl diver?

⭐

It Ain't Just Paint

You can't sit and not like this; for forty years he's been sit-
ting and spritzing, sitting and talking, sitting and nadling,
schmelling with the greats, the near greats, the ingrates, the
ne'er-do-wells, the good people. "I've had the young, the
old, the Weird Al Yankovics, the kids in the tight pants with
the hair, the guitars, things, I've seen it all, I've had it, I've
smelled it, I've touched it, and y'know what? It's fun."
  —Billy Crystal on Joe Franklin

Initially, my TV show aired from 12:30 to 2:00 P.M, ninety
minutes a day. It was the exact same format, the exact same talk
show, as Channel 7, with a tremendous lineup of guests. It was
still the golden age of movie press agents proposing people for
shows. Every day we had a star—Paul Newman, Ginger Rogers,
Jimmy Durante, Bob Hope, Jack Lemmon, Bill Cosby, Gene
Kelly, Jack Benny, Maurice Chevalier, all the big ones.

Just as at ABC, the show was called *Joe Franklin's Memory*
Lane, but I eventually dropped the words "memory lane." In
1970, we became *the Joe Franklin Show*. I felt that the term
"memory lane" had become overused, especially when Alan
Freed started to use it for rock-and-roll records that were six
months old; it diminished the value. Besides, it restricted me. We

weren't just memory lane, we were contemporary talk and talent. It was a way of reaching out to a new audience.

A second change came when I stopped showing silent-film clips. We were so jam-packed with guests, the roster was so full, that we felt it was best to go to the all-talk format. Many viewers were vastly disappointed. They missed the old movies, had associated them with me for so many years. Twenty-five years later, people still said to me, "Joe, why don't you show more movies?" In their eyes, I remained identified with the golden years of silent slapstick comedy. Even now people say, "I enjoyed the old movie you played the other night." It's so indelibly etched in their minds, it's unbelievable. "I saw the old Laurel and Hardy movie you played last week," when it was twenty-five years ago.

While the *Joe Franklin Show* still strived to keep its "Mom and Pop" flavor, we did reluctantly fall in step with new technologies. We were one of the last shows to employ color, and for many years I had fought going to videotape. I had felt that live television offered the audience a unique perspective and was crucial to a creative, spontaneous show. I loved live television. In the early days of television, I was watching a show called *Abe Lincoln in Illinois* on live TV, and the star was Raymond Massey, the most famous portrayer of Abe Lincoln. They were bidding the president farewell, and one actor said, "Good-bye, Mr. Massey." I never forgot the thrill of live TV. I was hoping those things would happen on my show. Even the most professional people in the world are prone to a blunder. I loved bloopers and blunders. That's one reason I hated to see the show go on tape, where it could be edited out. I loved the possibility of a blooper.

In the 1950s, there was little chance that our show would be taped. Videotape was prohibitively expensive, and only a very few network programs used it. But by the 1960s, the technology had fallen within the reach of every show. WOR at last began to suggest I go to videotape. I resisted, but when the station approached me about showing a repeat of the show at one o'clock in the morning, the only answer was to go to tape.

Our show was broadcast live at 12:00 noon to 1:00 P.M., then

re-broadcast at 1:00 A.M. This was before Tom Snyder, before
Letterman, before any of the late-late-night hosts. But again, I
feel I was a pioneer, a trailblazer. My staff worried that no one
would watch the show. I told them, "Don't say a word, we're going to make this work." When the rest of the stations were dark,
we were being broadcast, and we obviously filled a need. There
was a tremendous untapped viewership after midnight. Soon networks and local stations alike were scrambling to follow in my
footsteps. Today virtually every station broadcasts twenty-four
hours a day. After watching our performance, all of a sudden
other people decided, Hey, this is a viable spot; let's put something in there! When I went to late-late night I didn't suffer at all,
didn't lose a single sponsor, didn't lose an audience. In fact, it
brought me a new one that was to carry me for the next two
decades.

I've tried to estimate the number of guests I've had on the show
over the years. Sometimes I say 200,000, but the truth is, I really
have no idea. We've had plate twirlers, muscle men, politicians,
rock-and-rollers, scribes, rocket scientists. We've had stars, wives
of stars, sons of stars, daughters of stars, and mothers-in-law of
stars. Every important figure in entertainment at one time or another has graced my studios.

One of the great fallacies was that anyone could be on my
show. I learned, even recently, that I can turn on the radio any
time at night when I'm home in bed and somebody will say, "Ah,
Joe Franklin, what a nice guy; he puts everybody on his show."
In 1954, I was in my office fielding phone calls. I'd get, even
then, 200 calls a day from people wanting to be on TV. Later on,
by the time I got to WOR, it got to be 400 a day, 500 a day. But
for every one who comes on the show, I've turned down 400,
450. Despite the common misconception, I have had to turn
away the vast majority of would-be guests.

I would *like* to be able to let everybody come on. It hurts me
to reject anyone. I appreciate the desire, the incredible craving
to perform, to communicate with the public. I like to give people

that opportunity. But early in my career I learned something. If someone called and said they wanted to be on my show, my first question was: "What's your specialty?" They'd say finance or romance or nutrition. I'd ask, "What are your credentials? What are your qualifications? What's your background?" Nine times out of ten, they didn't have any. In the early days, out of my own inability to say no, I put on guests who didn't merit TV exposure. It turned out disastrously for all parties. Worst of all, I found out that if I put unqualified guests on the air, they didn't appreciate it. They said to themselves, Oh, Joe Franklin, he's hit rock bottom. If he put *me* on his show, he's hit the pits, the bottom. They had a need to be rejected. I didn't learn that until much later in my career. I found that there were ways to be nice without doing so at the show's expense.

Millions of people focus on the oddballs, the offbeat acts we've featured over the years. They think of our Dancing Dentist, the guy who whistles through his nose, fat ladies singing. Though I don't deny we've had more than our share of fringe performers—which did sell tickets—our reputation is overrated.

It was the Billy Crystal takeoff of me on *Saturday Night Live* that gave people the idea that I hosted a freak show every night. The truth is, I had Margaret Mead twelve times, the classical conductor Leopold Stokowski twelve times ("Sto-coff-ski! Sto-coff-ski!" he bellowed. "I am not a cow!"), Lou Rukeyser twelve times, William F. Buckley, Bob Tisch, Carl Icahn, Mario Cuomo, the leading figures in the worlds of business, finance, politics. I had Andy Warhol on the same show as Salvador Dalí. Bill Simon, secretary of the treasury, was on my show as a guest. Abba Eban, the foreign minister of Israel.

Some of the "offbeat" guests don't seem so offbeat anymore. We had Gloria Steinem on when nobody ever dreamed there would be such a thing as women's lib. Gloria Steinem and Betty Friedan talked about someday having a "crusade for women," and all of us were thinking, They're crazy! To show you how long ago that was, Gloria Steinem was still wearing makeup. I had the first transsexual, the first changeover, Christine Jorgenson. I was the first to investigate psychic phenomena in a TV forum. I've had more psychics than any other program—Uri Geller bending spoons, Jackie Stallone, Sly's mother and a top astrologer. I had a woman who opened up a restaurant in a former bordello where the ghosts of the girls would entertain the guests. Today what's the top infomercial? The psychic hot line. I once asked a believer in reincarnation if he thought he would come back in a future life as a part-time rabbi and fill in on the High Holy Days.

I was the first one to recognize the potential of cable TV as a powerhouse in the world of broadcasting. When most people hadn't even been hooked up yet, I was hosting people like Peter Abel, a cable pioneer and the publisher of cable's first listing. Peter Abel himself couldn't watch his show until six years after it began, when his Greenwich Village apartment was at last wired. The first cable audience was tiny, *tiny*. But I already saw that cable's origins paralleled, in many ways, the early days of radio. It was only a matter of time before the technology matured to reach the masses.

Along with Earl Wilson, I was one of the first to ever appear on a cable or public-access show; they were taped in only one location, the Teleprompter Studios on 178th Street in Manhattan. Most performers, most personalities, had nothing but contempt, dismissive contempt, for the fledgling medium. I went to Peter Abel's show, and half a dozen others, when very few people in the legitimate entertainment business gave them a second thought.

I had Howard Stern on the show long before he came to national prominence. The first time he came up to me out at the WOR studios and asked to come on the show, I said no, I'm not interested. I was relying on his reputation alone as a "bad boy of radio," a "schlock jock." But he kept asking, and finally his persistence won out. The interview was one of the most pleasant I've ever conducted. This guy was like a pussycat! We talked about his family, his father, a radio engineer who had worked at WHOM, the first station I had worked for. I thought, This is the guy they're all scared of? Only once did he emerge from the

☆

shell: Right before a break he leaped over the desk, gave me a big kiss, and started to rip my clothes off. I wouldn't have minded, but he was smearing my makeup.

Abbie Hoffman was on my show. He was considered wild, uncontrollable. He had just written *Steal This Book, Piss on This Book*; it was at the peak of his rebel days, when he was a yippie advocating burning, looting, stealing, down with the Establishment. When he was on my show, he was kissable, huggable. There's something about me that subdues rebels.

I had bodybuilders and strongmen in the days when the public thought they were all "fruitcakes." I've been told I helped popularize karate in the United States. On my show, a man named Aaron Banks was the first to give a demonstration of chopping wood blocks with the side of his hand. At that time, judo and jujitsu were virtually the only martial arts in America. "Karate" was six little black letters in the yellow pages. Joe Louis came on the show, and after his appearance, he walked out and said, "I don't feel too good, man, I don't feel too good." He collapsed in his car going home and landed in the hospital. It made headlines. I had Arnold Schwarzenegger on when he was promoting *Pumping Iron,* working out twelve hours a day at Gold's Gym.

I had Jack LaLanne, the fitness pioneer, on my show a hundred times. Jack offered a reward of $10,000 to anyone who could keep up with the same exercise he does every day. Arnold tried to do it; so did world champion Franco Columbu and many others. None of them could. When he turned seventy, Jack LaLanne towed seventy boats for seventy minutes with seventy people on them, to the *Queen Mary* for its seventieth birthday. He used to stay in a swimming pool with a harness and tread water for about four hours, and then he'd lie in a bathtub for about four or five hours and have his wife, Elaine, pour ice cubes on him to get his body used to the temperature of the water when he swam. Not long ago, I was on the elevator with Jack LaLanne in the Empire State Building. He asked me, "What floor are you going to?" I said, "Eighty-seven." He pushed my hand away and kicked the button with his foot, the toe going up to the right button.

"The Mighty Atom," Joe Greenstein, was ninety-four when he appeared on my show. He bent railroad ties with his teeth. He took a crowbar, put it over the bridge of his nose, and bent it. At ninety-four years old. I witnessed this. When he was younger, he used to tie women to his hair and drag them around. Lou Albano was on the show seventy-five times, Captain Lou. Very colorful man—wrestler, manager, movie actor. He goes on other talk shows and says, "Joe Franklin's the greatest!" I get embarrassed.

The only time we ever had a brawl on the show was when we had two physical-fitness experts. Susie Pruden, daughter of fitness expert Bonnie Pruden, was on the air promoting her new physical-fitness program for children. There was another physical therapist on the show, and the woman thought the program was not only of no benefit but harmful to children. The dispute grew to monumental proportions. It started politely with a discussion of physical therapy. It soon grew to a full-fledged war. The two women went at it like cats! We had to break for a commercial when they went to blows, so that we could break them up and lead them to separate corners.

I admit to having little knowledge of baseball, although I have been honored with Joe Franklin Day at Yankee Stadium. I've had all the baseball people as guests. I had Willie Mays as a guest in his heyday, accompanied by a fellow named Rudy Giuliani, who was then his lawyer. I had singer Theresa Brewer serenading Mickey Mantle with the song "I Love Mickey." That record, on the Coral Label, maybe sold ten copies. It wasn't a threat to Bing Crosby or Frank Sinatra. When I don't know whether our guest is an infielder or an outfielder, I let Richie Ornstein do most of the talking. A former New York City policeman who opened a chain of fitness centers, Richie has been on the air with me for about ten years and now cohosts my WOR radio show. Over the years he has brought me all the Yankees, all the Mets, the old-timers.

Despite my efforts to lift the show to a level of fine art, the most outrageous guests never failed to get the biggest ratings.

⭐

I've tried to analyze what appealed to the audience about them. Maybe it was the idea of seeing how far somebody would go to bring themselves to the attention of the world. Seeing what they'd do to get in the news, in the public eye. The offbeat performers were hardly original with me.

Nearly a century ago, impresario Willie Hammerstein booked the "man with the seventeen-foot beard," bicycle champions, runners, wrestlers, even lady sharpshooters, women he dubbed "Pistol Packin' Mamas." They created a sensation as Willie sold out the Palace Theatre, the hub of old vaudeville. Later, the great radio host Fred Allen introduced a segment on his radio program called "People You Didn't Expect to Meet," featuring lady blacksmiths, goldfish doctors, and sausage stuffers. Today that seems tame in perspective. Over the years, our level of curiosity has grown, our desire to watch the outrageous, the different. Whenever I featured an offbeat guest, I figured I was only following in a distinguished tradition.

My talent coordinator, Phil St. James, brought me an albino ventriloquist with an albino dummy. Everybody remembers the man who whistles through his nose and the singing undertaker. I always enjoyed Gloria Parker, a percussionist who played the rims of water glasses. Gloria had been a big band leader in the 1940s at the Hotel Astor, alternating on the bill with Vincent Lopez. Gloria was an artist with those water glasses; no musician was more nervous or sensitive than she. She would get upset and yell at us if the water in the glasses wasn't the right temperature. Then she would provide us a virtuoso concerto in B-flat. No Toscanini, no Sto-coff-ski, was more dedicated to her art. Ultimately, she got a part in *Broadway Danny Rose* after Woody Allen saw her on my program.

I've booked reverends, priests, rabbis, and cult leaders on the show. I had so many poets on—not that I have any great love of poetry—that they put me on the board of *Poetry* magazine. I don't remember any T. S. Eliots among them, but at least they received a venue. I would give them the chance to read one poem.

☆

Always considerate of the audience, I'd suggest to the bard, "Make it a short one."

I had jazz greats like Clark Terry, Oscar Peterson, Dizzy Gillespie. Even a great like Anita O'Day couldn't get on Johnny Carson, though Johnny knew her and loved her. To put her on the *Tonight* show or the *Late Show,* you'd have to go through some young producer who'd say, "Who's Anita O'Day?" I jumped at the chance to have her on. Once, we made American musical history when she was teamed with Duke Ellington and Sy Oliver, three swing-era legends.

Lest you forget our contributions to the realm of fine art, along with Dalí and Warhol and a few thousand others, allow me to introduce Morris Katz. Morris Katz, "beneath Picasso, the most prolific of all painters," first appeared on my show in 1968, painting a three-by-four-foot piece in fifteen minutes. Today it's undoubtedly in a museum someplace, a museum in somebody's attic. But truthfully, I knew Morris Katz was a genius from the moment he told me so. Since his 1968 debut, he's been on my show eight hundred times, more than any other guest. No one else is close. A distant second is Otto Preminger, who came on 155 times, then Georgie Jessel, at 125, and Rudy Vallee, at 85. There were fifty appearances by Tommy Rocco, who specializes in Russ Columbo songs. (At my suggestion, he went back to his original name and is known as Tommy Ritacco.) Fifty visits by Joe Marvullo, a very famous photographer; he's done many books. Brian Gari, singer, guitarist, Eddie Cantor's grandson, fifty times. Aaron Banks, the karate expert, whom I call "The Banks Who Never Fails," was on the show fifty times. Not the blood banks, not the banks of the Wabash, not the sperm banks, but Aaron Banks; that's how I describe him. Arthur Tracy, the "street singer" and star of *The Big Broadcast (1932),* was on fifty times. But Morris Katz, eight hundred! He would draw people, landscapes, anything in sight. He drew everything from banners to postcards. His special talent was painting on toilet paper. He warned, "Use this and my entire appearance is wiped out."

☆

Despite such rare lapses, we strived to remain a family-oriented show. I had nothing if not my wholesome reputation. From time to time we had women come into the studio who were dressed in ways that I felt were too revealing. I would personally help them cover up. I didn't want to be responsible for any heart attacks among our older viewers. I enjoyed being known as Mr. Clean.

Not that we were averse to guests in the adult entertainment field. I hosted Gloria Leonard, then publisher of *High Society* magazine. We had a woman come on from *Partner* magazine to tell us about the joys of swinging. Many of our viewers probably wondered, Swinging from what? I had cable-TV hostess Robin Byrd on. She was a very nice girl. Have you ever seen her show on TV? Al Goldstein, *Screw* magazine. I had porno actress Traci Lords on my show a few times, though I never made any movies with her. I wasn't built right, wasn't equipped.

I was the first to have dog acts, and that got me in more trouble than the porn stars. I had a man auditioning a dog act; he said he had a singing dog. But when the dog was about to audition for me, he made a mess on the floor. I said, "What's that all about?"

The owner quickly answered, "He's clearing his throat."

I had a plate-twirling poodle who could juggle plates, flip them in the air, catch them in his mouth, spin them on his nose. He was a marvel, but he got me in hot water. The Society for the Prevention of Cruelty to Animals said I shouldn't have dogs performing on TV. They lodged a protest with the management; it was against their policy. All the dog was doing was juggling plates. I said to the SPCA, "But this dog's father *wants* it to be in show business!"

Despite my warnings, some of the comedians who visited tried to perform their monologues. Five people laughing is not going to make you sound very funny. I finally knew what they meant by the sound of one hand clapping. But there was one notable exception. They were a duo who could've played to a wall and still gotten laughs.

☆

Two unknowns came into the studio in the early 1970s. They asked us to cue up the Jeanette MacDonald–Nelson Eddy song "Indian Love Call" on an old Victrola. One of the young men was wearing a dress, stockings and heels; in fact, it was quite a while before I realized it was a man at all. The other was dressed as a Canadian Mountie. They danced to the music, an old-time fox-trot. Later in the show, the Mountie was doing all the talking, funny little voices. We were all whispering, "Is that really how he talks?" Those two comics turned out to be Robin Williams—the one in the dress—and Andy Kaufman, with the funny voice. This was way, way, way before *Taxi,* before *Mork and Mindy.* Andy did all the talking, while Robin Williams never spoke. It was the quietest he's ever been.

I had Roseanne Barr on the show long before she was a star. She was just a heavy woman sitting there. She didn't have an agent, just herself; too nervous to talk about her career, she talked about the other guests. I put Richard Pryor on my show long before he was a star. One of my scouts, Hal Stone, was scouring the Village for potential talent when he saw Richard Pryor snoring at a counter in a diner, using a duffel bag as a pillow. His snoring must've cracked Hal up, because I got a call from him the next day urging me to put this new outrageous comic on the show.

Whoopi Goldberg was on the show many times. I had George Carlin on many, many times, before he got the beard and the cursing. Eddie Murphy was on our show many years back, along with the crew of *Saturday Night Live,* but he denies he ever made an appearance. That's okay. He'll live without me, and I'll live without him.

Dick Gregory and I remain very close. He was the first black comedian to cross the barrier, to enter the white man's world and make heavy money. He was the first to play Las Vegas and make $175,000 a week. But for some reason he walked away at the height of his success to become a crusader. He became a great pioneer. I've had him on the air many times both as a comic and as a health-food advocate. I had him on when he was working with that big fat man, the one who weighed two or three thousand pounds, the one they had to lift with the derrick.

Andrew Dice Clay got his start by winning a talent contest I sponsored. The prize was opening for Tiny Tim at the Fireside Inn in Queens and an appearance on my show. It's amazing he ever forgave me. Rodney Dangerfield was on my show maybe 100 times. Always sweating, always perspiring, always drenched. The first time Dangerfield appeared, he came on with his sister. I was shocked, did a double take, a triple take. She looked just like him! Rodney never learned not to do shtick on the show. Like the corpses of the other comics, his jokes just laid there. Whenever one of his laugh lines would die, he'd poke me and say, "Hey, Joe, is there anyone else watching this show beside you and me?" Rodney used to say he got more exposure in his synagogue than he did on my show.

Woody Allen was discovered on my show, coming on to plug his first record, "Woody Allen Live at the Bitter End." He had been a writer for Sid Caesar's *Show of Shows* and was branching into stand-up comedy. I had him on with Jack Warner, the famous movie producer. Jack came on my show holding his Oscar for *My Fair Lady* (which, incidentally, he left in my studio by mistake. We had to track him down and give him back his Oscar). Jack liked Woody so much he invited him to a press junket in California for the opening of Warners' new movie *The Great Race,* starring Jack Lemmon, Natalie Wood, and Tony Curtis. Woody went and became the host of the affair. Playing that audience didn't hurt his career. Since then, Woody has been on my show maybe fifteen or twenty more times. He spent quite a bit of time visiting at my offices or in my studios. One of my thrills is whenever he asks me to make an appearance in his movies. I love pretending to be an actor. In fact, in high school I tried out for the dramatic club but couldn't remember my lines. Woody is more forgiving than my drama teacher was. He gives me a little Hitchcockian, roundabout cameo sequence in which I play (who else?) myself. My most well known appearance is in *Broadway*

☆

Danny Rose, where I host an interview segment with the star of the film. We actually shot that segment in the WOR studios, as if it were an everyday show. Woody collaborated with Bob Diamond to make it absolutely authentic. I admire Woody's touch, his nuance, his savoir faire. He'll someday be recognized as the modern-day Charlie Chaplin.

Because of Billy Crystal's classic impersonation of me on *Saturday Night Live* ("I've had the greats, the near greats, I've had it, smelled it, touched it"), many people think Billy and I are old friends. The truth is, I didn't meet Billy until recently. I was reluctant to meet him because I remembered what Dick Cavett had told me about Groucho Marx. For many years Cavett had been dying to interview Groucho Marx. Groucho was his idol; Cavett worshiped him as a divinity. At long last he finally got Groucho Marx on his show. And Dick Cavett was very, very disillusioned, for Groucho turned out to be just like anybody's old grandfather, quiet, not funny. He could have been a matzo ball. So I said to myself, God forbid that I should get Billy Crystal on my show and he finds out that I'm just an ordinary guy not worthy of satire, not worthy of all that press. Then it would be good-bye, so long, to all that great media hype! I'd see Billy frequently— we'd shake hands at cocktail parties—but I was always afraid to have him on the air. He was submitted to the show many times after he was already a star, already on *Saturday Night Live.* But I turned him down as a guest each time, even though he was a big, big star, because of my own insecurity. He was only on the air with me once, on my 40th Anniversary Special. Whenever anybody asks what I think of his impersonation of me, I always answer, "One of us is lousy!"

Bill Cosby is the nicest guy in the world and one of the few who came back on my show after achieving true celebrity. He rarely does talk shows anymore, but in 1993, at the height of his superstardom, he came on mine. His press people stared at him and said, "Why *that* show?"

He answered, "I don't want to forget the man who gave me my first break, when I didn't have carfare to come to the studio."

★

Bill Cosby called up our show and asked to come on, and one of our production assistants, Virginia Engasser, answered the phone. At first, she thought it was a gag. She was one of many who worked for me for many years who, even though I was the star, didn't think I was worthy of getting the top performers. Even though they were with me around the clock, down deep, subliminally, they still thought I was grade B. It's almost pathetic that they could be with me for years and still think I was second-rate. Despite her initial disbelief, Virginia followed through, and we booked Bill Cosby.

The result was a brilliant hour. Bill Cosby brought tears to my eyes when he said, simply, "Joe, I have to come back here to say thank you." He lightened the moment when he said, "The only problem with you, Joe, is that you keep saying, 'We're going to make this show a classic.' You're putting more pressure on me than you put on me when I was that young twenty-four year-old."

I told him, "Bill, I tell that to everybody on every show! I meet them in the purple room, the orange room, I say today is a masterpiece. I say this is one for the archives."

Bill laughed. "You scared me, Joe! I thought you were gonna be upset with me. You wouldn't have me on anymore!"

I hate to use the word "discover" in terms of talent, as if somebody is a continent. If anybody discovers them, it's their parents. But I did give thousands of performers their first exposure. As with the comics who have come through the studio, I've been in on the first appearances of major talent. I gave Al Pacino his first television booking. His film and stage career skyrocketed, and he hasn't made a television appearance since. I had Michael Jackson on the show when he was with the Jackson 5. I told the cameraman to "focus on the little guy." Liza Minnelli came on my show when she was still a teenager. She was not known; she was still "Judy Garland's daughter." Diana Ross was on with and without the Supremes. Peter Dean came on with his young niece Carly Simon. A teen-aged Whitney Houston appeared with her mother, Cissy Houston.

☆

I was the first to put a young cowboy boot salesman named Garth Brooks on the air. He had been struggling, working odd jobs to make ends meet. He was chubby, not especially sexy, and several people around me said, "Joe, we're booked full. Let's pass." But for some reason I felt Garth Brooks had something special, and we put him on. He became the nation's number-one country star. But along with the Woody Allens, the Pacinos, the Garth Brookses, possibly the most remarkable young guest to debut on my show was Barbra Streisand.

Frank Campana was a public relations man who used to bring me Jerry Vale, Tony Bennett, Mitch Miller, Johnny Ray, Guy Mitchell, and Jill Corey. One day he brought me in a rather un-photogenic Brooklyn girl named Barbra Streisand. When I shook her hand, for some reason I noticed her long, sensuous fingers. She told me she'd been auditioning for months but couldn't get hired as a beatnik. She had been turned down by every agent in town because of her nose. Frank Campana begged me to put her on my show. I was hesitant, but he insisted she was a brilliant singer. I said, "Frank, if you want it, I'll do it, but I don't think it means anything."

A week later, she was on my show, and she sang. She was all the superlatives Frank had said and more. She asked me if she should have her nose fixed. I told her, "Don't ever change, because then it wouldn't be you anymore."

Rudy Vallee was on the panel with her that day. I guess he didn't care for her, because although everyone else was raving, Rudy told her she'd never make it in show business. He said, "Quit. You haven't got the face or the voice."

I told her after the show that I might be able to help her get a couple of Catskill hotel jobs. Even then, when she had yet to achieve any kind of fame, she declined the job, saying, "I don't want to be known as a Catskills singer." She was very strong; she knew what she wanted from the start and how to go about it.

A few days after her appearance I got a phone call from the owner of a nightclub-cabaret called the Bon Soir on Eighth Street in the Village. Ernie Scroy asked me where he could get in touch

☆

with "that big-nosed singer from Brooklyn" I'd had on my show. I gave him her number, and he signed her up for a one-week gig at the Bon Soir. That was her first important appearance any-where. Incidentally, on the same bill was a young comedian named Dick Cavett who was in the unfortunate position of trying to entertain the throngs that had come for one reason and one reason alone: to hear Barbra. It was one of those bookings all co-medians dread.

Barbra's new manager, Marty Erlichman, wanted to put out an album and call it *Barbra Streisand at the Bon Soir,* but the club's management or their lawyer—I forget which—wanted $500 for the use of the club's name. That was an all-time boo-boo, all-time bad judgment. That album would've kept that club in busi-ness until the next millennium.

Barbra got into her first Broadway shows, *Another Evening with Harry Stoones* and *I Can Get It for You Wholesale;* then *Funny Girl* became a smash, and she hasn't stopped since. Once her career got into high gear, she never came back to my show. Or any other talk shows for that matter. But I was—and she has confessed this many times—her earliest advocate. That's how she says it; I was one of her earliest advocates.

Bette Midler recently performed at Radio City at $100 a ticket, for thirty-six nights. But many years ago an agent named Dick Miller sent her to me, asking me to use her as a guest on my show. After her first appearance, she ended up working as my receptionist.

I remember her singing for me a cappella in the office. She would sing to amuse me. She was very sweet, quiet, calm. Hear-ing her sing, seeing her style, I sensed she would take off. My wife agreed, and when she met her at the office once, she sug-gested Bette change her hair color, which she did. I helped get her into the chorus of *Fiddler on the Roof,* her first job. Her next one was singing at a gay club, the Continental Baths, with Barry Manilow as her arranger and accompanist.

Everyone in my office is a critic. They all think they know who is going to make it and who isn't. One of the office crew, a public relations man named Dick Falk, told Bette Midler she'd never have a career. He was insistent on the matter and, I must admit, rather rude. He'd tell her she was ugly, had no looks, no talent, on and on. After weeks of abuse, she finally had had enough. She burst out, "Excuse me, but fuck you."

Bette Midler used to go through my collection of sheet music, and one time, before she left, she picked out a song called "The Boogie Woogie Bugle Boy of Company B." It put her on the map, her first big hit. I tease her now, she should bring the sheet music back.

A lot of people think I stopped listening to music in 1950, but we've probably booked more rock groups than anybody but Dick Clark. I've always surprised people who thought my musical awareness stopped with Tin Pan Alley. We put on a group called They Might Be Giants when nobody would touch them. The Ramones were on many times. Joey Ramone just loved to do the show, and he'd bring on his friends. They'd come just to chat. The New Kids on the Block came on the show, and their singer shouted, "I can't believe it! We're on the *Joe Franklin Show*!" And they all cheered.

The J. Geils Band gave us a show that was different from any other we ever did. In 1983, they were the hottest band in the country. They had two platinum records at one time, "Freeze Frame" and "Centerfold." They were number one at that moment in the world. *Saturday Night Live* wanted them, the *Tonight* show wanted them—and the J. Geils Band called us, the *Joe Franklin Show*. David Letterman offered them all kinds of money to go on his show, but they said, "No, we want to go on Joe Franklin. Joe is a real man." Who was I to argue?

They said they wanted to come on and do a whole sixty-minute show, "their" show. We had meetings, rehearsals, which we never did with anybody else. We blocked out how the show was going to go. We staged the show, set up the numbers, scripted everything but the interviews. We had an audience for that show, one of the few times we had one. We ended up turning away hundreds, since the studio was only allowed to seat

☆

seventy-five people. Moreover, the J. Geils Band brought their own entourage, and the place was packed.

At the time the sponsor was Martin Paint. The band members said they wanted to do a tribute to Martin Paint. I asked what they had in mind. Their lead singer, Peter Wolf, said, "I'd like to be *bathed* in Martin Paint. Drenched in it."

"Go on," I said, listening patiently.

He told me his scheme. The band would form a human pyramid, and then, dropped from the scaffolding above, would be gallons and gallons of paint. The colors would pour from the sky, creating a visual kaleidoscope, a rainbow of rock-and-rollers.

I said, "Why not? Whatever makes you happy." Georgie Jessel used to like hookers; these kids liked paint.

Bob Diamond was the voice of reason. He discouraged this plan. But the group was insistent. At last Bob said, "Well, at least if you drop paint on yourselves, make sure it's tempera paint." Their road manager, who obviously didn't know much about paint, said, "No, no, we want your Martin *latex* paints!"

Martin Paint was more than happy to accommodate, and they provided the paints. Down to the last minute, I still couldn't believe they wanted to do this, but they said they did. The cameras were rolling, they formed a human pyramid, and the paint came streaming down. The paint went everywhere, gallons of it poured from above. It just went everywhere. It was the biggest mess you've ever seen.

They had a concert that night and the next day, but they were destined to do it in living colors. As you know, latex paint is washable, but not if it dries. Their wardrobe was ruined, they were stuck with a huge cleanup fee for their limo and damage charges at the Waldorf, where they were staying. They later told me they were washing paint out of their hair for two weeks. Even our studio charged them for cleanup. I thought the studio sort of looked like an abstract painting, splatters over everything, but the station didn't have the same aesthetic sense. The band, however, kept its sense of humor through it all, and it became a classic show.

☆

I was on the air twice in those days. The first show was broadcast in the morning, and I went to see the J. Geils Band in concert at night. Somebody walked up to me and said, "You wanna buy a hot tape of the J. Geils Band on the *Joe Franklin Show*?" It was already being pirated, and who did this guy want to sell it to? Me! That was a hot, hot tape!

John Lennon was brought to my show by a record-promotion man named Pete Bennett. Pete, a former musician who had had a hit with an instrumental version of "Fever," had been a frequent guest on my show himself. But he really made his name not as a drummer but by pitching records by the Rolling Stones, the Beatles, Herman's Hermits, all the top groups, to deejays and station managers around the country. He was responsible for breaking in many, many groups, getting them on the charts. Nobody knew the ins and outs of the business like Pete. To show you how prominent he was, he helped CBS president Tommy Mottola break into show business back in 1969.

Pete was a big fan of mine and brought me some of rock's top talents. One of them was John Lennon. It was one of those things, like the Marilyn Monroe appearance, the James Dean appearance, the Barbra Streisand appearance. In some ways, it hurts me, because when authors and researchers do chronologies of appearances through the years, so very carefully detailed and researched, I'm left out. Because I was local, never had a press agent, never made too much noise. But John Lennon made one of his only television appearances ever on my show. He came on because I agreed to put Yoko on *three* times to talk about her pet causes—women's rights, air pollution, penal reform—whatever it was at the moment. She read from a book called *Grapefruit.* John loved her and wanted to give her career a push. It was a lot like Bing giving his wife, Kathryn, a nudge.

When John Lennon announced his visit, there was tremendous excitement. Big crowds gathered around the studio. We had a big, big turnout, big ratings. Oddly, I knew how big he was, but I was not that excited down deep. I knew the reputation of the Beatles, the importance of their music, mainly through what my son Brad told me. But my great sentiment and affection weren't there.

The only time anyone ever "put one over" on me was a rock-and-roll band called Spinal Tap. I only knew they were in a new movie, *This Is Spinal Tap*. As the interview proceeded, I had sneaking suspicions about them. But I wasn't sure, so I had to play it straight. After the show, I asked Bob Diamond, "Do you get the feeling there's something wrong about that group?"

He said, "Joe, they're not a real group! They're a put-on!"

"Oh."

John F. Kennedy

I don't know if I told you I met John F. Kennedy just before he became president. His hair was brick red. When I met him later, about a year and a half into his presidency, his hair was all gray. So I said to myself, I don't want that job. I turned it down twice.

Tony Curtis

Tony Curtis went through a bad period; it's in his book. We lost touch for about fifteen years. I knew something was strange because during that period, when I used to ask him to be on my show, he'd say, "Joe, I gotta get paid!" I knew, with all his money, if he was asking to get paid, something had to be wrong.

I was a big fan of Tony's. Loved his movies. People used to make fun of his accent; you know, "My faddah da caliph waits yondah." But he didn't care. He loved it.

I was surprised to be left out of Tony Curtis's book. His cowriter spoke with me for half an hour. I think I gave him some things too revealing.

☆

Ray Milland and Vincent Price

I'm probably the only host who had Ray Milland on the air
without his toupee. Everybody was stunned. He was just in a
good mood that day. Friendly. He was absolutely unrecognizable
without the toupee.

He was busy to the end. He was most famous for his role in
The Lost Weekend. Remember that movie, about being a drunk?
He made some Hitchcocks, and was a fine actor. I had him on
without his toupee. It was one of my all-time TV highlights. He
didn't care.

He was on with Vincent Price. It was a hot, hot summer day,
and Vincent Price came in wearing shorts and sucking an ice
cream cone. Just a fun, fun day.

Bob Kane

Bob Kane was an articulate, well-dressed man, but he never
got the money he should have gotten for creating the character
Batman. He somehow sold the rights at an early age, and when
he got divorced, his wife tore up all the comic books. Now
they're worth ten, twelve, eighteen thousand, apiece.

Jerry Lewis

I almost lost Jerry Lewis as a guest when I asked him about
his breakup with Dean Martin. He said, "No wonder they call
you 'The Nostalgia Kid'! Don't you know we broke up ten years
ago?"

☆

The Kennedy Assassination

One of my saddest days was when I did my show and a stage-hand said to me, "Joe, our president just got shot." I was on that day with Margaret Whiting and Troy Donahue, the actor. I figured that the stagehand meant the president of the network. But it was John F. Kennedy. It was a very sad day. Word came right after my show that day; I was on Channel 9 from 12:30 P.M. to 1:30 P.M.

José Ferrer

José Ferrer was talking about an out-of-body experience, of watching himself from an external vantage point. Things were told to him while he was out there about what was going to happen to him and to his family. It was very strange, a very, very strange show. It was José Ferrer's last public appearance. He died not long after.

Rosemary Clooney

Rosemary Clooney walked off our show. At the time, she and José Ferrer were in deep trouble, divorced, and he was not paying alimony. Ferrer was doing a show off Broadway at the time, and I kept mentioning what a good actor he was. Rosemary Clooney kept saying, "We're not talking about him; we're talking about my nightclub act." I kept bringing up José Ferrer, and she got upset, annoyed, and irritated and just walked off the show. She later apologized, saying she had major problems at that time. I pushed a little too hard.

Pearl Bailey

Pearl Bailey used to come on the show and talk, just talk—
I'm here, let's talk. At that time she was in *Hello, Dolly!* the first
black version. She told me, on the air, that all the kids were running around naked backstage. She warned them, "If you don't
stop running around naked backstage, I'm going to leave the
show, and the show's going to flop." After that, they put on their
pants and underwear. She was a very proper lady, even though
she sang double entendres.

Liberace

One night I was walking with Richie Ornstein to the radio station at midnight, and we saw two guys holding hands. One of
them was Liberace, in a jumpsuit. At the time, he was appearing
at Radio City Music Hall, making half a million dollars a week,
staying at a $4,000-a-day suite at the Plaza. We followed him two
or three more blocks, and he went into a tiny little hallway, under the stairs. You have a luxury suite in the greatest hotel in the
country, and you've got to go to a kinky place.

Sammy Davis, Jr.

Sammy Davis: I loved him. My saddest memory was on the
Jerry Lewis Muscular Dystrophy Telethon with him. I could tell
by the way he was talking and singing that he was dying; the
voice was forced and strained. I said to him, "Sammy, do me a
favor, stop, don't do the Louis Armstrong, the gravel voice. The
gravel voice plus the smoking is going to get you in the vocal

cords." I knew, however, that it was already too late when I said that. The vocal cords are very, very thin, thinner than the thinnest hair on your head, and if you irritate them, you get cancer. He smoked five or six packs a day, and he did a Louis Armstrong imitation every day. I said to him, "Sammy, look, Nat King Cole died from smoking five packs of cigarettes a day." Davis was discovered by Eddie Cantor—the Will Mastin Trio, featuring Sammy Davis. He liked the girls. He would always make a date with one of the girls on my show.

Dennis and Harry Belafonte

I had a friend, Dennis Belafonte, who claimed to be the brother of Harry Belafonte—I never knew for sure if he was just bragging. Dennis and I were inseparable as movie collectors. He wrote several movie books. One day he was going to help me do a book on Eddie Cantor called *Eddie Cantor: The Man Who Made Whoopie.* I gave him sixty of my priceless Eddie Cantor photographs. That's how much I trusted him. But before it came to fruition, Dennis Belafonte got killed in a bar. Because he was light-skinned, he apparently made a remark that he was lighter than some other black people. One of them went home, got a gun, and killed him.

After Dennis died, I wrote Harry many, many letters and called him on the phone, begging him to get me back my rare Eddie Cantor shots. They were one of a kind. Harry Belafonte never responded. Who knows, maybe he had no idea what I was talking about.

One day, at a nostalgia convention, I saw them on sale. That really made me sad. I was shocked to see they wound up at that show. It made me very sad.

That was one of the few times I was really disillusioned. Sixty of my best Eddie Cantor shots, many of which Eddie *gave* me.

⭐

They were on sale for ten or twenty dollars at a nostalgia convention in a church. They had my initials on the back.

George Shearing

We had a major setup for the great white jazz pianist George Shearing, who is blind. "Fat" Jack Leonard, that notorious insult comic, said, "George, by the way—you're black."

Sylvester Stallone

I had Stallone on before he was big, when he was in *The Lords of Flatbush*. When he was peddling his *Rocky* movie, he couldn't even pay his rent. Stallone used to come to Richie Ornstein's health club when he didn't have enough money to pay the membership—fifty dollars back then. He was working as a butcher in Brooklyn; that's where he got the punching scene for *Rocky*.

Jennifer O'Neill and Carole Lombard and Alfred Hitchcock and Otto Preminger

Jennifer O'Neill was on my show with Otto Preminger on the panel, and she mentioned that Alfred Hitchcock used to call actors and actresses "cattle." She recalled how Carole Lombard

☆

was making a movie with Alfred Hitchcock and walked out onto the set with three cows just to tease him. Otto Preminger took severe umbrage at her story. "No! That happened to *me!* On *my* set, not Hitchcock's!"

He wanted to be known as mean, even though the story really did apply to Hitchcock. He wanted the credit for being the cruel one. He tried to play the part of a nazi or villain in real life, but down deep he was a softie.

Dustin Hoffman

I did radio every night from 9:15 to 10:00, a straight talk show, no nostalgia. Just a plain interview show. My wife produced it with me, and we had guests like Lawrence Welk. I remember one day I kept him waiting because we used to tape in the afternoon; he was very impatient. We'd tape the radio show at about three, right after my TV show, so I could stay at home at night and listen to the radio or else go to opening nights. I didn't have to be there at nine at night. Then again, I was on till midnight on radio.

I had Dustin Hoffman on one time; he was in a Broadway show called *Eh?* E-H. He said, "Please, Joe, get me on early, because I have to go to an audition for a movie called *The Graduate.*" He said his agent said, "Don't bother, you're too short for the part," because Anne Bancroft is a few inches taller than he. But he went, anyhow, and he got the part, and of course that was the turning point of his career.

I used to meet him every Sunday morning at a place called Barney Greengrass's—they sell sturgeon—at Eighty-sixth Street and Amsterdam Avenue. He was with his wife.

Elliott Gould

I've had some great shows with Elliott Gould on TV. He's very bright, fiercely bright. He read poetry for us—"Casey at the Bat." People forget what a big star he was, but it was once a joke that it was hard to find a movie Elliott Gould *wasn't* in. He was very big in the 1960s and 1970s.

One of the gauche things I did over the years was to have Elliott Gould on the show and ask him, "In case Barbra Streisand is watching, is there anything you want to say?" The odd thing is, he always had something to say about his ex-wife. I'm sure they still have deep feelings for each other.

Muhammad Ali

I had Muhammad Ali on four times: he was very cultured, dressed beautifully, did magic tricks after the show, and levitation, picked people up in the air, held them up in the air for over an hour, a very, very jolly, happy man. Later on, I sent over a book of Dunninger's magic tricks to Ali. Dunninger was before your time.

Robert Wagner, Sr.

Robert Wagner, Sr., the mayor of New York City for many years, was a close friend of mine. We both greatly admired Fiorello La Guardia. There were many TV shows when he would talk about the former mayor. Mayor Wagner wanted to be remembered the way La Guardia was, as a humanitarian more

than a politician. He was able to balance the budget the same as
La Guardia. He was a good man, beholden to nobody. What you
call a man of the people.

Abraham Beame

Abe Beame is a mild-mannered, very short fella. When he was
mayor, we always used to kid that he could walk under the turn-
stiles and wouldn't have to pay the fare.

John Lindsay

I thought Mayor Lindsay was going to become the president
of the United States someday. He had the great John Kennedy
charisma; he was on my show many times. There were big arti-
cles in *Look* magazine—that was the big magazine in those
days—about his being on my show in those days. They mentioned me, saying his appearances on my show brought out the
"housewife vote." I used to joke that if he became president, I'd
be something big in Washington, D.C.

Roy Cohn

I knew Roy Cohn very well. I sent somebody to his house
once with flowers for his birthday. I couldn't make it. The deliv-
ery guy told me Roy Cohn opened the door in his shorts and

made a lunge at him. Did it right away, fast; the guy ran out the
door. Very, very, very aggressive.

Ronald Reagan

The last time Ronald Reagan was on my show, he brought me
his autobiography called *Where's the Rest of Me,* which is a line
in a movie called *King's Row.* I didn't even bother getting an autograph, because it was just an ordinary visit of an author plugging a book. A year later, Ronald Reagan ran for governor of
California and then, later, of course, president. I always felt
funny that I didn't even ask him for an autograph, but to me he
was just another working actor with a book.

Tiny Tim

Tiny Tim is probably the only living person who adores people that I admire whom nobody else even remembers. Who else
cares about Henry Burr, Billy Murray, Irving Kaufman, Arthur
Fields, Charles Hart, Elliott Shaw, Louis James, maybe twenty-
five old-time recording stars? Tiny Tim and I get together in lim-
ousines when we're traveling to a benefit together. We spend
hours and hours privately singing duets to old songs, made famous on old Victor records by the aforementioned stars. We sing
"Old Pal, Why Don't You Answer Me," "Was There Ever a Pal
Like You," "Every Night I Cry Myself to Sleep Over You," "You
Know You Belong to Somebody Else, Why Don't You Leave Me
Alone," "Midnight Rose," "Broadway Rose"—hundreds and
hundreds of old songs. This is my greatest relaxation, my ther-

★

apy, my medicine, my release. Whenever I can get together with Tiny Tim, we sing.

Tiny Tim is for real. He is not a put-on. He's almost like Michael Jackson or Elvis Presley in that he craves his seclusion. He cannot eat if anybody's watching him. He must dine in private. He must take about twelve showers a day. He's impeccably clean, immaculate.

Tiny Tim's been on my show maybe eighty-five times. When *Newsweek* did an issue with David Letterman on the cover, they said how I started all the unusual, off-the-wall acts. The picture they chose out of a thousand that they went through here in my office was of me with Tiny Tim. So I guess he's a symbol of the Joe Franklin–type guest. I love Tiny; he's great.

PART IV
The Great Joe Franklin

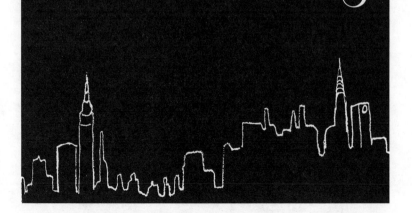

Family, Friends, and Enemies

People always ask me all kinds of indiscreet questions about Joe. Is he clean, messy, is he cheap, is he gay? I say, "None of your business; why don't you call Joe Franklin?" This is my business. Joe to me is a wonderful guy; how much more can I say? What he is, he is. He's my friend; that's my answer. And the morning he comes to the barbershop, I fix his tie. I fix his necktie for thirty years. You see that tie? I make the knot in it.

—Roger deAnfrasio, Joe's barber

I think my one happiness about my son is that he didn't want to be an actor. It's the world's worst business. You're always insecure. Every time the phone rings you're afraid it's bad news, you're afraid you're going to be canned. I helped get Brad his own TV show for two weeks, when he was seventeen. He was sensational. Then he said, "Daddy, that's it." I was so happy when he walked away from it.

Brad and I were always close. I would take him out every Sunday when he was little, buy him salami, and he would say, "Buy me lanali, lanali!" When he was six, seven, eight, we would buy comic books for twelve cents apiece. I am very close to him. I spoiled him. My wife was good to him, but I spoiled him. Even though we had bars on the fifteenth-floor apartment windows, I would still stare at the kid all night long so that nothing would happen. I was a crazy father.

My father, M.F., taught my son how to count money when he was very little. I used to bring Brad down to the store, where M.F. took in hundreds of dollars every day in coins, in change. When Brad was about two, he could already make little stacks of pennies, nickels, and dimes. My father died in 1960, when Brad was three years old.

Ironically, M.F. never started watching my show until he got sick, a few years before his death. He used to call me up and congratulate me on my shows. He became warmer to me. But he never apologized, never regretted our distance when I was growing up. He was too much of a man, too unemotional, to ever apologize, to ever cry. But as he got older, he got mellower toward me, prouder.

It was a famous test case, a medical freak, when he died. He was in the hospital and wanted to live so badly. He had no heartbeat, no pulse, but his eyes were open, and he was mentally aware for several hours. He was alive, but he was dead. That's how much he wanted to live. They sent all the doctors around his bed to study him.

My mother, Annie, died many years later, in 1977. She was my biggest fan; she called every day at work to critique my show. Which guest she liked, which she didn't, how I should run the show. When my mother used to call me up and say, "Great show," I knew it was lousy. When she said lousy, I knew it was a good one. She was not a very good critic.

When my father died, Annie had the chance to marry very wealthy men. She wouldn't do it. She was loyal to his memory and, much to my wife's horror, turned her attentions toward me. Many days, Annie would come down to the office. She was a vigorous, vital woman. She had been been a health-food addict all her life. Ironically, she died from an undiagnosed potassium deficiency. All the potassium was being lost from her body, and

☆

a good doctor should have recognized the signs. We could have gone for a malpractice suit, but the doctor claimed it wasn't indicated that she was on diuretics. A few simple potassium supplements could have saved her life.

I was there the day she died. The police came, and they put her in a black bag. As they were carrying her out, I remember looking at the bag and shaking my head sadly. I said, "That's Annie." I was profoundly sad. It was a big loss for me. She was my biggest fan. She loved me. I still get cabdrivers now who say, "You know, your mother used to tell me you were her son." Now she's gone, sixteen years.

I used to dream a lot that my mother was leaning out the fifteenth-floor window—we lived on the fifteenth floor on East Eighty-fourth. She would slip and I would grab her. We would go back and forth over the windowsill. I was falling, she was falling, I was trying to pull her in. I dreamed that a few times. I called a friend of mine who's a psychiatrist and asked him to help me interpret the dream. He said it meant that I wanted to be with her in life or in death. It was kind of a simplistic, basic, almost gauche interpretation, but it made me happy. I liked the thought that I wanted to be with my mother in life or in death.

I named Bradley after my grandmother, whose name was Betty. We kept the same first initial. It was an unusual name at the time. And now every Tom, Dick, and Harry is named Brad. I miss the days when kids were named Sol and Moe and Hymie. They were better days, Moishe.

Sundays we went to the penny arcades to play Skee-Ball. Young Brad spent many weekends in my office getting to know Pops, Happy, and the other characters. They were an offbeat version of everybody's favorite uncle. But our biggest thrill together was our trips to Coney Island, where we indulged in our favorite activities for the day, throwing darts at the balloons and riding the Ferris wheel. Brad was tireless as the wheel went around and around. At home, he grew up watching Charlie Chase and Harold Lloyd silent comedies when everybody else was watching *The Jetsons*. The two of us spent endless hours screening old 16-millimeter movies on an antique film projector in our living room.

As a young child, Brad was bothered by bad allergies. For years we tried to find out why he had so many colds. This became a source of conflict between my wife, Lois, and my mother, Annie. Annie would blame Lois for giving Brad too much orange juice or not enough clothes. Lois thought Annie and I were conspiring against her, accusing her. Every time he had a cold he would get an ear infection.

One time, when he was two, he had an infection that didn't go away. Nothing would help him. Antibiotics weren't working. His fever raged for eight weeks. We sent for every top pediatrician, but nobody could figure it out. Finally, Annie suggested, "Joe, maybe it's his ears." We sent for an ear, nose, and throat doctor and found out he had a mastoid condition. It took my mother to diagnose him.

One night, we had to race him to the hospital in the middle of the night for a double-mastoid operation. Later, we were told that you could either die or go deaf from this operation. Thanks to Dr. Harry Talbot, our son came out 100 percent healthy and lost no hearing! I've known people in the old days who were devastated by mastoid operations. Happy the Clown was one; he lost 90 percent of his brain and his hearing. In those days they did the operation on the kitchen table with a rusty coat hanger. I was so incredibly lucky. But the night of Brad's mastoid operation was one of the most horrible experiences of my whole life, far and away.

Our domestic life was marked by periodic separations. Lois has always been an astute businesswoman, and she convinced me to buy a country home in New Hampshire. She and Brad enjoyed it tremendously, but I never went up. They spent weekends and summers there, while I stayed in the city. Later, she bought real estate in Florida, which I never visited.

☆

In the city, Lois and I did spend time together, socializing with couples like Suzanne Pleshette and her boyfriend; the singer Connie Boswell and her husband, Ben Levy; Alice Faye and Phil Harris; with Shirley Jones and Jack Cassidy; or Rudy Vallee and his wife, Eleanor, when they were in town. Lois and Eleanor used to go to exercise and acting classes together. At films or in the theater, I would often fall asleep and depend on Lois to help with my reviews. She was an astute critic and was gracious about giving me the credit.

I think Lois's biggest regret was that I was never more of a mingler, a hobnobber. But after a full week of being "on" at the studio, I was more inclined to spend my free hours in front of a projector watching my silent-screen favorites or culling items at out-of-the-way flea markets for my nostalgia collection. I know I should have been honored to have been invited to so many parties and galas, but I don't feel comfortable at those kinds of affairs. Lois was annoyed that I always tried to duck out of Park Avenue soirées and cocktail parties before the pâté was served. I would have been more at ease with matzo balls.

Lois never cared for my office or my office crew. She told me she once tried to clean it up, but I messed it up in between. She warned me, "You'd better not mess up the house the way you mess up the office! Make all your messes there." She was not fond of Pops or Happy or Phil Schindler or the rest. She called them "the dregs of society."

She freely admits to taking many, many swings at me. Over little things. One time I commented that our baby-sitter was working too many jobs, and was too tired by the time she got to our house. *Thwack!* Lois warned me, "Don't ever say anything about the sitter!" "Okay, okay!" One time she belted me so hard I ended up in the hospital. It turned out my eardrum was ruptured, a part of the inner ear called the stapes.

Despite our tumultuous relationship, I could never, ever get divorced. I'm just a creature of habit. I found out that when men get divorced, for many reasons they are more shattered than the woman. I've seen big TV executives get divorced, and one year later, they're down in the Bowery drinking wine. Some people are happiest when they're unhappy. It's like the song Fanny Brice sang, "I'd Rather Be Lonely Without You Than Happy with Somebody Else." "I'd rather be blue, thinking of you / than happy with somebody else."

At the age of fifty-five, Lois was struck with multiple sclerosis. It's rare that it hits at that age, but that was the diagnosis. Lois had always been active—skiing, dancing, exercising three times a week. I think about my wife, who used to walk like an antelope; she used to be able to read a movie marquee from six blocks away. Now she can't. She walks with a cane, but she walks, she walks! For health reasons, she moved down to Florida, where she currently maintains five houses. We talk frequently, and whenever she is back in New York, she stays with me. Her mind is still sharp, she has a brilliant mind. She has a lot of my money; she's got to be smart.

My son Brad is now in the mail-order business, hugely successful. He is bright, fiercely bright. We talk almost every day; whenever I have a question, I call Brad. He is everything to me. Out of great respect for my wife, if not for her, Brad probably wouldn't have turned out as well as he did. Because I indulged him, I spoiled him, I was a lousy father by being a good father. Lois evened the scales by being stern. She would yell, "You're a bastard!" I would always say that she was not maternally inclined, but then, later on, I realized she probably was.

My extended family includes friends like Richie Ornstein and Leon Charney. I met Richie when he was a cop on Tenth Street, Greenwich Village TPF—Tactical Patrol Force. I was a guest in a parade, and Richie was doing security. I asked him if he might moonlight as a personal security man. I was going to nostalgia conventions, shows, and carrying $2,000 or $3,000 cash with me at a time. Richie said sure, and I joined his elite list of clientele, stretching from Bob Guccione to Richard Nixon.

On the show, Richie's brought me great guests, provided a

☆

steady anchor, and we have a nice rapport. Perhaps our most famous feature is a trivia game that we played on our TV show and
is now on the radio. Richie digs through the record books and
nostalgia guides and tries to stump me about old-time movie
trivia. The trivia became so big from our show on radio that even
Pat Sajak in California was using the same questions on his
show—in California. More often than not, I get the correct answer, and Richie's smile can practically be seen over the radio
waves, "That's rigggght, Joe! That's riggggght!"

Leon Charney, a lawyer who got rich when he brokered the
sale of Rockefeller Center, has been one of my closest friends
for many years. Up from the streets of Elizabeth, New Jersey, he
owns over 2 million square feet of real estate in Manhattan. He
always handled show business cases, like when his client Abe
Margolies sued the critic who fell asleep at his Broadway show
I'm Solomon, with Dick Shawn. Jackie Mason was his client,
too, and he defended him against censorship. The Smothers
Brothers had him on their show, and he did some tough material
about Vietnam. As a result, the show got taken off the air. He
claimed censorship. His line was: "Why are we worried about
the Vietnamese? They'll never get past Central Park." Leon and
Jackie Mason sued and won, beating CBS.

Leon is tough. He represented the columnist and writer Earl
Wilson when he was being sued by Frank Sinatra after the publi-
cation of Wilson's unauthorized biography, *Sinatra.* Wilson was
sick, he was so afraid of the pressure from Sinatra. Leon tells
how he was riding in a limo with one of Sinatra's lawyers from
Los Angeles to Palm Springs. Leon was there to take Sinatra's
deposition, and the lawyer was nervous because Sinatra didn't
want to sit through a deposition. Sinatra didn't want to be asked,
"Did you ever have an affair with Juliet Prowse?" Or, "Did you
ever have an affair with Marilyn Monroe?" It would've been a
no-win either way; it would've gone right to the tabloids.

The lawyer was smoking a big fat cigar, and Leon hated
smoke. He said, "Put the fuckin' cigar out. I hate it."

☆

The lawyer, who talked like a longshoreman, said, "Who in the fuck are you talkin' to. It's my fuckin' car, it's my cigar, I'll do what the fuck I want."

Leon said to the driver, "Stop the car, I want out."

The lawyer said, "You're in the middle of the fuckin' desert; we'll stop and let you out right here."

Leon dared him. "Do it."

At last the lawyer relented, "Ah, fuck, all right, here's the cigar." As soon as he said that, Leon knew the case was over.

Even after he called Earl Wilson and told him that everything was all right, Earl was quivering, he was such a wreck from that case. He wouldn't believe his own lawyer; he kept calling because he couldn't believe that the case was over.

An avid, fervent supporter of the state of Israel, when the Yom Kippur War broke out, Leon Charney was working in Washington at the time with Sen. Vance Hart of Indiana. But even with that kind of connection, he couldn't get behind the battle lines. Leon became my first and only foreign correspondent, using the *Joe Franklin Show* to acquire a press pass. Leon traveled to Egypt, Syria, and reported directly, exclusively, to us. Even with typical press passes from normal people you couldn't get through. Somehow my name and my press pass—Leon was twenty-four years old—got him through. Leon told me there was a guard who said,"You work for the *Joe Franklin Show*?" That allowed him to move around and report back to the U.S. government about the infiltration of Soviet arms to the Egyptians and the Syrians. At Golda Meir's press conference, the whole world was watching when Leon raised his hand and introduced himself, "I'm Leon Charney, from the *Joe Franklin Show,* WOR, New York City."

Although I'm probably not his biggest client, Leon has helped me out many times. Leon gave me a certain feeling of security or boldness; if somebody attacked me or bothered me, it was good to know he was there. Richie and Leon have that in common; they're both my protectors.

The *Joe Franklin Show* has been sued only a couple of times

☆

that I know of. WOR was taken to court once when we played the *Beverly Hills Cop* theme song without acquiring the rights properly and another time when a woman fell off a stage. I've been sued, personally, a few times. I'm like Eddie Cantor, who always got sued after he got friendly with cabdrivers, the man on the street. He made promises he couldn't keep. Intimacy is the worst thing a public figure can get involved with, it always backfires. I've been sued a couple of times by people who have come to me with an idea, people with whom I promised to coproduce projects. I'd get sidetracked by not being able to say no, and then the projects never came off. But the cases are always thrown out long before they get ugly.

I tend to be litigious, but Leon Charney curbs my appetite for confrontation. Usually, when I feel unusually affronted, Leon will tell me to swallow it. After a nasty jab in the press, he often reminded me, "Remember that time LBJ was on the phone to Louis Nizer? LBJ was yelling, 'The *Saturday Evening Post* says I used the word nigger. I never said the word nigger! I wanna sue!' So Louis Nizer said to LBJ, " 'Forget about it, swallow it.' " Leon used to tell me all the time, "Swallow it."

But we did sue Stewart Klein, the critic, once. He libeled me, said something sarcastic on the air, and *bing*! There was a letter, and Stewart Klein retracted in ten seconds.

I've been attacked by the press, had cheap things written about me many, many times. Once when I was on TV there was a column written by George Frazier, a former major jazz critic and the music editor of *Life* magazine. George Frazier was then living in Boston, music critic for the *Boston Globe*. He wrote a big article with a blaring headline: "What Is a Schmuck?" And the whole column was about me. In the same column, down the line, he included Johnny Carson and a couple of other people, but I got the top billing among the schmucks. The reason for that was that George Frazier had been signed by George Wein to host the Newport Jazz Festival at Carnegie Hall and was replaced by me, so he held a little grudge. He wrote a really nasty column, so I went to a lawyer who also happened to be the attorney for the

Globe. He told me there were so many lawsuits against George Frazier already that if I sued him, he'd lose his job. I held back. I got the word six months later that he died of cancer. I think it was cancer of the tongue.

Soupy Sales got angry at me once when I put out a book called *Encyclopedia of Comedians.* The publisher arbitrarily took out about two hundred names because the book was too long, too thick. Soupy Sales was caught in the overset, along with two hundred other comedians. He called up, shrieking, shrieking hysterically. I was never yelled at by anybody the way he yelled. "How could you leave me out . . . You got Phil Silvers, but you don't got me? Who the hell cares about Lum and Abner? What's a Tommy Chong? Everybody knows Soupy Sales!" Before that we had been the closest friends in the world. I'd given him a quote: Joe Franklin says, "Funniest Man in the World, Soupy Sales," and he'd been using it in all his ads. He opened up on me full guns, and we haven't spoken to each other since that book came out. We can live without each other. But I really felt bad. I explained to him that the publisher arbitrarily took out all those names, but he didn't want to know that. I still think he's a funny man.

You ever hear the name Uncle Floyd? You know that I sued him? A classic case. Made front-page news all over the world. Uncle Floyd did a takeoff on me called the "Joe Frankfurter Show . . . Sponsored by Martian Paint." I love satire—*except* he got very vulgar. He had four guys on with yarmulkes and Jewish accents, me with a Jewish accent. He had "guests" on my alleged panel blowing snot into a glass. It was at the time I was doing *Broadway Danny Rose* for Woody Allen. Woody advised me, "Joe, you gotta do it. You gotta sue him. This guy is gonna hurt you." I took the advice.

I used the best process servers in the city, but they couldn't track Uncle Floyd down. Finally, I asked my friend Arnold Wachtel, of the Magic Shop, to help. He finally tracked Floyd down before a One-to-One telethon at Studio 54. As a result of that, he was taken off the air. Floyd and I have since become

☆

very good friends, very close. He's been on my show numerous times. He does comedy clubs; he packs 'em in. But I feel bad that I hurt his career. He's probably going to hate me again for bringing it up, but I had no choice.

A few years back an artist drew what I considered a libelous caricature of me in a magazine called *Heavy Metal.* I filed a $40 million libel suit against the magazine and the artist. The artist claimed he was a longtime fan of mine; nevertheless, I found it offensive and hurtful. His father was an author who had been on my show many times and told me he was ashamed of what his son had done. I lost the suit but put an end to the caricature.

Georgie Jessel was always getting hit with paternity suits. Women were always coming out of the woodwork, accusing him of being the father to their newborns. His answer to them was: "It's not true that I'm the father, but I'm very flattered." Although I've never had any paternity suits, I've had three different women who, at different times over my career, had a fixation on me.

Judy used to go around saying she was my wife. I actually went to her house a couple of Saturday nights for lamb chops, maybe twenty-five years ago. But that was all—just lamb chops. She just liked the sound of my voice. After two nights of chops, she told me she was in love with me. I asked how that could be possible. She told me she "knew." We were meant to be together. She was the "real" Mrs. Franklin. Soon she felt it was necessary to call my wife and break the news. She expected me to divorce her and marry my "true" wife. She called my office thousands of times a day. She went to department stores and told them she was my wife. She thought she was more my wife than my wife was. She was completely deluded.

An artist named Helen had the same problem. She, too, announced she was in love with me and made it impossible for Lois or me to answer the phone. We never knew what she would say. Sometimes she was sweet; at other times, she spit venom. I don't know why she had a fixation on me; we had never "done" anything. Probably because of my being on TV, my voice. She was lonely, I suppose. I don't know what it was.

☆

A third, Anne, was a very tall English artist—I seem to inspire or excite artists. Anne was very cultured, dignified, proper, and British, and boy, she had a thing on me! I sat in her studio one day while she did my portrait. She couldn't keep her hands off me! I was flattered, but then she started to call my wife at three in the morning, threaten suicide, the works. Anne insinuated that I was going to leave Lois; it was very embarrassing. I was put in the position of trying to explain something that wasn't happening. Anne got pregnant, by the way, when she knew me. But not by me. She didn't try to blame me, but that's when that one ended. But she had a big crush on me. She told me one night that when she was getting pregnant that night, she was visualizing me, fantasizing about me. I never forgot that, I said that's the sweetest thing I ever heard in my life. I really felt very touched by that remark.

With Judy and Helen, I was forced to get a restraining order from the courts to stop their harassment. Whenever Leon Charney and I went before a judge for these cases, the judge would stop the case, take us into his chambers, and reminisce about show business. One time, after talking about silent-screen comedies for forty-five minutes, the judge asked, "Well, what do you want me to do to her?"

I said, "A restraining order, Your Honor."

The judge replied, "Done." As an afterthought, he asked, "Tell me, this girl. Is she good-looking?"

☆

A Night at
WOR-AM

I saw Mommy kissing Santa Claus / Underneath the mistle-toe last night

—as sung by Jimmy Boyd, 1952

Every Saturday night/Sunday morning, from midnight to 5:00 A.M., fifty-two weeks a year, I can be found over the airwaves of WOR-AM (710). It's been a ritual for over thirty years and has become the highest-rated program in its time slot in America. WOR-710—*Where Your Friends Are*—can be heard in thirty-eight of the fifty states, and as John Sanders, the show's engineer, will tell you, the worse the weather is, the better it travels.

Eleven o'clock on a Saturday night. I am a figure among thousands in Times Square. I clutch my shopping bags filled with records, the playlist for the evening. The Broadway throngs are just applauding the final curtain and will head back home, through the crowd of traffic on the bridges or in the tunnels. In a building on a quiet side street on the cusp of the Garment Center, I occupy Newsroom number 2, where I present the only nontalk show in an all-talk radio format.

The record selections directly reflect my personal taste. I am a great fan of Connie Boswell and Russ Columbo, always Al Jolson and Eddie Cantor and Kate Smith, and songs like "Around the World in 80 Days," "How Much Is That Doggie in the Window." I love the novelty hits of Spike Jones, Tony Bennett doing "True Blue Lou," the young crooner named Dick Haymes, the up-tempo songs of Eddie Fisher, his singing "Oh My Pa Pa!" I like the Andrews Sisters and the Dorseys, the kids from Hoboken, Jimmy Roselli and Frank Sinatra; Guy Lombardo and Louis Prima, the operatic warblings of Jeanette McDonald and Nelson Eddy.

Entering the studio, my producer, Ed Gollin, takes charge of the collection. I take a seat at the desk to study the spots for the evening, make my own personal notes, and prepare for what is ultimately an impromptu, spontaneous, and improvisational show. At two or three in the morning, I will just about be able to decipher my hieroglyphics.

My friends are here in force every week. Ed Gollin keeps the logs, times the commercials, and lists the songs played for ASCAP and BMI reporting purposes. John Sanders is the engineer. A disk jockey in his own right, John sits across from me, behind a pane of glass, cueing up records and working magic on a technical system that has changed very little over the years. A trumpeter and card-carrying member of the musicians union, John has told me his dream was to have played in the brass section for the old Guy Lombardo band and "toured the country fifty-four weeks a year in Pullman cars."

In a waiting area outside the glass-enclosed rooms is my office entourage. Here are mainstays Johnny De Maria and Wally Banks sprawled side by side, asleep on a sofa, sawing loudly enough to be heard in twenty-six of the thirty-eight states I'm heard in—without the mike. They are joined in slumber by an elderly epic poet named Wolfe, who is eager to discuss his theories of the upcoming messianic age, when he awakes.

Ben Dasaro, in the control room with John Sanders, gives me great moral support. He's been coming to my show for the last five years. A Madison Square Garden ticket taker, he bears a slight resemblance to Lou Costello. He tells the story of how at a "Def Comedy" jam he was working at the Garden, one of the patrons began hounding him and his girth, "Hey, Abbott! Hey, Abbott!" At last, tired of the jibes, Ben gazed directly in the eye of the heckler and said, "Listen, buddy. If you're going to do it, at least do it right: *Heyyyyy Abbbbbbboottttttttttt!*" Section B gave him a standing ovation, and the heckler slinked back into his seat.

As my show begins and the ON-AIR light flashes, I cozy to the mike and introduce myself. "I am with you . . . wandering through . . . Memory Lane. The big party is just beginning." Songs of the greats set the mood as we slowly enter the past, the realm of singers, songwriters, and entertainers gone by. I introduce the hits of days past: "This one is for the archives. This one we're going to put in the time capsule, and we'll play it again in the year 2200."

Richie Ornstein comes into the studio around one—"It's a quarter to one; let's have some fun"—taking his seat directly across from me. Richie picks up the pace, the tempo of the show, with books and lists of questions for one of our most popular segments, celebrity "significa." Not trivia, *significa*. Every radio show has sports trivia, movie trivia, gefilte fish trivia. We decided to be a little different and call it significa, because it's significant. And if the others decide to abuse significa, we're going to call it "magnifica."

Whenever I get a correct answer to his puzzlers, Richie is effusive with his congratulation: "Joe, that's right!" and, "Very good, Joe! Great!" Even when I get them wrong, Richie always gives me the benefit of the doubt. "Good guess, Joe!" Even when I don't answer at all, he says, "Good try!" He asked me a question once where the answer was Marilyn Monroe, and I answered, "Richard Nixon." Richie still said, "Good guess." I said, "What do you mean, 'good guess'? The only thing they ever had in common was that they were both human!" But if Richie wants to stump me, he doesn't have to try hard. Just give me something from 1970 on.

Our sponsors include Powervites; Sonny Bloch and his real estate seminars ("from your birthplace to your resting place");

Coat World ("Get your coat at Coat World!"); one of my favorite restaurants, the 37th Street Hideaway, in a town house where John Barrymore once lived; and an assortment of lawyers, will writers, life insurance vendors, and pain clinics. And don't forget Martin Paint.

We get calls from listeners that would bring tears to your eyes: Dozens of calls light up the phones throughout the show. People all over the country, with their kind words: "Thanks, Joe, for the lovely memories," or, "We're just calling in to tell you how much we enjoy the show." I played a Frank Sinatra from the 1940s, and a man called in: "Joe, my cousin was the sax player on that record, Hymie Schoetzer. I had to call up and say thank you." But the most touching was a woman who called and said, "Joe, I want you to know that your show is my reason for living. I don't have any family anymore, and I listen to the music of Joe Franklin. It keeps me going; it brings the past back to me on my radio. Those five hours with you enhance my life."

I'm always amazed when people call in at three to find out the song we played at one. I think, Why didn't they call at one? They answer, "I just didn't think of it till now." But our listeners are great, no wise guys, no pains in the ass.

Around three in the morning—"it's a quarter to three, and it's just you and me"—I'll present a guest. I might introduce Arthur Tracy, the accordionist and singer known as "the Street Singer," enormously popular in his day and currently playing Barbra Streisand's father in a new movie. I'll feature the crooner Russ Columbo; George Gee, America's only Chinese-born big-band leader; or Joe Sannuto, a young Jolson imitator who has been called "more like Jolson than Jolson"; Stan Edwards, who does a Bobby Darrin tribute—now let me comb my mind—Chip Deffaa, jazz critic from the *New York Post*. Once in a while I'll hand the mike to Chip and let him play his favorite jazz and swing recordings. He scours his archives to find something I haven't heard before, an obscure radio broadcast or big-band date. I give equal time to Jeff Weingrad, the TV editor of the *Daily News*; and Adam Buckman, the *New York Post*'s television and radio

★

editor. I'll host Richard Johnson of the *Post*'s page 6; Cindy Adams and her husband, Joey. I had Jilly Rizzo, Frank Sinatra's best friend, on shortly before his death in a car accident; and comedian Joey Faye, the man who made sneezing fashionable in slapstick movies. Barry Gray, the golden voice of radio, who paved the way for the Bob Grants and Rush Limbaughs, is a compulsive listener. He calls in at three to play trivia. Sometimes Richie will even give me a question about Barry.

By the end of the night, I'm exhausted but exhilarated—"It's quarter to five and I'm still alive." Five hours on the air after midnight is more than enough even for a man three months younger than I. I sign off and prepare to hit the predawn streets of New York City, the flea markets on Sixth Avenue as they are about to open, where untapped jewels of nostalgia await like hidden treasure.

☆

Lord of Hosts

You just feel all sweetened up all over your insides when Joe begins his injections of compliments. I fall for it every time. Every time Joe Franklin sees you and goes into that clubhouse crouch and says, "Holy mackerel, you were really terrific the other night," then you're under the spell. You actually stand at parade rest and beam with pride. He unwraps each word as though he's been saving that word for you and he wasn't going to give it to you until the moment you deserved it, and this is the moment. And it feels good, and exclusive. And the explanation is—you have been Franklinized.

—Barry Farber

I started on television in the days of *Ozzie and Harriet,* the *Ruggles,* and *A Date With Judy.* I remember the debut of the *Flintstones* in 1960. I was on in 1965, when TV's ratings leaders were *Bonanza, Get Smart, The FBI,* and *The Man from U.N.C.L.E.* I remember the debuts of *Laugh-In* and *Gomer Pyle.* In 1973, I saw the nature of TV change as sitcoms became socially redeeming, shows assumed a new seriousness, and leaders were *All in the Family, The Waltons,* and *Sanford & Son.* I've known talk-show hosts from Wendy Barrie and Steve Allen to Ricki Lake and Montel Williams. I've known Dr. Joyce Brothers,

Dr. Ruth, Dinah Shore, a thousand more. From early morning Dave Garroways to late-night Conans.

My hours jumped around at WOR as wildly as they had at Channel 7. My daytime slot was shuffled every other year, mainly because of the acquisition of syndicated shows—the *Hawaii Five-O*s—that were taking over daytime. Not that I was suffering; I'd always had consistently high ratings, threes, fours, always respectable numbers. But I felt the need for more security, and I found that security by taking the boldest leap of my career: moving to after midnight.

While most people saw it as broadcast Siberia, I recognized an opportunity after midnight. Up until that point, screens were blank. "The Star-Spangled Banner" played and signaled the end of the road. Insomniacs were forced to watch test patterns, and few pioneers were willing to survey the territory. Most television executives completely wrote off the potential after-midnight audience. After all, *they* were asleep. Wasn't everybody?

I didn't think so. I saw a potentially huge audience in completely virgin territory—and best of all, no competition. There were headlines— "Franklin Breaks New Ground!"—when I first made the leap. People debated the issue; 99 percent thought it would never work. Most of them thought I was crazy to move to those hours. They thought it would be the end of me. They told me only hookers would watch. In truth, it brought me to a totally new audience and opened the floodgates for twenty-four-hour programming. And what was wrong with hookers? They bought ginger ale, too.

In the beginning, I was on *live* at 1:00 A.M. That was actually a great time slot to do a live show. The Broadway curtains went down at 11:00 or 11:15, and the stars would go out, have a drink or sandwich, and then make an appearance on my show. I had Ethel Merman, Robert Goulet, Debbie Reynolds, great people.

But that only lasted a few years. I started taping my shows in 1972. I did miss the spontaneity of a live show, and I liked the quality of our late-night guests. But I had no choice. The station couldn't afford to pay the crews the late-night differentials; it boiled down to a financial decision. I began taping my shows in the afternoons for the late-night showings, twice after midnight, from 1:00 to 2:00 A.M., and then the same show repeated from 6:00 to 7:00 A.M. And for at least three or four years, I *owned* that 1:00 A.M. time slot in New York. I was up against virtually nothing. Johnny Carson went off at 12:30 A.M.; there was no David Letterman, no Tom Snyder.

I always had a theory that the number of people watching, the bulk numbers by the ton in New York from one to two in the morning, was equal to or larger than prime-time audiences in about two hundred major American cities. From one to two in the New York metro area you have as many people watching as in Dallas, Detroit, Cleveland, Cincinnati, and Weehawken, Illinois. My only regret was that some of my older viewers couldn't watch anymore. I told them I'd come to their house and perform for them privately. (A couple of them took me up on the offer. I really *did* go to their houses!)

Almost by accident, that late-night time slot thrust me into prime-time television for the only period of my life. During the 1980s, WOR became a cable superstation, and I went national for the first time. What was "fringe time" in New York became *prime time* on the Pacific Coast. People in Los Angeles, San Francisco, and Seattle could watch me at 10:00 P.M. It was the first time in my television career that I was on in major markets, prime time. Yet while my audience multiplied, I never got paid extra for it. It always amazed me that I was seen by so many more people but never paid a nickel more.

I've got to confess that I watch very little TV. I still have a black-and-white set at home. The only show I ever watched regularly in my whole life was *The Ed Sullivan Show*. I used to watch it every Sunday night at 8:00 P.M. I rarely even watched my own shows, because I always agonized—what I should have said, done, asked a guest—no matter how good it was. I was reluctant to watch other talk shows because I didn't want to be swayed by other hosts, their style, their way with guests. I thought I'd pick up their techniques, their mannerisms, their line of questioning—and I didn't want that.

But over the years, if I were to compare myself to anyone, it would be Jack Paar and Steve Allen. Like me, they have their origins in radio. Everyone else on television began on television or is a child of television. The radio background gives an entirely different flavoring. The hosts on radio were creators, storytellers. We developed our styles as verbal communicators. We painted a picture, as Martin Block did, of our "Make-Believe Ballrooms." On television, everything is out in the open, before your eyes. There is no need for a running narrative, a mental image. On radio, we relied on the imagination. In some ways, I think we all lose something on TV.

Johnny Carson was the greatest television talk-show host of them all. He had the benefit of something called "venerability." When you're on that long, you're great. You become a habit, as I did. You become a part of people's lives. I like how his biographer, Lawrence Leamer, put it: "He never swung for the fences. He peppered the field with base hits, turning even bloopers into singles. . . . He had learned what worked and what didn't." Nine-tenths of the battle is sticking it out. Carson knew how.

Not all hosts did. There was a program called *The Little Rascals,* got a gigantic rating. One Friday I heard that the host asked for a raise; he thought he was the reason kids were tuning in. He didn't realize it was the series. By Monday, the station let him go. Without him as the host, the program got the exact same rating. That taught me a lesson: Don't let a little bit of fame go to your head.

I think one of the reasons I lasted in those days was because I was never bold, never got cocky. I realized that without the station, without the camera and the microphone on me, I'm nothing. You're only as big as your affiliation. There was a columnist once named Louis Sobol who had a very important column in the *New York Journal-American.* Along with Winchell, Earl Wilson, and a few others, he was a major power broker. He told me that one year, at the height of his clout, he received sixteen thousand Christmas cards. The next year, the *Journal-American* folded. That Christmas he got *four* Christmas cards, all from relatives. Four—from sixteen thousand down to four. That's why I never took it seriously. I knew that when people wined and dined and romanced me, it was all just for the power of the microphone. That can be so frustrating, so devastating, if you're not really detached and aware. It can destroy you.

So many people who came on my show later became hosts of their own TV talk shows. Gypsy Rose Lee was a famous stripteaser and eventually a film actress—also the subject of a big Broadway show called *Gypsy*. She was on my show about twelve times, then went out to California and got her own TV talk show called *Gypsy*. Bill Boggs came on as an author before he became a host. Chauncey Howell was writing for *Women's Wear Daily* when he wrote a piece about me. He was picked up by NBC after I plugged that article. Sally Jessy Raphael was with WMCA radio and had just opened a Puerto Rican restaurant on the East Side when she first appeared on my show. She came on to plug the restaurant. She was charming. Kathy Lee Gifford was on the show long before she was Kathy Lee Gifford, before she was ever a talk-show person. Joan Rivers was on my show about thirty or forty times as a comic. She was first a guest hostess, then got her own show, called *That Show,* which bombed. Then she got with Johnny Carson, and her career took off. Frankly, I have never been able to analyze her success, and over the years she has publicly questioned my reputed success.

When I was a guest on *David Letterman* about eight years ago, I found David to be a good interviewer but somewhat restless. His mood "read" on camera. I gave him my own tips on interviewing: Make eye contact, act interested, and stay sincere. I'd like to think that part of his long-term success was thanks to my suggestions.

Everyone asks me what I think of Howard Stern. One time, Howard was shooting his own Channel 9 show in the Secaucus studios when I was working there. He came running across the hall and, with everybody there in the media, put his arm around

⭐

me and said, "This is a real star." Exactly his words: "This is a real star." Then he grabbed me and kissed me. That's a good way to win me over.

I put him on when he was an unknown, when he was just battling to get his name out there. I liked him from the start. I called him "How-weird" Stern, and we hit it off great. He would ask me to plug his persona, plug his name, plug his radio show back in those days. Dial-a-Date, Dial-a-Lesbian, Dial-a-Homo. I give him credit. No one I've known really compares to him. He's *the* trailblazer in that kind of broadcasting. He talks about masturbation, a whole hour about his going to the toilet, how many times to wipe. You ever hear that? Incredible.

Mike Douglas came on my show when he was a piano player in a local New York City hotel. He had been a vocalist with Kay Kyser and the Orchestra, then got a job here as pianist in the Hotel Lexington. He was also selling insurance at the same time, but he got his break. Westinghouse needed somebody to host a show, and he did a great job. In his heyday there was nobody like him.

I was a guest on his show in Philadelphia, and the comedy team of Allen and Rossi were on the show. Marty Allen tapped Mike Douglas on the shoulder and said, "Hi, Mike!" Mike totally lost control. He became wild, swinging his arms, yelling, "Nobody can touch me on the shoulder!" People were stunned, he was completely overreacting, but then, it was *his* shoulder.

Dick Clark and I began virtually at the same time in the basement of ABC, in the Leonard Goldenson days. Dick and I also share our admiration for the great disk jockey Martin Block. Dick never worked for Martin Block but admired him as the man who paved the way for all the radio personalities who followed. We used to sit in the lobby, talk and have coffee, chat about music, show business.

Dick Clark took over a local Philadelphia show called *Bandstand* from a guy named Bob Horn, who had a series of troubles. First he was fired from the station after a drunk-driving charge. This was followed by a statutory rape charge involving a fourteen-year-old girl. There was talk that he was making dirty movies at a Pennsylvania farm. Then Bob Horn was arrested a second time on charges of drunken driving. He went to Texas and died in obscurity. Dick Clark took over, added the word *American* to the show's title, convinced ABC to broadcast *American Bandstand* nationally, and became a billionaire. He's a master salesman, a conglomerate.

Oddly, one image comes to mind when I think of Dick Clark. There was an announcer then, a pioneer in TV named Jimmy Blaine, who had epilepsy. He used to fall down on the floor. Dick and I used to pull out his tongue and pick him up from the floor.

Merv Griffin was another who parlayed a talk show into an empire—casinos, developing and producing many TV shows, *Dance Fever, Jeopardy*. I was never too close to Merv Griffin, but I always admired him as a host, admired his saccharine, homey, friendly style. I was always close to Arthur Treacher, Merv Griffin's sidekick. He was on my show many times, maybe twenty times. He was the only guest I had on my show in my whole life who, when he was tired or bored or cranky, would simply get up and start to walk off. In the middle of the interview, he'd say in his elegant British accent, "Ooh, Joe, the old man's getting cranky now, the old man's getting grouchy, the old man's getting tired," and he'd just get up and walk away! So natural, so organic, so lifelike!

The *Joe Franklin Show* was unique for one primary reason. We were a two- or three-man operation. You can go to see Conan, Johnny Carson, Letterman, and find hundreds of people behind the scenes. We got right down to the basics. Host and guest. Host and guest. That was it. We didn't have to put all kinds of trimmings out there. The show was Joe Franklin, sink or swim. For the show to work, it was up to me to bring out the best in every person, no matter who.

Merv Griffin is great, but Merv had to show you he was once a major singer. Same with Mike Douglas. Dick Cavett was a stand-up comic; Jay Leno, a comic; Steve Allen, a jazz pianist, composer, singer, dancer, matzo ball maker. I'm not a comic, a singer, a pianist. On my show, everybody else is the star. I put myself in the background and let the other person shine.

I believe that the best way to do that is to treat everyone on the panel as an equal. Whoever is the guest, whoever sits in the chair, is the star. It doesn't matter whether they're a "known" or an "unknown," they get equal time and equal attention. I had a cowboy star come on, R. J. Coldwin, a country singer. He's a very good singer, but he's not really well known. He came off the set and told me, "Joe, you're the greatest. I never met you until today, but you made me feel like Johnny Cash. I was never so thrilled in my life."

Bobby Buttafuoco, Joey's brother, came to us. This was when the Amy Fisher case was red hot, in every paper in the world. Every talk show wanted Bobby—but only to talk about Joey. But Bobby, who's in the music business, managed a group called Virgin Steel, and he wanted to promote their video. All the other shows had turned him down. They wanted to hear about Amy. I invited him on the show. I didn't talk about Amy or anything to do with the case. I just spoke about Bobby and his group. The show was phenomenal.

One of my greatest compliments came when Bill Cosby said, on the air, "Joe, when so many people can get a reputation for tearing *down*, it is now time to go back to the people who don't have to get a reputation for tearing down; then we can sit around and have a good time." That's my point: to make the guest the king, to make them think, for that fifteen minutes in the chair, when they're talking to me, that they're on top of the world. That they're the hottest things to ever cross Broadway, Hollywood, Shangri-la.

Kirk Douglas's son Erik laid the rules down when he came on my show. He didn't want to be the subject of yet another "children of the stars" piece. "Don't talk about my father; talk about me only. I'm a stand-up comic." He told me all the rules. I thought they made perfect sense and agreed to all of them. When we got to the studio, all we spoke about was his father. I said, "Listen, Erik. I know everybody asks you about your famous family, your brother Michael and your father Kirk. I don't want to ask you about that. I want to talk about you, about what you're going to do, your future, where you want to be, your long-term, short-term goals."

As soon as I said that, Erik held up his hands. "No, no! I want to talk about how I got my name! My name came from *The Vikings*. My father did that movie with Tony Curtis, and 'Erik' was the name of Tony Curtis's character. Tony Curtis was my father's best friend, and that's why he named me Erik. I was born around the time the film came out, and my father's the greatest, he motivated me!" All he spoke about during the entire show was his father.

Sean Connery's wife came on in the 1960s after writing a novel. She explicitly told me she did not want to discuss what it was like being married to "James Bond." As the show began, she was nervous, watching my every move. She wanted to make sure I didn't say a word about her famous husband, who was then at the height of his fame. To make my point, I got around it by saying, "I guess we're the only talk show in town that would have Sean Connery's wife, the wife of the famous James Bond, on our show *not* to talk about her husband. How do you think James Bond would feel about being the husband of a famous author?"

Most hosts want to talk about what *they* want to talk about. As soon as they ask a question, the talk-show host is thinking about his next question. When I ask a question, I want to know the answer. If you say something to me about your mother, I want to find out more about that. I don't just try to jump into something else. If for some reason my charm isn't working, I do get stuck; if I find myself at a loss for words, I'll always resort to my standard lines. The first: "When were you first bitten, smitten, by the show business bug?" This usually opens them up. If not, then I'll bring up a matter of current events and ask, "What is your informed assessment? Your educated appraisal? Your considered opinion?" And if things get really bad, I'll want to know what their favorite word is. I got "warm" from Elliott Gould. Dorothy

☆

Lamour's was "sarong." She never got bored talking about sarongs. Bing Crosby's favorite was "Fore!" I would say my favorite word was, hands down, "nostalgia." It could start me talking for hours.

I was once on a TV show with a man who was very popular for a while here in New York, Stanley Siegel. Remember the name vaguely? He was very big for a while, at 9:00 A.M. As a matter of fact, when I left ABC to go to Channel 9, he took my 9:00 A.M. spot. He had a routine where he would lie down on the psychiatrist's couch. He would have the psychiatrist sit alongside him and analyze his woes.

Stanley and I used to have a friendly rivalry cooking. One day we planned a program, a *High Noon* kind of confrontation. I went on his show as a cohost, and at each station break, they'd show him walking toward me and me walking toward him. In the last segment, we had a little duel. It was a lot of fun.

However, Stanley complained about an author who had been a guest on the show. During the interview, the author had just said yeah, no, yeah, no—dull, boring. Stanley bawled out his staff. I sat in the back watching him berate his staff for booking such a "lousy guest." When the smoke had cleared and all the personnel had gone their way, I took him in the corner and said, "Stanley, let me tell you something. I'm not that much older than you, but let me tell you one thing. When your guest flopped, he didn't flop, *you* flopped. You've got to bear in mind one thing: That man was an author who previously had a couple of big books. His last couple of books didn't do so well, so what happens in a case like that? His editor or his publisher says, 'Irving, Maxwell, Dick or Harry—you want to sell books? You gotta go on talk shows.' So begrudgingly, belligerently, he's got to make the rounds of talk shows. Whereas in his heart, he'd rather be in his ivory tower just writing books and making money." So I said, "If your guest flopped, which he did, you flopped. You've got to look in his eyes. I'm not saying you've got to hypnotize him. I'm not going to say mesmerize. But enchant him. Make him forget he's on TV. Do whatever it takes, whatever the technique might be to open him up and make him fascinating to the viewer at home. What makes a good guest is not the guest. It's the host."

Garry Moore

I like those "Where Are They Now?" books. I was very upset today to see that Garry Moore died. Originally named T. Garrison Morfit, the five-foot-six—my height—Moore came in from Chicago, and I got very friendly with him. I was about fourteen and he was about twenty-five, I guess. I used to go to see his radio show, then he teamed up with Jimmy Durante. I always admired him because he reminded me of myself: No great talent, he got by on charm and affability and just being pleasant. And nobody mentioned in the obituary that he was number one at the time he was on the air; his was the number one, highest-rated show in all of TV. He was the host for an hour every Wednesday night on the *Garry Moore Show*. Carol Burnett, Alan King, Jonathan Winters, Don Knotts—he broke them all in. Fame is fleeting.

You know, Garry Moore was part of that one big fell swoop where they took off all those people whose demographics they figured were older people, even though they had the highest rating in their time period. So they took off Garry Moore, Danny Kaye, Lawrence Welk, Red Skelton, Jackie Gleason, Ed Sullivan, Arthur Godfrey. Now they want the old people back. Ed Sullivan, same reason. Twelve or fifteen people like that. The *Dean Martin Show.* They just wanted to put something on for younger audiences.

John Cameron Swayze

John Cameron Swayze goes back to the days when newscasters were on for fifteen minutes, with absolutely no production value. The program was called the *Camel Caravan. Camel News Review*—that's when you could have cigarette sponsors. It was just called "rip and read." Rip the news off the wire and read it on the air. I always liked John Cameron Swayze's speaking voice; it was always mellow, therapeutic, to me. For me, he was the only newscaster. There was no other newscaster.

Dennis James

He started by announcing boxing. Now he does telethons. He goes from city to city doing telethons. A charming guy. Dennis had a long-ago TV show called *Hi, Mom.* His secretary was Mary Higgins Clark. Mary, a dear friend of mine, guested on my show forty times.

Jack Paar

Jack, of course, was a complainer, always griping about something. He would gripe anytime he didn't get his name in the newspaper. At one time, he had a feud with Dorothy Kilgallen after she rapped his daughter. He came on the air, muttering, "That chinless thing!" meaning Kilgallen, knowing she was very sensitive. Dorothy Kilgallen went to war, building up the attack on his daughter. She called her a "fat, pudgy little thing." It was almost a visceral attack against the kid; it was undeserved. They went into personalities instead of just performance. It was sad.

Al Capp and Joe Pyne

One time I had Al Capp, the cartoonist, on the show, with Joe Pyne, the very acid, acerbic talk-show host. Each had an artificial leg. Joe Pyne got upset over the politics of one of the characters in L'il Abner, and they started shouting at each other on the air, so I said, "Listen, boys, why don't you take off your wooden legs and fight a duel?"

Jack Eigen

Jack was a blatant Winchell imitator. Not an impersonator, an imitator. He was originally on the radio late at night, providing mostly Broadway and Hollywood gossip. What he would do is read the items in the paper and change them a little bit. I was always a little jealous of Jack Eigen. I was always jealous for some reason that the great Fred Allen liked him and used him as a guest on his radio show and always worked his name into the script.

I remember that he was the first one ever to use the telephone on a radio program or TV show. He called his program *Meet Me at the Copa.* In those days, you could only hear the host; you couldn't hear the other end of the phone. He had to repeat the conversation. You had to visualize what the other person was saying. It was a great leap of faith for the listeners. He could've faked it, but he didn't.

One night I was there with him when he was broadcasting and the columnist from *Radio Daily*, Sid White, called the station. White said, "Jack, I'm going to give you an exclusive. I'm going to marry Ethel Thorsen, a showgirl, and it's for you, personally." Jack was all breathless and said to the audience, "I just got a call from Sid White! *Radio Daily!* He's gonna get married! Congratulations, Sid! Now, remember, folks! You heard it here!"

☆

Mike Wallace

Mike Wallace was on my show many times in the olden days, long before *60 Minutes*. He was married to a lady named Buff Cobb, and they had a TV show called *Buff and Mike*. He then got his first local talk show, called *PM*. Or was it *AM*.

Mickey Rooney

Mickey is my second-closest show biz pal, after Tony Curtis. Mickey was number one at the box office from 1939 to 1943. Mickey told me that the film studio moguls were never as evil as depicted in most movie books.

Alan Burke

I admired Alan Burke. He was on my show many times. He was the original of all these hard-hitting guys, all these Rush Limbaughs. He would cross-examine people, be very severe on them, call them hypocrites, superhawks, superpatriots, challenge them, always challenge them. But that was good TV. He was very big for a while. He was like Morton Downey, Jr., two big years, then he plummeted. Burke went to Florida and broadcast locally after that. As big as they become, they plummet the same way. The public is fickle.

Dick Roffman and Robert Taylor

Dick Roffman was a big PR man. He represented really odd-ball Broadway Danny Rose–type personalities. But he was very articulate, a lawyer with a nimble mind. Besides handling off-the-wall characters—the eighty-six-year-old belly dancers—he also represented financiers, musicians, authors.

Dick was the kind of guy who would have rather made a nickel than $100,000. Combination sadist and masochist, but an interesting man, very complex. He was the only one in my whole brain trust I used to pay. I'd give him a token honorarium every Friday of about twenty dollars, and a couple of books to read, a couple of record albums, some fig newtons and maybe a banana.

He told me one time when he was working on the *Journal-American* that there was a rumor that Robert Taylor, the matinee idol, had always worn a chest wig. Robert Taylor wanted to set the record straight once and for all. He invited Dick Roffman to pull the hair on his chest. It was real; Robert Taylor was at last vindicated. It made the front page. Dick was a very colorful guy, one of my very closest friends.

David Susskind

David Susskind had a program called *Open End*. It was on at 10:00 P.M., but the station would let it run, if required, until five in the morning. I always admired that format, that's a dream.

After graduating from Harvard, David Susskind got a position as an agent with MCA. When television came in, he pushed himself right into Channel 5, WNEW, with his Sunday night show. I remember the time he had Khrushchev on the show. Khrushchev kissed him on both cheeks, and Susskind didn't know what to do or say.

There was a time buyer at an ad agency who met a girl in my office one day. They had a five-year romance. He told me, "I don't know, Joe. She can't have real sex; she can only have oral sex."

I said, "Well, then, have oral sex."

One night, this ad man is watching David Susskind, his subject that night is "Sex Changes and Transvestites." He sees his girlfriend on the air; she's a transvestite! The ad man got furious at *me!* He dropped me as an account; his agency wouldn't buy any more time.

Howard Cosell and Bud Greenspan

Howard Cosell and I both began at ABC at about the same time, 1950 or 1951, and I always liked him. He introduced me to a fellow in the sports department named Bud Greenspan. One day Bud came to my house. He was putting out an album of sports legends, and he asked if I could help him with material from my collection. I gave him all of my rare, rare sports memorabilia, recordings, film clips, and photos of Babe Ruth, Lou Gehrig, hundreds of Hall of Famers. I never got them back. I called him once or twice, but he ignored my phone calls. I felt terrible about that. That was my one recollection of Howard Cosell, that he introduced me to Bud Greenspan, who was doing this project and never returned the material he borrowed.

Johnny Carson and Sandy Dennis

I was on the Carson show several times in New York City but never in Los Angeles. Once I was visiting L.A. and was guesting on Tom Snyder's *Tomorrow* program. Johnny saw me on the way to the studio and asked me why I wasn't appearing on his show. Why was I doing Tom Snyder's? I told Johnny that nobody asked. He became furious.

Toward the end, when he did a thing with Christian Slater, he really gave me a big, big send-off. In his last six months he talked about me several times.

☆

I don't think Johnny was anybody's good friend, in an intimate sense. He was always distant and cold, aware of his power. As untheatrical and pretentious as I was, he was the exact opposite. Aware of his power. But I've always had a theory about show people: If they act aloof and conceited, many times it's required; it's protection. There was an actress named Sandy Dennis who was considered so high-hat that she would never answer people when they spoke. She was supposedly very conceited and aloof and cold. But she told me that the reason was she was very nearsighted. She couldn't see people to say hello to them on the street. Sometimes you have to bend the other way and overlook people's outward behavior.

Freddy Roman and Henny Youngman

While we were taping for my 40th Anniversary Special, we had a comedians' round table at the Friars Club. We had Joey Adams, Bob Melvin, Mickey Freeman, Henny Youngman, and Freddie Roman. Freddie made the remark that when he was a kid, he broke in at the Copa.

Henny interrupted and said, "You're a liar! You never played the Copa!"

Freddy Roman got angry. "You son of a bitch, I played the Copa."

"You never played the Copa!" Henny insisted. They just about came to blows; they shrieked, spat; it was the end of the whole sequence. Henny tended to irritate him. Henny is one of the funniest men in the world, but he irritates some people.

☆

Reflections on Collections

Joe became involved in collecting memorabilia because of his family. His father was rejecting. There was something missing in Joe's early childhood where his own personality wasn't really working. He was rejected for being natural. Joe's real self was not really accepted by his parents. His first early interest in nostalgia was looking for a way to get around in life.

—Dr. Elan Golomb, psychotherapist

Memorabilia is my number one love. After I get off the air on Sunday morning at 5:00 A.M., I walk down Sixth Avenue to the flea market. The vendors are just setting up their wares. I like to be the first one to see what they have to offer.

The other day Richie and I saw some ladies' dresses from the 1930s. Excellent renditions, perfect condition. We held them up for inspection. People on the street saw Joe Franklin and his bodybuilder / producer holding up dresses. They're looking at us with pocketbooks and dresses in the morning, saying, "Wow, Joe goes that way!" "I didn't know Joe was gay!" It was the funniest thing in the world! Women were giggling.

My favorite dealer was the Record Collectors Exchange on

Fifty-third and Seventh. It was run by a man named Jack Caidin, and there were frequent visitors like Billy Murray, a top recording star of the old days. The Record Collectors Exchange brought together a network of collectors, myself included. Jack found me many of my most precious 78s, the singers I loved.

When I started buying up old movies for my show on Channel 7, I became equally fanatic. I went to dealers with names like Abby Films, Peerless, a place called Mogul. I felt it was important, essential, to save the crumbling old classics. There was an actress once named Marguerite Clark, the second most famous actress in the silent movies after Mary Pickford. There isn't one print in the world of Marguerite Clark. She was close to Mary Pickford in popularity, but you couldn't watch her in a film nowadays if you paid all the money in the world.

Buster Crabbe, who played Buck Rogers in the movies, played Tarzan and Flash Gordon, came over to my house all the time to watch movies. I idolized him. We were very close. Just a nice, nice guy. He knew I had films of him that no one else had.

I watched, and still watch, the old films at home on a 16-millimeter projector. I'm the last of the purists. I've got three VCRs in my house and have never used one in my life. I don't even know how to turn one on. I can't even insert the tape. With me, I only want to watch 16-millimeter films, to play machines that you wind up with a crank, a Victrola, a gramophone.

I've known many collectors who have been forced to make a choice: the collection or the wife. The collection always wins. I have not met many women who share the nostalgia bug. Mainly men. Very few women.   I know that many fellow collectors let their attachment to their archives wreck their married lives: their wives say it's either your junk or me. I was always able to keep my junk and my wife. She just overlooked it. She was always understanding, very docile and tolerant.

One of my best friends died some years ago; his name was Mark Ricci. He owned a place downtown called the Memory Shop, on East Twelfth, I'd go browsing in there. I wanted to buy

☆

the shop's archives when he died. He had a reputation of being a
necrophiliac for a long time. I don't know if we want to get into
that. He was a very peculiar guy, but we shared a great love of
memorabilia. I don't think he ever got married. He wore a
toupee. I've known a bunch of interesting people. But most collectors of memorabilia are a little bit off the wall. That goes with
the territory. It's always commendable that the money we spend
on this kind of stuff at least is not being spent on prostitutes,
horse races, or drugs or whiskey, so that's one semiconsolation.
I'd take memorabilia over a love affair. You can always find romance, but you're not always able to purchase the exact memorabilia you're seeking. At least that's a theory of mine.

Almost every weekend I go to trade shows. Memorabilia
shows. I spend a fortune. I never stop buying; I buy like mad. I
look for anything old, but it must be in mint condition. Lobby
cards, photographs, movie programs, souvenir programs, but if
one edge is a tiny bit torn or bent over, I won't buy it. I'm a fanatic. When I buy a magazine from 1907, it's got to be exactly in
the mint, pristine condition of 1907. Otherwise, I won't buy it.
When I do buy something, I immediately wrap it all in cello-
phane to preserve its condition.

Do I read the old magazines, the old programs, do I handle the
antique lobby cards? The big word in my vocabulary is "someday." Someday, leaning back with a mint julep, I'll open them
up. I'd love to read old magazines, old souvenir books, but just
hope the day will come and I can do that. But I'm sure I'll keel
over before that. I treat them like butter.

A film producer named Sam Sherman became a great friend because he shared my interest in old records and old movies. In the
mid-1950s he came down and saw me at the studio, proudly
bringing a handpicked collection of 78s as a gift. I looked at them
and flipped through them as though I were flipping through baseball cards. "Got it, got it, got it, got it, got. Well, thanks very much
for bringing these, but I have all these, anyway, but I appreciate
it." It's amazing we still became friends, but we are to this day.

★

We've spent many nights together screening old movies. The star of *Dillinger*, Lawrence Tierney, once joined us in my apartment to watch his film classic. Sam and I like the "B" companies of the 1930s: Tower, Majestic, Imperial, Invincible, Chesterfield, Mascot, Equitable, known as the "poverty row" companies of the thirties. We'll discuss George R. Batchelor, the head of Chesterfield; Maury Cohen, the head of Invincible; C. C. Burr and E. E. Derr. We talk about Edwin Maxwell—we're always kidding around about him, a great character heavy of the 1930s—and Noel Madison. We always figured these guys died forty years ago, but once I sent a lady to Sam who wanted to do a syndicated program. She turned out to be the daughter of Noel Madison, who died not long ago on Long Island. We thought that the ghost of Noel Madison sent her to us—here we'd been kidding about him for twenty-five years.

I talk about the big stars, but I really love the Toby Wings, Pinky Tomlins, Lila Lees, Dixie Dunbars, everybody who's small and obscure, who's maybe talented in the B movie sense but didn't make it in the A movies. It's liking the underdog. I've always remembered an expression—I don't know where it originated: "For those who understand, no explanation is necessary. For those who don't understand, no explanation is possible." Those of us who love the old films, the old stars, and the old music, speak a certain kind of language. There's no need to explain.

My nickname is "the Nabob of Nostalgia." Somebody coined that. I'd like to say that if there weren't practical considerations, I'd spend all my time watching old films, listening to old records. I wouldn't do anything else. It's not practical to be that way, but I would do it.

I've almost never met anyone who won't sell. That's rare. Somebody's always willing to sell for the right price.

I had Rudy Vallee's megaphone; lent it out, never got it back. I found Charlie Chaplin's bowler. I had two. That stuff can't be appraised. What do I tell people? You don't know what the traffic's going to bear, right? Who knows what some Arabian oil sheik wants to pay for Greta Garbo's shoes? Right?

One time I went to a memorabilia show and a guy had a utility check—a bill to an electric company—from Mae West. Crisp. Mint. He wanted $125, $150 for it. After a few minutes of rapping—the guy knew me—he said, "Give me a hundred dollars." I walked away and said, "I'll be back." I came back and it was gone. I learned that sometimes you have to grab a thing when it's hot. How many times are you going to be able to get a check from Mae West in that condition?

Serious stamp collectors are usually introverted, usually to some extent loners, very bright people, usually well-educated people.

With stamps, a fifty-cent Columbian is worth the same thing in New York as it is in California. You take a New York City history book, a New York City postcard, the farther you get from the source, the lower the value.

Richard Selkowitz, a collectibles dealer, found a little book by Eddie Cantor published in 1929. It was relatively scarce, and he figured I might want it. He was proud of himself for making the find. I looked at it and said, "I'll take it, but too bad it doesn't have a dust jacket."

His eyebrows raised. "Dust jacket?"

I said, "Yes, and by the way, I already have twelve of these."

A lot of memorabilia was taken out of garbage cans initially. In difficult economic times, people turn to cheaper things. In times of turmoil, people feel their youth was much better than the present.

I keep my collections in houses all around town. I'm in about six or eight different vaults or storage places around town. My overhead is about $2,000 a day. Just overhead.

I envy Hal Stone. When Hal Stone went to the coast, he just took one sock. One sock.

☆

Where Am I Now?

I'm a great man for canceling and blowing hot and cold.
I'm the world's number one hot-and-cold blower in his-
tory. I'm amazed that I'm finishing this book. Through the
years I've taken down payments from several publishers
and always gave them back.

—Joe Franklin

The *Joe Franklin Show* was part of my life, my routine, for many, many years. Everybody on the set would take vacations but me. I didn't like them. I would run cruises using my name but wouldn't go on the boat. I'd stand at the dock, shake hands with the passengers, then greet them on their arrival. They never knew I wasn't on board. Once in a while I would travel to Los Angeles to visit my friend Rudy Vallee at his Mulholland estate or scour the state searching for collectibles—Eddie Cantor memorabilia, particularly.

I hate the old cliché workaholic, but I was one. I always worked Sundays, always worked seven days a week, *seven days a week.* When I wasn't doing the show, I was hosting hospital fund-raisers, benefits. I never learned how to say no for fifty years in show business. I went to fairs, chose the winning raffle numbers, judged dance contests, beauty contests, spelling bees.

I was like Jimmy Durante. I always said yes. I could never say
no to a good cause. Sometimes I wonder why I enjoyed it. Why
didn't I want to go home more often? I had a nice son, a nice
wife. Why didn't I go home more often?

Retirement was something I considered for many years. I didn't
need to keep working for the money, although it was always
good. I had my first thoughts when *Donahue* came on in the
early 1970s. It was a signal of a new time in broadcasting, a new
type of host. I wasn't sure if I could fit in with the new format,
the issue-oriented structure. I began to feel almost like a di-
nosaur. I used to be sponsored by big national companies. Now
my sponsors were the phone sex lines and Hair Club for Men.
The money was the same, even better, because the sponsors felt
privileged to have air time. But it's not the matter of money
alone, sometimes it's the prestige and dignity, too.

I just felt that the parade was passing me by. I was very severe on myself. The world was changing, but I wasn't. I didn't
change; I never did. I saw slicker talk shows, with more production value, more planning. The shows were less haphazard, not
as free-flowing as mine. I voiced my doubts to management.
They told me that the public didn't want me to change. They
looked at me as an anchor in their lives, a steady constant amid
all the change. I was ready to stop working and enjoy life, but
they urged me to continue.

But eventually the grind began to get to me, and more and
more frequently, I recalled newsman John Kiernan's line "Getting the body to and from the studio gets to be a drag." In the late
1980s, WOR's station headquarters moved from Manhattan to
Secaucus, New Jersey, former swampland turned into an island
of offices between the Meadowlands and the heavy industry
along the turnpike. The station had been having licensing problems with the FCC in New York. They moved to New Jersey,
which resolved the problem through the state legislature. But
everyone moaned when we left Manhattan. It was only a fifteen-
minute ride through the Lincoln Tunnel, but it felt like light-years

away. God, I hated that schlepp. Despised it. Stars of most network shows get limos to pick them up at their home, their hotels, Coney Island, but we had to scramble to form carpools. We not only had to worry about getting ourselves out there, but also our guests, who automatically resented the inconvenience.

When at last my staff was able to come to an independent deal with a limo company, getting the cars free in exchange for promotional considerations, the station management promptly put an end to it. I think they resented that we were able to make a better deal than they were. So we were back to Share-a-Ride. It was enormously frustrating. At one point we were shooting five days a week, going out every day. One thing that really upset me was—and it happened maybe twenty times over the years—that we had stars of Broadway shows as guests. I promised their PR people emphatically, unequivocally, that they'd be back in time to get to the theater at seven-thirty at night. At least twenty times there was traffic, or the car got stuck in the tunnel. Everyone would call me from the theater, the PR: "Joe, you promised! The show can't go on without the star!" I had twenty near thromboses. It's not like a movie where you can show the star on-screen. If the player's not there— And who's the culprit? Me.

But for me the very worst feeling was that I would get to Secaucus in the morning and never be able to get back into town. I had an anxiety attack every single day. We might as well have taped the show in Kankakee.

The transportation issue, of course, was only part of it. Being on a talk show is one of the most draining things a person can do. Putting together a show five days a week, sixty or ninety minutes a day. You're meeting dozens of guests a week, interviewing countless others, dealing with the day-to-day production problems, the transportation, the thousand and one details that you always seem to forget about. For some reason, everybody wants to do it and thinks they can. But it's like anything else, whether you're a clown or a ballet dancer or an ice skater. If you make it look hard, nobody's interested. To perfect it, you've got to look as if you're not working. You've got to stay relaxed, calm, before the

★

cameras. Nothing can rattle you. If you throw tantrums, if you scream and yell, you won't last long. Jack Paar was brilliant, a master, but with his temper, he burned himself out from television after a relatively brief career. Those with longevity pace themselves. I had been able to keep that pace for many, many years. But at the end I was taping five shows in one day. That would mean interviewing twenty to twenty-five people in one day. When we got in the car to come back to the city, I was beyond tired. As my fortieth anniversary on television approached, I felt physically and emotionally drained. I spent more time contemplating the past and less considering the future. I'd had nearly every guest I'd wanted to have. Today's stars did not hold as great a fascination for me as those of yesteryear. As Eddie Lopat, the great Yankee pitcher of the 1930s and 1940s, said on my show, "I knew it was over when it wasn't exciting anymore."

As much exposure as the Billy Crystal *Saturday Night Live* skit got me, it had its downside as well. To many millions of people who had never had the opportunity to see my show, I became known as the person who only put on oddball, kooky guests. The truth was that I very rarely had the "oddball" guests, the "kooks." My panels were very respectable, in some ways equal to or better than so-called quality programming. But the *Saturday Night Live* audience wanted to see me as they knew Billy. They tuned in to watch not the Bob Hopes and Bill Cosbys but the amateurs, the freaks. While I thought it was good show business, it wasn't the direction I wanted my career to follow.

Above all, there was no one I was aching, yearning, to have appear on the show. Almost everyone I'd ever wanted to interview, to chat with, had been on. Without my asking, over the years, all the greats had come to me—Frank Sinatra, John Lennon, Lauren Bacall, and thousands more. Over my entire span, besides Greta Garbo, there were only four people I was sorry I'd missed. The reason was not because they wouldn't have appeared but because of my own timidity. I didn't ask them because I was afraid they might turn me down. I was worried that I wouldn't be able to get them, afraid of the rejection.

☆

George S. Kaufman, Bert Lahr, Groucho Marx, and Fred
Allen were the four greats I wished I'd had, and I found out in
every case that they had wanted to be on the show. All four men
scared me; they all looked so dour and sour and grim. They really frightened me. And in every single case, after they were
dead I found out that they were only yearning to be invited. It
was a lesson I'll never forget.

Bert Lahr played the Cowardly Lion in *The Wizard of Oz*.
His great popularity stemmed from doing a Wise potato chips
commercial. Groucho Marx wrote a book—*Hello, I Must Be
Going*—with a woman who was to become a very dear friend
of mine named Charlotte Chandler. They sat together in her
apartment and watched my show every night. Many years later,
she told me he would say, "I wish Joe would invite me on the
show; I love Joe Franklin!" I'd meet Groucho around town, but
I was like a shy eighth-grader at a school social. I'd be afraid
he'd turn me down. I heard the same later from Bert Lahr's son
and from Portland Hoffa, Fred Allen's widow, and the same
with George S. Kaufman. His maid told me he wondered why I
never invited him on the show.

When I made my decision to retire, my biggest fear in the last
year or so was disappointing the people who depended on me.
First, I recognized the tremendous void that would be left in the
cabaret scene, the New York music scene. There are no other
venues to showcase young performers. Nothing gave me greater
pleasure than to be in on the dawning of a great talent. Many
club owners, cabaret owners, have written and phoned again and
again, begging me to return to the air, to provide a launch for
their talent. Where will they get their openings? Where will they
find their borscht belts? And what about the old-timers, the stars
of yesteryear? Will the Arthur Tracys, the Anita O'Days, the Jes-
sica Dragonettes, ever find a stage again? Or will a young talent
coordinator come along—as one did in my office a few years
back—and ask, "Who's Jimmy Durante?"

Along with the performers, young and old, I was concerned

⭐

for the futures of those who had worked with me over so many years. Both management and crew depended on the show as a career, and many came to love the show as much as I did. We all knew the time would come to move on, but we thought we could put off the reality forever. Finally, I felt most for my fans. I didn't want to let them down.

But the decision was in the air. The office mood was a little different, the environment nervous. There was a sense that something momentous was going to happen. Yet when I actually made up my mind to give up the *Joe Franklin Show,* I didn't feel sad. Instead, I felt a tremendous sense of relief. After forty years, I had been afraid to cut the cord. When I did, I didn't feel as if I were losing anything. Instead, I felt as if I were embarking on a new phase in life, where anything would be possible.

When I made the announcement about six months before I actually retired, I got the media blitz of modern times. It was covered on *Day One* and *Current Affair* and on page 1 of every newspaper in town, AP, UP, IP, *Parade* magazine, double spreads. That was flattering and good for the ego. But little by little, as time goes on, I'm beginning to realize what all the headlines, the columns, meant and what they were talking about when it came to my career. It's even mind-boggling to me now, it's creeping up on me now, what I did! Forty-three years! *Of a talk show!* There's never been anything to equal it; there never could be, ever, ever again. It's occurring to me more and more lately, what a fantastic thing I've done. I'm the icon of the aeon in this kind of scenario. At the time, I just sort of glazed over it, but now, in retrospect, it's catching up with me. It's supercataclysmic, super-Herculean. I didn't really appreciate myself or what I had accomplished until then.

When I quit after forty-three years, I was concerned about the void, the devastation or the trauma. How much of my identity and existence were wrapped up in the show, in being that personality? What would happen? My son was wondering, Would I die? You want to know what? After all the fanfare, all the write-ups, the following Monday, it was as if those forty-three years had never happened. There was no trauma! What surprised me most after I made the decision was that there was no trauma! Isn't that amazing? How do you analyze that?

I've watched the careers of other talk-show hosts after they've left their shows. Johnny certainly retired with dignity, but not all of them have. Mike Douglas, after a tremendous track record for Westinghouse, went to cable—to a show I felt was not worthy of his talents. I'm sure that Mike Douglas, a good friend, a close friend, will agree with my theory: quit while you're ahead.

If I go back to TV at all, it's got to be a good move; it just can't be something that could undo the four decades of greatness. It's a question of being very cautious, picky, choosy, exclusive. As of now, I'm turning down more and more spoofs of myself. I don't want to undignify myself.

Despite my plethora of sponsors over the years, I never wanted to be known as a pitchman off the show. I continue to turn down commercials. I did one for a margarine once, called Imperial, and it turned out I had a margarine sponsor on my own show. I lost it through the conflict. I turned down big sponsors, heavy money, with a few exceptions, like the one I did for Burger King where I impersonated a hamburger. Recently, I made two infomercials, one for a motion picture company and one for my dentist.

I've got a public company, Joe Franklin Productions, which markets nostalgia, T-shirts, cheesecakes. I merged my memorabilia collection with Sports Heroes, one of the country's leading marketers of memorabilia collectibles. We're venturing into TV and film production. I have two radio shows, the Saturday night show on WOR-AM and the five-time daily show on WBBR-AM. I've got *Saturday Night Live, Conan O'Brian:* I'll be doing other episodes. I just got an award from the Radio Hall of Fame. I'm giving lectures at schools and universities, I'm talking to a thousand people at the Museum of Television & Radio in New York City.

☆

Many people want to see the "Joe Franklin" as portrayed by Billy Crystal, the effervescent ham, the cornball TV pioneer who still wears his first polyester suit and mines the trades for hot new singing undertakers. Well, that's me, too. I know they'd like to embellish that and blow it out of proportion for the sake of their ratings. I'll do a little of that.

But the real Joe Franklin is into classic old records, vaudeville, the greats—everything else is just a facade. I still am a fanatic collector of photographs, sheet music, magazines, lobby cards, postcards—anything from 1890 up, in mint condition. I'm a compulsive collector. I can't stop. The real me is the old-timer. A young old-timer. I never gave up the image of the joker. I love to go along with that, because for me, it's financially prudent. But that image helps finance the collector, the curator; one supports the other. I played a Nat King Cole record one time when he was on with me, called "Romance Without Finance Is a Nuisance." That could be my motto.

The Saturday night WOR radio show has a huge following. What I love about radio is that it's the theater of the mind; you can create a personality on radio that you can't on TV. I'm a different kind of host on radio. You've got five hours on radio; on TV, thirty minutes. I don't have to worry how I look, I don't have to shave, I can be casual. I love the calls that come in from people who love the music, the "musically disenfranchised," as I occasionally call them. They want to hear the old songs. I give them memories. To some, and they tell me this, I am their lifeline. To use Elliott Gould's favorite phrase, that makes me feel warm.

I suppose my path could have gone differently. I could have taken the networks up on their offers in the early decades of TV. I could have gone into syndication earlier. I might have followed a career as a concert promoter and impresario or gone into TV production at the dawn of the era. But while Dick Clark and Merv Griffin ventured into production, syndication, distribution, I remained a "Mom and Pop" candy store. It was my own choice. I didn't want to be MCA of America. I've got enough to buy vit-

☆

tles, I have my Cheerios, and I always wanted to quit before I got evicted.

I'm like the Rock of Gibraltar. I represent permanence and peace of mind to a lot of people. The world changes, values change, meanings of words change. But I'm still there, symbolizing something that lasts. They say, if Joe Franklin still sits there with the collar and the tie, even though the world is changing, some things still endure.

Dear Diary:

Well, 1940 is all over. No more diary, I presume. It was a nice year—went fast. But I've been noticing lately how time flies! It's not wrong to plan five weeks ahead;—five weeks pass before one realizes it!

I'm listening to Al Jolson sing.

Good night!

★

A Joe Franklin Chronology

1926   **March 9** Born to Anna and Martin, Echo Hill Sanitarium, the Bronx, New York
1943   Contributes gags and special material to Eddie Cantor, the *Eddie Cantor Show*
1944   Military, Fort Dix, New Jersey; Camp Hood, Texas
       Hosts first radio show for military radio station
       October, honorable discharge, return to New York City
       November, fifteen-minute radio program, *Vaudeville Echoes*, WHOM
1945   Technical adviser to Ted Collins and Kate Smith, *Kate Smith Sings* and *Kate Smith Speaks*
       Assistant to Martin Block, *Make-Believe Ballroom*, WNEW
       Joe Franklin's Antique Record Shop, WMCA radio, 8:00–9:00 A.M.
1947   *Echoes of the Big Time*, WMCA radio, nightly
       Supplies records for the *Paul Whiteman Club*, five afternoons a week
1948   Hosts *Echoes of the Big Time,* WMCA, 8:00–8:30 P.M.
       Joe Franklin's Antique Record Shop, WMCA, 8:00–9:00 A.M.
       Vaudeville Isn't Dead, twenty-five-minute radio program

1949   Impresario, "Echoes of the Big Time" concert, Carnegie
Hall, January 21, 1949, benefit for March of Dimes
Main Street Memories, WMCA radio (nationally
syndicated)
Joe Franklin's Antique Record Shop, WMCA radio,
8:00–9:00 A.M.
December, *Joe Franklin's Record Shop,* WJZ radio, Monday–Friday, 6:30–7:00 A.M.; 11:30–11:55 A.M.; Saturdays
at 11:30 A.M.

1950   March 21, 1950, produces Eddie Cantor live performance
at Carnegie Hall, "My Forty Years in Show Business"

1951   *Joe Franklin's Record Shop,* 11:35 P.M.–12:00 midnight
nightly, Saturdays 11:00–11:30 A.M.
January 1951, the *Joe Franklin Show* (originally titled *Joe
Franklin—Disc Jockey*) first airs via WJZ-TV (Channel
7), Monday–Friday, noon–12:30 P.M.
Impresario, Al Jolson Remembrance Night, Carnegie
Hall, October 23, 1951

1952   *Main Street Memories*: radio show heard by 102 stations
May 12, 1952, *Spotlight to Stardom* airs, WJZ-TV,
10:00–11:00 A.M. "Gives new faces in show business a
chance to exhibit their wares before the TV cameras."
September 21, 1952, *Joe Franklin's Memory Lane,* Sundays, 10:15 P.M.
December 13, 1952, Marries Lois Meriden (Knoblock)

1953   *Memory Lane,* on WINS Monday–Saturday, mid-
night–1:00 A.M.
June, *Memory Lane,* Wednesday nights, 9:00 P.M. ("Joe
Franklin emcees a nostalgia review.")
October 6, 1953, *Joe Franklin's Memory Lane* debuts,
daytime, WABC-TV, 1:00 P.M.

1954   *Joe Franklin's Memory Lane,* WABC-TV, 2:00–3:55 P.M.
(Show airs at 3:30. Hosts a program of feature film, Monday, Wednesday, and Friday, 2:00–3:30 P.M. and Thursday, 2:30–3:30 P.M.)

☆

Stories for You
Main Street Memories

1955 Host, *Movies for You,* WABC-TV, 2:00 P.M.
Host, *Romantic Interlude*
Joe Franklin's Memory Lane, 3:30–4:00 P.M.

1956 *Joe Franklin's Memory Lane,* WABC-TV, Monday, Tuesday, Thursday, Friday, 12:30–1:30 P.M.; Wednesday, 1:00–1:30 P.M.
March 3, 1956, "10th Anniversary in Broadcasting" show, with Eddie Cantor, Tony Curtis, and others

1957 February 21, Bradley's birthdate.

1958 *Joe Franklin's Memory Lane,* 12:30–1:00 P.M.
September 17, 1958, moves from 12:30–1:30 to 10:30–11:00 A.M. and 1:30–2:00 P.M.; show run in two parts.

1959 *Joe Franklin Junior*, until 1961

1961 9:00 A.M. time spot, WABC

1962 October 1, switches from WABC to WOR (Channel 9)
Joe Franklin's Memory Lane, 11:30 A.M.–1:00 P.M.
Begins WOR-AM radio program

1967 Joe Franklin drops *"Memory Lane"* from show title
Joe Franklin Show, WOR-TV, Monday–Friday, 12:30–2:00 P.M.

1968 *Joe Franklin Show*, Monday–Friday, 10:00–11:30 A.M.

1970 *Joe Franklin Show*, 12:00 noon–1:00 P.M., rebroadcast from 1:00 A.M. to 2:00 A.M.
June 28, 1971, on at 10:00 A.M.

1971 WOR-TV, Monday–Friday, 10:00–11:00; 1:00 A.M.–2:00 A.M.; Saturday night at 1:00 A.M. *Best of Joe Franklin* repeat
WOR radio, every evening Monday–Friday, 8:15 to 9:00

1972 January 24, 1972, *Joe Franklin Show* moves from 1:00 P.M. to 3:00 P.M., Monday–Friday, and 1:00 A.M.

1973 Airs 9:00 A.M., repeated at 1:00 A.M.

1974 Showtime: 8:30 A.M., repeated at 1:00 A.M.

☆

1977 Showtime: 9:00 A.M., repeated at 1:00 A.M.
1979 Release of Joe Franklin's *Encyclopedia of Comedians,* Citadel Press
1981 September 14, moves to 6:00 A.M., rebroadcast at 2:00 A.M.
1982 Show moves to Secaucus, New Jersey, studio
1984 Show is aired twice, at 5:30 A.M. and 2:00 A.M. Weekly radio show, 12:00–5:00 A.M.
1987 November 22, Joe Franklin Productions becomes a publicly held company.
1988 Aired at 1:00 A.M.
1991 40th Anniversary Show and party at Club "21"
1993 **August 6,** Last show, after 21,425 shows

☆

Index

Abbott and Costello, 20, 77
ABC, 35, 47, 86, 88–89, 90, 93, 106, 129, 160–61
Abel, Peter, 177
Abe Lincoln in Illinois, 174
Adams, Cindy, 221
Adams, Joey, 221
Adamson, Al, 144
Adelman, Linda, 169–70
Albano, Lou, 179
Ali, Muhammad, 199
Allen, Fred, 17, 44, 78, 90, 129, 145, 180, 234, 248
Allen, Leroy, 148
Allen, Steve, 41, 89, 225, 228
Allen, Woody, 147, 180, 184, 214
Allen and Rossi, 32, 227
Ameche, Don, 116
American Bandstand, 86, 227–28
"Am I Wasting My Time on You?," 28, 110
Amsterdam, Morey, 87
Andrews, Lois, 49
Anna, 135–36
Ann-Margret, 88, 98
"Anytime," 91

Appleton, Eleanor, 128
Arbuckle, Fatty, 57
"Are You Lonesome Tonight?," 28, 110
Armstrong, Louis, 35, 63, 195–96
Astaire, Fred, 47–48
Astor, Mary, 55
Autry, Gene, 52, 69, 112–13

Back Street (Hurst), 90
Bailey, Mildred, 36
Bailey, Pearl, 195
Baker, Belle, 27
Baker, Carroll, 134
Ball, Lucille, 45, 134
Bancroft, Anne, 98, 198
Bankhead, Tallulah, 63
Banks, Aaron, 178, 181
Banks, Wally, 151, 218
Barker, Katherine, 171–72
Barnouw, Eric, 160
Barr, Roseanne, 183
Barrie, Wendy, 87
Barry, Jack, 29
Barrymore, Ethel, 32
Barrymore, John, 220
Baruch, André, 19

Baruch, Bernard, 53
Batchelor, George R., 242
Beame, Abraham, 200
"Because of You," 22
Belafonte, Dennis, 196
Belafonte, Harry, 99, 196–97
Bells of St. Mary's, The, 47
Bennett, Pete, 191
Bennett, Tony, 22, 110, 218
Benny, Jack, 11, 17, 50, 72
Berle, Milton, 43, 50, 85, 91, 98
Berlin, Irving, 19, 41
Bernie, Ben, 27
Bess, Herman, 27
Bess, Jerry, 101
Bevan, Billy, 93
Beverly Hills Cop, 213
big bands, 21, 35–36, 135
Big Top, 163
Blackstone, Milton, 91
Blackwell, Earl, 78
Blaine, Jimmy, 228
Block, Martin, 20–25, 26, 29, 34, 35,
    42, 87, 103–4, 163, 225, 227
Blood and Sand, 97
Bloom, Madeleine, 164–65
Bloomberg, Michael, 152
Blue Dahlia, The, 122
Blue Network, 34–35, 47
Bob Crosby Show, 105, 106
Bob Howard, the Jive Bomber, 84
Body and Soul, 95
Boggs, Bill, 226
Bolger, Ray, 37
Bontempi, Pino and Fedora, 162
"Boogie Woogie Bugle Boy of Com-
    pany B, The," 189
Boone, Pat, 30
Borden's Musical Review, 35
borscht belt, 95–96, 248
Bova, Joe, 89
Boyd, William, 89

Brando, Marlon, 116
Braunstein, Bob, 168–69
Brewer, Theresa, 179
Brice, Fanny, 62, 210
Bride and Groom, 129
"Bring Back the Thrill," 91
Broadway Danny Rose, 180, 184–85,
    214
Brooks, Garth, 187
Brooks, Phil, 143
Buckman, Adam, 220
Burbank, Luther, 66
Burbig, Henry, 89
Burke, Alan, 235
burlesque, 76–77
Burns, Davey, 147
Burns, George, 50, 96
Burr, C. C., 242
Burr, Henry, 27, 110, 143, 201
Busse, Henry, 36
Buttafuoco, Bobby, 229
Butterworth, Charles, 97
Buttons, Red, 96, 128
Byrd, Robin, 182

Caesar, Irving, 78
Caesar, Sid, 96, 147, 184
Cagney, James, 67, 88, 114, 129
Cahn, Irving, 30, 98, 118
Caine Mutiny, The, 155
Campana, Frank, 187
Canada Dry, 104, 106
Cantor, Eddie, 17, 26, 31, 35, 36–41,
    44, 45, 49, 55, 67, 72, 77, 88, 91,
    98, 144, 145–46, 196–97, 213,
    217, 243, 244
Capp, Al, 233–34
Captain Blood, 59
Captain Kangaroo, 89
Captain Tim Healy's Stamp Club, 68
Captain Video, 147
Carlin, George, 183

Carmichael, Hoagy, 36
Carney, Don, 71
Carpetbaggers, The, 134
Carroll, Diahann, 107
Carson, Johnny, 98, 104, 181, 213, 224, 225, 226, 237–38, 250
Caruso, Enrico, 27, 33, 37
Castro, Bernie, 103
"Cathedral in the Pines," 30
Catskills on Broadway, 100
Cavett, Dick, 185, 188, 228
Celebrity Service, 78
Chaffee, Suzy, 147
Chance for Romance, 160
Chance of a Lifetime, 107
Chandler, Charlotte, 248
Chaplin, Charlie, 51–52, 57, 152, 155, 185, 242
Charney, Leon, 148, 211–13, 216
Chase, Charlie, 58, 208
Chase & Sanborn Hour, The, 37
Chayefsky, Paddy, 146
Cher, 136
Chesterfield Supper Club, 21, 22
Chiti, Morrow, 153
Chiti, Pam, 153
Claire, Ted, 67
Clark, Dick, 86, 189, 227–28, 251
Clark, Marguerite, 240
Clark, Mary Higgins, 233
Clarke, Mae, 55
Clay, Andrew Dice, 184
Clooney, Rosemary, 194
Cobb, Buff, 235
Coca, Imogene, 147
Cohan, George M., 33, 41
Cohen, Maury, 242
Cohn, Roy, 95, 200–201
Colby, Marion, 89
Coldwin, R. I., 229
Cole, Nat King, 196, 251
Collins, Ted, 17–20, 34, 44, 77

Colonna, Jerry, 55
Columbo, Russ, 220
Columbu, Franco, 178
comedians, 76–77, 95–96, 182–86
Como, Perry, 21, 87
Connery, Sean, 230
Connolly, Walter, 97
Cooper, Jackie, 59
Corio, Ann, 76
Cornell, Joseph, 110–11
Cosby, Bill, 99, 147, 185–86, 229
Cosell, Howard, 237
Cott, Ted, 25
Cowboy Tom's Gang, 69
Cox, Wally, 116–17
Crabbe, Buster, 240
Crawford, Joan, 58–59, 132
Crosby, Bing, 26, 35, 46–47, 48, 115, 191, 231
Crosby, Kathryn, 48, 191
"Cry," 115
Crystal, Billy, 12, 93, 173, 176, 185, 247, 251
Cured by Excitement, 93
Curtis, Tony, 74–75, 116, 184, 192, 230, 235

Dagget, "Uncle John," 71
Dagmar, 87
Dalí, Salvador, 176, 181
Dangerfield, Rodney, 184
Dasaro, Ben, 218–19
Davis, Bette, 132–33
Davis, Sammy, Jr., 38, 99, 195–96
Day, Shannon, 111
Day in Court, 160
Dean, James, 116, 191
Dean, Peter, 186
deAnfrasio, Roger, 147, 205
Deffaa, Chip, 220
De Maria, Johnny, 141, 151–52, 154, 166, 218

DeMille, Cecil B., 111
Dennis, Sandy, 238
Denny, Joan, 30
Dent, Vernon, 93
Derr, E. E., 242
Diamond, Bob, 166–68, 185, 190, 192
Dick Van Dyke Show, 87
Dietrich, Marlene, 131
Donahue, 245
Donahue, Troy, 194
Donaldson, Walter, 41
Dorsey, Jimmy, 35
Dorsey, Tommy, 35, 98
Dorsey Brothers' Show, 98
Douglas, Erik, 229–30
Douglas, Kirk, 229–30
Douglas, Mike, 227, 228, 250
Downey, Morton, Sr., 36
"Downhearted," 91
Downs, Johnny, 58
Do You Trust Your Wife?, 104
Dr. I.Q., the Mental Banker, 71
Dua, Mimi, 142–43
Dudelheim, Hans, 92–93, 107
Dumont, Charles A., 84
Dumont Network, 84, 98
Durante, Jimmy, 30, 43, 64, 74, 147, 232, 245
Durbin, Deanna, 132

Early Bird Matinee, 86
Eban, Abba, 176
Eberle, Bob, 165
Ed Sullivan Show, The, 31, 98, 224
Edwards, Cliff, 52
Edwards, Stan, 220
Eigen, Jack, 234
Ellen, Vera, 48
Ellington, Duke, 114, 181
Eltinge, Julian, 77
Encyclopedia of Comedians (Franklin, ed.), 214

Engasser, Virginia, 186
Erlichman, Marty, 188
Everything Goes, 89
Extract, Howard, 144

Fairbanks, Douglas, 59
Falk, Dick, 189
Farber, Barry, 222
Faulk, John Henry, 94–95
Faye, Alice, 135
Faye, Joey, 77, 221
Felix the Cat, 93
Ferrer, José, 194
Fiddler on the Roof, 188
Field, Rudolph, 119, 120
Fields, W. C., 41
Fine, Jack, 34
Fisher, Amy, 229
Fisher, Eddie, 38, 43, 91–92, 108, 218
Fitzgerald, Ella, 143–44
Flav-r-Straws, 107
Fletcher, Tex, 69
"Flowers That I Picked for Her Wedding Are the Flowers I Placed on Her Grave, The," 69
Flynn, Errol, 59
Ford, Art, 55–56, 87
Fortgang, Anna (mother), 66, 67, 69, 70, 128, 129, 148, 206–7, 208
Fortgang, Martin (father), 66, 67–71, 89, 100–101, 152, 206, 239
Fortgang, Meg (sister), 67, 80
Francis, Connie, 90, 110
Franklin, Art, 29–30, 32–33
Franklin, Bradley (son), 80, 148, 205–6, 207–8, 210, 245
Franklin, Joe:
  birth of, 66–67
  childhood of, 66–77
  chronology of, 253–56
  comedians admired by, 76–77
  as critic, 100, 127, 209

diary of, 66, 125, 252
drama as interest of, 71, 75–76
earnings of, 88, 128–29
education of, 67–68, 75, 76, 78–79
fans of, 58–59, 220
as father, 70, 205–6, 210
fundraising by, 145–46
as gag-writer, 17, 72, 77
height of, 120
as impresario, 40–44
lawsuits of, 213–15
love affairs of, 118–30, 215–16
marriage of, 129–30, 208–10
memorabilia collection of, 11, 33,
    45, 46, 68, 97, 108, 128, 147, 155,
    221, 239–43, 250
mentors of, 17–26, 34–41
military service of, 79–80
name of, 33
nostalgia as viewed by, 7, 28–29,
    69, 231
office of, 85–86, 141–58, 209, 249
part-time jobs of, 77–78
personality of, 11–12, 34, 130,
    165–66
"phone etiquette" of, 154, 156–58
press coverage of, 12–13, 29–34,
    213–14, 249
as record collector, 26–28, 37, 69, 80
retirement of, 244–52
sexual experiences of, 67, 76
in show business, 20, 73–74
style of, 95–97
suspensions of, 94
as talk show host, 11, 86–108,
    222–32, 246–48
tall blondes preferred by, 67, 120
trivia knowledge of, 142–43, 211,
    219, 221
Franklin, Lois Meriden (Knobloch)
    (wife), 101, 126–30, 188, 198,
    205, 208–10, 216, 245

Frazier, George, 213–14
Freed, Alan, 101, 163, 173
Friedan, Betty, 176
Fuller, Samuel, 103
Funny Company, 162
Funny Girl, 188

Gable, Clark, 18
Galiber, Joe, 79
Gambling, John, 161
Garbo, Greta, 60–61, 108, 131, 132,
    155, 243, 247
Garfield, John, 95, 96
Gari, Brian, 172, 181
Garland, Judy, 125, 134
Gary, Harold, 50–51
Gary, Sid, 50–51
Gee, George, 220
Geller, Uri, 177
Gentleman's Agreement, 95
George White's Scandals, 52–53
Georgian, Linda, 147
Gershwin, George, 78
Gershwin, Ira, 78
Giffen, Ralph, 165
Gifford, Kathy Lee, 226
Gillespie, Dizzy, 35
Giuliani, Rudolph W., 179
"God Bless America," 19
Goddard, Paulette, 45
Godfrey, Arthur, 52, 116, 232
Going My Way, 47
Goldberg, Whoopi, 183
Goldenson, Leonard, 88, 163, 227
Gold Rush, The, 51
Goldstein, Al, 182
Gollin Ed, 102–3, 218
Golomb, Elan, 239
Gone With the Wind, 133
Good Earth, The, 110
Goodman, Benny, 23, 114–15
Gordon, Bert, 39

Gould, Elliott, 199, 230, 251
Grable, Betty, 45, 135
Graduate, The, 198
Graham, Virginia, 87
Grant, Cary, 39, 60
Gray, Barry, 221
Great Dictator, The, 152
Great Laughter (Hurst), 90
Great Race, The, 11, 184
Great Ziegfeld, The, 110
Greenspan, Bud, 237
Greenstein, Joe, 179
Gregory, Dick, 183–84
Gribbon, Harry, 109
Griffin, Merv, 228, 251
Gromyko, Andrei, 95
Grossinger, Jenny, 96
Gunsmoke, 102
Gunty, Morty, 162
"Gus Edwards' Kid Kabaret," 31, 37

Hall, Jon, 171
Hammerstein, Willie, 180
Happiness Boys, 109, 125
Happy the Clown (John Kuhley),
    148–50, 208
Hare, Ernie, 109
Harris, Phil, 135
Hart, Kitty Carlisle, 46
Hart, Margie, 76
Hart, Maurice, 24
Hart, Vance, 212
Haymes, Dick, 218
Hayworth, Rita, 48
Heavy Metal, 215
Hecht, Ben, 56–57
Heller, Aaron, 70
Hello Dolly!, 50, 195
Hellzapoppin, 32
Hemingway, Ernest, 103
Henie, Sonja, 40
Herbst, Johnny, 168

"Here Comes Santa Claus," 112
"High Noon," 69
History of Hair, The (deAnfrasio),
    147
Hitchcock, Alfred, 197–98
Hobart, Rose, 55
Hodge, Al, 147
Hoffa, Portland, 248
Hoffman, Abbie, 178
Hoffman, Dustin, 198
Hollander, Xaviera, 48
Holtsworth, Saxi, 149
"Honeycomb," 98
Hope, Bob, 12, 20, 62, 72, 88
Horn, Bob, 227–28
Hospital, 146
Houseboat, 60
Houston, Whitney, 186
Howard, Joe, 78
Howard, Willie and Eugene, 61,
    66–67
Howell, Chauncey, 226
*How to Succeed in Business Without
    Really Trying,* 54
Hughes, Rush, 21
Hurlock, Madeline, 93
Hurricane, The, 171
Hurst, Fannie, 90
Hutton, Betty, 130

"I Can't Get Started with You," 62
"I'd Rather Be a Lobster Than the
    Wise Guy," 12
"I'd Rather Be Lonely Without You
    Than Happy with Somebody
    Else," 210
"If You Knew Susie (Like I Know
    Susie)," 37
"I Love Mickey," 179
"I'm Sorry I Made You Cry," 28, 143
"I'm Walking Behind You," 91
Inherit the Wind, 48

I Remember Mama, 75
It's a Wonderful Life, 38
"It's de-Lovely," 62
I've Got a Secret, 87
"I Want to Be Happy," 78
"I Wish I Had My Old Gal Back Again," 28, 110
"I Wonder Where My Baby Is Tonight," 28, 110
"I Wonder Who's Kissing Her Now," 78

Jackson, Chubby, 89
Jackson, Michael, 186
Jacobson, Max, 91–92
James, Dennis, 107, 233
James, Harry, 22, 23, 135
Janis, Elsie, 27
Jarvis, Al, 21
jazz, 34, 35
Jazz Singer, The, 41, 44
Jessel, Georgie, 18, 27, 31, 37, 41, 48–50, 67, 74, 88, 105, 108, 112, 144–45, 170, 181, 190, 215
J. Geils Band, 189–91
Jim the Wrangler, 89
Joe Franklin—Disk Jockey, 86
Joe Franklin Junior, 107
Joe Franklin Productions, 250
Joe Franklin Show, 173–92
    early version of, 83, 89–90
    final season of, 244–52
    guests on, 173, 175–92, 229–32, 247–48
    ratings for, 179–80, 191, 223
    sponsors of, 245, 250
    taping of, 174–75, 223–24
    time slot for, 174–75, 223
    title of, 173–74
Joe Franklin's Memory Lane, 83–108
    bookings for, 98–100
    crew of, 165, 168–70

early shows of, 89–92
films shown on, 92–93, 94, 174
guests on, 96–100, 146–48, 161, 168–70, 173–92
producers for, 164–65
program directors for, 166–68
ratings for, 105–6, 160
sets used by, 89–90, 168
sponsors of, 99, 100–107, 164
studio audience for, 95
as talk show, 96–100
time slot for, 160–61
title of, 90
typical show of, 171–72
Johnson, Grace, 93, 94, 101
Johnson, Lyndon B., 213
Johnson, Richard, 221
Johnson, Van, 96
Jolson, Al, 23, 27, 29, 41–44, 72–73, 217, 252
Jolson, Erle Chennault Galbraith, 43
Jolson Story, The, 41–42, 43
Jones, Billy, 109
Jones, Spike, 218
Jorgenson, Christine, 177
"Judy," 144
"Just a Gigolo," 78
"Just a Girl That Men Forget," 28, 143

Kahn, Gus, 41
Kamarr the Magician, 147
Kane, Bob, 193
Kate Smith Hour, 17–20
Katz, Morris, 147–48, 181
Kaufman, Andy, 183
Kaufman, George S., 248
Kaye, Danny, 96, 232
Kaye, Sammy, 23
Kayser, Robin, 172
Keaton, Buster, 74, 97, 152
Keeler, Ruby, 43–44

Keeshan, Bob, 89
Kelly, Gene, 48
Kennedy, John F., 106, 192, 194, 200
Kennedy, Joseph P., Sr., 131
Kenny, Nick, 29, 30, 31–32, 34
Keogh, Jack, 71
Khrushchev, Nikita, 236
Kid from Spain, The, 38, 45
Kid Millions, 38
Kiernan, John, 245
Kiernan, Walter, 163
Kilgallen, Dorothy, 115, 128, 233
Kimbai, Michiki, 172
kinescopes, 83, 98, 117, 129, 155
King Kong, 162
Kirkland, Sally, 135–37, 147
Kirschner, Claude, 162–63
Kitchen Kapers, 86
Klein, Stewart, 213
Kleinsinger, Shirley, 125–26
Koch, Ed, 97
Kollmar, Richard, 115
Kuhley, John (Happy the Clown),
    148–50, 208

La Guardia, Fiorello, 199–200
Lahr, Bert, 248
Laire, Judson, 75
Lake, Veronica, 121–22, 145
LaLanne, Jack, 55, 178–79
Lamour, Dorothy, 171, 230–31
Lancaster, Burt, 97
Langdon, Harry, 57
Lanza, Mario, 88
La Rose, Rose, 76
Laughton, Charles, 87
Laurel and Hardy, 75
Leamer, Lawrence, 225
Lebow, Guy, 161
Lee, Gypsy Rose, 76, 226
Lemmon, Jack, 97, 184
Lennon, John, 191–92

Leno, Jay, 228
Leonard, "Fat" Jack, 197
Leonard, Gloria, 182
Lester, Jerry, 87
Lester, Lance, 151
"Let's All Sing Like the Birdies
    Sing," 149
Letterman, David, 189, 202, 226
Levant, Oscar, 31, 132
Levey, Ethel, 33
Levine, Joseph E., 134
Lewis, Jerry, 88, 172, 193
Lewis, Robert Q., 116
Lewis, Ted, 41
Liberace, 195
Lindbergh kidnapping trial, 21
Lindsay, John, 200
Linton, Charles, 143–44
Little Rascals, The, 89, 225
Livingston, Margaret, 36
Lloyd, Harold, 208
Loesser, Frank, 54
Lombard, Carole, 197–98
Lombardo, Guy, 63–64, 218
Lopat, Eddie, 247
Lopez, Vincent, 84, 180
Lords, Traci, 182
Lost Weekend, The, 193
Louis, Joe, 178
"Love Letters in the Sand," 30
Loves of Sonja, 131
Loy, Myrna, 18
Lucas, Diane, 86
Luncheon at Sardi's, 98, 108, 118–19

McCarthyism, 94–95
McCormack, John, 37
McGinnis, Maureen, 20
McMahon, Ed, 163
MacMurray, Fred, 98
McNeil, Claudia, 65
McNeill, Don, 87

McPhillips, Mary Helen, 163
Madison, Noel, 242
Main Street Memories, 27, 34
Make-Believe Ballroom, 21, 22
Manilow, Barry, 188
Mann, Claire, 89
Manners, Zeke, 87
Man on Fire, 48
Man on the Street, 85
Mansfield, Jayne, 121
Mantle, Mickey, 179
Margolies, Abe, 211
Marilyn Monroe Story, The (Franklin and Palmer), 120
Marjorie Morningstar, 48
Marks, Johnny, 112–13
Martin, Dean, 193
Martin, Freddy, 23
Martin, Joe, 37
Martino, Richard, 33–34
Martin Paint, 99, 190, 220
Marty, 146
Marvullo, Joe, 181
Marx, Groucho, 37, 42, 185, 248
Marx Brothers, 75, 152
Mason, Jackie, 129, 169, 211
Maxwell, Edwin, 242
Maxwell, Marilyn, 36
Mays, Willie, 179
Mead, Margaret, 176
Meir, Golda, 212
Melton, James, 89
Memory Lane Cavalcade, 107
Memory Lane Jr., 108
Mercer, Johnny, 36, 58
Merry Melodies, 37
Mets, *see* New York Mets
Michel, Martin, 102
Mickey Mouse Club, 89
Midler, Bette, 188–89
Milkman's Matinee, 55–56
Milland, Ray, 193

Miller, Arthur, 50
Miller, Dick, 188
Miller, Glenn, 21
Miller, Marilyn, 41
Million Dollar Movie, 162
Mineo, Sal, 116
Minnelli, Liza, 48, 186
Minnelli, Vincente, 48
Mix, Art, 144
Mix, Tom, 144
Monroe, Marilyn, 108, 116, 118–20, 191, 219
Montez, Maria, 171
Moon Is Blue, The, 94
Moore, Dickie, 132
Moore, Garry, 87, 232
Morehouse, Ward, 40–41
Morris, William, 144
Mottola, Tommy, 191
movies:
    "B," 242
    Franklin's early interest in, 74–75, 76
    silent, 57–58, 92–93, 94, 97, 174, 209, 240
    TV vs., 84–85, 92–93, 94, 102–3, 159, 162
"Movin' Man, Don't Take My Baby Grand," 42
Moynihan, Daniel Patrick, 78–79
Mullins, John, 47
Murphy, Eddie, 183
Murphy, George, 114
Murray, Ken, 72, 78
Murray the K, 163
Myerson, Bess, 97
"My Way," 11

Nagel, Conrad, 128
Naldi, Nita, 97
NBC, 17, 35, 47, 84, 165
Nebel, Long John, 104

Nelson, Harriet Hilliard, 135
Nelson, John, 129
Nelson, Ozzie, 135
Network, 146
New Kids on the Block, 189
Newman, Paul, 97
News, Views and Reviews, 98
Newsweek, 85, 202
Newton, Wayne, 13
New York Mets, 163, 164, 171, 172
Night at the Opera, A, 152
Nixon, Richard M., 106, 210, 219
Nizer, Louis, 95, 213
Noble, Ernest J., 35
No, No, Nanette, 43
Normand, Mabel, 46
Norris, Kathy, 86
Novak, Kim, 98
Nutrition Center, 104, 108

Oberon, Merle, 133
O'Brian, Jack, 30–31, 34
O'Day, Anita, 181
Odd Couple, The, 1176
Odets, Clifford, 110
Oh, Calcutta!, 135
"Oh My Pa Pa!," 218
Oliver, Sy, 181
O'Neill, Jennifer, 197–98
One Man's Family, 105
Ono, Yoko, 191
On the Beach, 48
"Operation Daybreak," 160–61
Ornstein, Richard, 59, 136–37, 153, 179, 195, 197, 210–11, 212, 219, 221, 239
Our Gang, 57, 93

Paar, Jack, 94, 225, 233, 247
Pacino, Al, 186
Page, Patti, 22
Palmer, Laurie, 118, 120

Parker, Colonel, 18, 98
Parker, Gloria, 180
Park Row, 103
Parks, Larry, 42
Parrish, Mitchell, 113
Parsons, Louella, 45
Patriot, The, 75
Patton, 54
Paul Whiteman Club, 35–36
Peck, Gregory, 103
Penny, Oliver, 84
"Penthouse Serenade," 62
Peterson, Otto, 147
Pickford, Mary, 109–10, 240
Pignatore, Mike, 36
Porter, Cole, 64
Poston, Tom, 89
Powell, Eleanor, 37, 48
Powell, Jane, 132
Preminger, Otto, 94, 170, 181, 197, 198
Presley, Elvis, 18, 88, 98
press agents, 29–30, 32
Price, Georgie, 27, 31, 112
Price, Robert, 116
Price, Vincent, 193
Pruden, Susie, 179
Pryor, Richard, 183
Psychic Friends Network, 147
public relations (PR), 97–100
Pyne, Joe, 233–34

quiz-show scandals, 104

radio:
    announcers on, 73–74
    disk jockeys on, 21–25, 26, 35–36, 86
    Franklin's career in, 11, 17–44, 79, 80, 107, 128, 131, 251
    Franklin's early interest in, 68, 71–74, 76
    live, 47

records played on, 21, 35
sponsors for, 23–24, 26
studio audience in, 37–39
TV vs., 24, 44, 47, 84
Radio Hall of Fame, 250
Raft, George, 64
Rainer, Luise, 110–11
Ramone, Joey, 12, 189
Rand, Sally, 126–27
Randall, Dick, 85–88
Randall, Tony, 121, 147
Ransky, Frank "Pop," 150
Raphael, Sally Jessy, 226
Ray, Charles, 57
Ray, Johnny, 115
Reagan, Ronald, 44–45, 201
"recips," 30, 31–32
Record Collectors Exchange, 239
Reddy, John, 129
Reed, Alan, 147
Reider, Lola, 124–25
Remick, Lee, 97
Reynolds, Debbie, 91, 108
Ricci, Mark, 240–41
Richman, Harry, 112
Ritter, John, 69
Ritter, Tex, 69
Ritz Brothers, 75, 126
Rivers, Joan, 226
Rizzo, Jilly, 221
RKO, 159, 162, 164
Roach, Hal, 108
Robbins, Sophia Orculas, 153–54, 156
Robinson, Edward G., 18, 52–53
Rocco, Tommy, 181
Rockefeller, Nelson, 128
Roffman, Dick, 98, 235–36
Rogers, Ginger, 48, 55
Rogers, Jimmy, 98
Rogers, Will, 41
Roman, Freddie, 100, 238

"Romance Without Finance Is A Nuisance," 251
Roman Scandals, 38
Romantic Interlude, 107
Romper Room, 83, 162, 168
Rooney, Mickey, 125, 235
Roosevelt, Eleanor, 95
Rose, Billy, 44, 53
Rosie, Grandma, 152
Ross, Diana, 186
Ross, Dorothy, 36
Rubin, Sid, 98
"Rudolph the Red-Nosed Reindeer," 112–13
Ruffner, Tiny, 86
Rukeyser, Lou, 176
Rumpus Room with Jimmy Olson, 85
Russell, Bill, 147

St. James, Phil, 99, 180
Sajak, Pat, 211
Sales, Soupy, 214
Sanders, John, 217, 218
Sannuto, Joe, 220
Saturday Night Live, 176, 183, 185, 247, 250
Savalas, Telly, 56
Schindler, Phil, 150–51
Schoetzer, Hymie, 220
Schwartz, Manuel, 75
Schwarzenegger, Arnold, 178
Scott, George C., 54
Scott, Sandy, 133
Scroy, Ernie, 187–88
Second Avenue Pushcart Mart, 68
Selkowitz, Richard, 147, 243
Sennett, Mack, 45–46, 109
Shaw, Artie, 22
Shaw, Stan, 56
Shawn, Dick, 211
Shearing, George, 197
Sheen, Charlie, 153

Sheen, Fulton, 97–98
She Loves Me Not, 46
Shelton, John, 125
Sherman, Sam, 241–42
Shopping News, 86
Shore, Dinah, 23, 38, 39
Siegel, Stanley, 231–32
Silvers, Phil, 77, 96, 214
Silver Streaks, 75
Simon, Bill, 176
Simon, Carly, 186
Simon, Neil, 87
Sinatra (Wilson), 211–12
Sinatra, Frank, 11, 23, 34, 43, 211–12,
　　218, 220, 221
Sing Along with Mitch, 86
Singing Fool, The, 41
Six Bridges to Cross, 116
Skelton, Red, 77, 232
Slater, Bill, 119
Smith, Bob, 24, 163
Smith, Kate, 17–20, 29, 52–53, 87,
　　217
Smith and Dale, 27
"Smoke Gets in Your Eyes," 62
Smothers Brothers, 211
Snows of Kilimanjaro, 103
Snyder, Tom, 237
Sobol, Louis, 29, 225–26
Southern, Georgia, 76
So You Think You Know Music, 25
Spellman, Francis Cardinal, 49
Spielberg, Steven, 147
Spinal Tap, 192
Spotlight to Stardom, 107
Squillante, Daniel, 104, 108
Stack, Robert, 132
Stallone, Jackie, 177
Stallone, Sylvester, 197
"Stardust," 113
starlets, 118–19, 122–24, 152–54
Steinem, Gloria, 176

Stern, Howard, 11, 177–78, 226–27
Stevens, Gary, 98, 118
Stevens, Inger, 48
Stewart, Jimmy, 129
Stockman Joe, 144
Stokowski, Leopold, 176
Stone, Ezra, 20
Stone, Hal, 114, 183, 243
Stone, Sharon, 153
Streisand, Barbra, 114, 147, 155,
　　187–88, 191, 199, 220
Strike Up the Band, 125
Sugar Blues, 131
Sullivan, Ed, 29, 31, 32, 68, 100, 232
Sullivan, Sylvia, 100
Super Circus, 162
Susskind, David, 236–37
"Swanee," 78
Swanson, Gloria, 97, 131
Swayze, John Cameron, 232–33
Sweet Charity, 100
Switzer, Carl "Alfalfa," 57

Taft, Robert A., 19
Talbot, Harry, 208
Taylor, Elizabeth, 57, 91
Taylor, Robert, 236
"Tea for Two," 78
Teagarden, Jack, 36
Telethon, 146
television:
　　cable, 177
　　censorship on, 93–95, 102
　　daytime, 85, 86–87, 89, 101, 104,
　　　159–61, 162
　　early days of, 83–108, 174
　　Franklin's career in, 44, 85–108,
　　　244–52
　　fundraising on, 145–46
　　movies vs., 84–85, 92–93, 94,
　　　102–3, 159, 162
　　network, 160–61

prime-time, 84–85, 224
radio vs., 24, 44, 47, 84
Temple, Shirley, 112, 132
"Tennessee Waltz," 22
"Thanks for the Memory," 62
"That's the Kind of Baby for Me," 35
"There's a Gold Mine in the Sky," 30
Thorsen, Ethel, 234
Three Stooges, 62–63, 75
Tierney, Lawrence, 242
Time for Fun, 89
Tinker's Work Shop, 89
Tiny Tim, 149, 184, 201–2
Todd, Mike, 76, 88
Tonight, 87, 181
Towering Inferno, The, 48
Tracy, Arthur, 181, 220
Tracy, Fred N., 73–74
Tracy, Maude, 73
Treacher, Arthur, 228
"True Blue Lou," 218
Tucker, Forrest, 91
Tucker, Mrs. Richard, 171, 172
Tucker, Richard, 172
Tucker, Sophie, 27
"Turn Back the Hands of Time," 91
Turner, Lana, 125
TV Guide, 85, 93
TV Shopper, 85
20th Century-Fox, 102–3
20 Questions, 98
"Two Sleepy People," 62

Ubangi Dance Company, 94
Uncle Don, 71
Uncle Floyd, 214–15

Vagnoni, Frank, 90
Vale, Jerry, 168
Valentino, Rudolph, 66, 97
Vallee, Rudy, 27, 29, 54–55, 155, 168,
    181, 187, 209, 242, 244

vaudeville, 27, 31, 37, 49, 85, 145, 180
Vaudeville Echoes, 20
Vaudeville Isn't Dead, 25, 27
"Voice of Experience," 72
Von Zell, Harry, 39

WABC, 24, 83, 97, 101, 104, 163, 168
Wachtel, Arnold, 154–55, 214
Wagner, Robert, 97
Wagner, Robert, Sr., 199–200
Walker, Danton, 29
Walker, Nancy, 56
Wallace, Mike, 235
Walsh, Jack, 146
Walters, Barbara, 87
Walters, Lou, 87
Warhol, Andy, 176, 181
Warner, Jack, 184
Wayne, John, 60, 69, 74, 88, 129
WBBR, 250
WBNX, 98
Webb, Chick, 143–44
Webb, Fay, 54
Wein, George, 213
Weingrad, Jeff, 220
Welk, Lawrence, 198, 232
Welles, Orson, 65
West, Mae, 130–31, 243
We Who Are Young, 125
We Won Today (Barker), 171
What! No Beer?, 74
What's My Line?, 119
Where's the Rest of Me (Reagan), 201
Where Your Friends Are, 217–21
White, Frank, 20
White, Sid, 29, 234
Whiteman, Paul, 26, 34–36, 73, 90
Whiting, Margaret, 194
WHOM, 20, 25–26, 98, 177
Whoopee, 38
William, Warren, 97
Williams, Bert, 26, 41

Williams, Robin, 183
Williams, William B., 21, 101
Will Mastin Trio, 38, 196
Will Success Spoil Rock Hunter?, 121
Wilson, Earl, 34, 177, 211–12
Winchell, Walter, 21, 29, 30, 31–32, 34, 37, 128
Wingate, John, 86, 163
WINS, 163
WJZ, 86, 89
WMCA, 27, 84, 104
WNBC, 22
WNEW, 17, 20, 22, 24, 25, 27, 55, 103, 163, 236
Wolf, Peter, 190
Wood, Natalie, 184

Wood, Peggy, 75
WOR, 24, 25, 74, 101, 154, 159, 161–64, 168, 170, 174, 185, 213, 217, 223, 224, 245–46, 250, 251
WPAT, 27
Wyler, Jim, 89

Yankee Doodle Dandy, 114
"Yes Sir, That's My Baby," 37
"You'll Never Walk Alone," 172
Young, Sara, 123–24
Youngman, Henny, 19–20, 238

Zanuck, Darryl, 84–85
Ziegfeld Follies, 48, 62
Zimmerman, Mr., 77–78
Zussman, Irving, 100

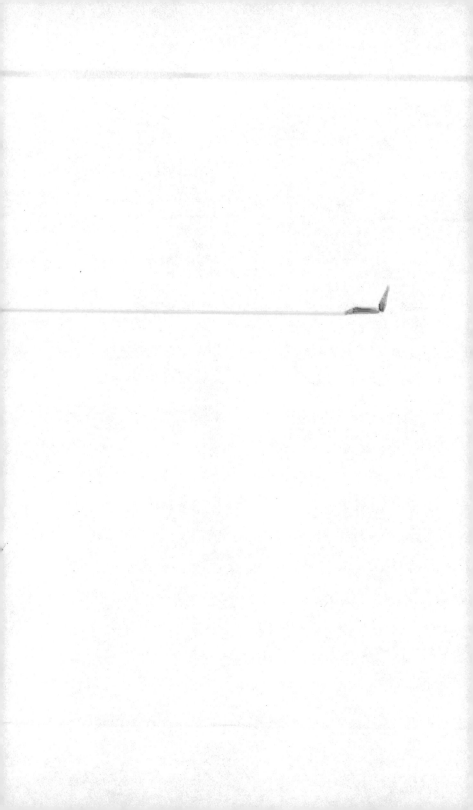